Wooden
Ships
from
Texas

NUMBER SEVENTY-SEVEN:
The Centennial Series
of the Association of Former Students,
Texas A&M University

To Donald Kay
with best wishes
April 3, 1999

Wooden Ships from Texas

A WORLD WAR I SAGA

Richard W. Bricker

TEXAS A&M UNIVERSITY PRESS
COLLEGE STATION

The paper used in this book meets the minimum requirements
of the American National Standard for Permanence
of Paper for Printed Library Materials, Z39.48–1984.
Binding materials have been chosen for durability.

Library of Congress Cataloging-in-Publication Data
Bricker, Richard W., 1925–
    Wooden ships from Texas : a World War I saga / Richard W. Bricker.
—1st ed.
       p. cm. — (The centennial series of the Association of Former Students,
Texas A&M University : no. 77)
    Includes bibliographical references and index.
    ISBN 0-89096-827-6 (alk. paper)
     1. World War, 1939–1945—Naval operations, American. 2. Ships, Wooden—
Texas—History—20th century. I. Title. II. Title: Texas wooden ships, 1916–1994
III. Series.
D589.U6B75   1998
940.54'5973—dc21   98-13742
                                                        CIP

To Janie Salinas Bricker
I always wanted to paint but could not,
I always wanted to write
but had nothing to say.
My wife and constant supporter
said otherwise.

Contents

Illustrations

PLATES   *following page* 142

Tables

Preface

One day in 1992, in a restaurant near Winnie, Texas, I noticed a large framed black-and-white photograph of a square-rigged ship. She was sailing very smartly with all sails up and several hands in the rigging. The title on the picture was *Off Sabine Pass*, and, according to the proprietor, the ship was a Texaco tanker. This I found hard to believe, but it started me on an intensive research program that has included trips to various museums along the Texas coast and study in research libraries all the way to Biloxi, Mississippi. In 1992, I started obtaining copies of various documents on Texas vessels from the National Archives in Washington, D.C. I spent a week there in January, 1996, obtaining copies of official documentation and correspondence on Texas ships that were the major finds of this research. And, in September of that year, I spent another week at the National Archives, obtaining more documentation on Texas vessels.

Texas books contain a wealth of fact and fiction concerning oil, cattle, and cowboys. Books about the Texas Navy and Civil War battles, from Sabine Pass to Brownsville, are in most libraries. This book tells little known and significant events in Texas that are mostly unrecorded.

Missing from most historical accounts are the tremendous accomplishments of Texans in both the construction and utilization of marvelous sailing vessels all along our lengthy coast. These are the boats and ships that people built out of necessity, as the only way to move people and cargo around and across our numerous bays and estuaries.

In a grand finale to Texans' long career of building vessels, fourteen wooden sailing ships were built in time to make a significant contribution to World War I. The design and construction of this number of large sailing ships in three years was a tremendous achievement, never equaled by one yard anywhere else in the world.

While looking for pictures of Texas sailing vessels at the National Archives Pictorial Library at College Park, Maryland, I found numerous photographs of wooden steamships. Texas shipyards, from Sabine Pass to Rockport, built several of these ships for the government during and right after World War I. Both sailing ship and steamship programs occurred for the same reason—the shortage of shipping caused by World War I.

The major objectives of this book were to document the major sailing shipbuilding accomplishment, discuss the ships' careers until the last vessel was salvaged in 1994, and review the wooden steamship program.

Why is this book needed? Accounts of American sailing ships ignore Texas maritime history. Pictures and written material are plentiful for East Coast vessels. One can find data on almost all vessels built in Maine starting as early as 1783 with some listings of vessels as early as 1748. The same is true, to some extent, for the other northeastern states.

Limited references and comments in books by eastern maritime experts regarding the larger Texas sailing ships were sometimes derogatory, frequently erroneous, and almost never substantiated by in-depth research. This book, primarily based on official vessel documentation and correspondence and on a limited number of firsthand accounts, is, I believe, about as close to the true story as is possible to achieve sixty to eighty years after the events occurred.

Acknowledgments

Acknowledgments are thanks, and I owe them to many people for their contributions to this book.

My wife, Janie, she encouraged me to paint and write and also helped with the NA research, along with sacrificing a lot of her activities. She was also very helpful with the tedious task of installing the many editorial corrections required.

The painting training at San Jacinto College came first, and I must credit William C. Balusek who taught with considerable and necessary starch, no slop, drip, or splash allowed. Doug Sweet taught me Drawing and Design and Composition and provided critiques of my later painting efforts. Also, college librarian Sue Gale Mock Kooken led me to some book references that were of much value.

The late George Griffith of the NASA/Johnson Space Center tried to teach me something about scientific writing, about the need for proof always, and about never, but never, assuming anything. He also taught me that he who positively knows that something is true is frequently wrong. Research for this book has demonstrated the truth of that axiom several times.

Carolyn Rose, administrator of the Heritage House Museum, Orange, Texas, introduced me to Frank Karppi's paper, which led to the revelation that a total of fourteen ships were built, and the fact that the Bludworth family had a photo album of the barentines constructed at Orange. This is when the book was conceived and the project took direction. Dr. Howard C. Williams, Orange County Historian, provided the only available picture of the ship *City of Orange* and several other significant photographs.

The Bludworth family provided many construction and launch pictures and information on John L. Bludworth, the master carpenter. His sons, Harold and John L. Jr., and a grandson, Johnny Bludworth, were very helpful. Johnny also provided the panoramic view of the International Shipbuilding Company shipyard.

Mindy Durham, director, and Robin Moran, curator of the Texas Maritime Museum at Rockport, Texas, provided newspaper information on the Bludworths' racing activities, pictures and photographic information, and articles on the Heldenfels Brothers shipbuilding during World War I.

Researching fourteen ships made it mandatory that I go to the National Archives, in Washington, D.C., where I was greatly helped by Richard W. Peuser and Angie S. VanDereedt of the Archives I Reference Branch. Additional thanks to Peuser, because he led me to other files besides ships' documentation, thus adding some human interest to the history. He also went to considerable extra effort to determine the Spanish American War veteran status of one of the key individuals in the book.

About this time, I was put on the right track regarding organization of the book by Richard Hanneman, who does nonfiction book reviews for the *Houston Chronicle*.

Murella Hebert Powell, local history and genealogy librarian at the Biloxi, Mississippi, library researched and provided most of the Gulfport, Mississippi, area information on Henry Piaggio.

Jerry W. Harris, granddaughter of L. E. Weaver, provided the only picture found of internal wooden sailing ship construction at a Texas yard.

Very rewarding was the opportunity to talk to and exchange information with a charming connection to the Piaggio shipbuilding era, Mary Anna C. Anderson of Beaumont, Texas, who, at the age of nine, was sponsor for the *City of Beaumont* and christened the ship when it was launched. She has followed the ship's history ever since.

Robert Haas, a ship model builder, of Lumberton, Texas, was very helpful, and his model of the *City of Beaumont* was most useful in my painting of that ship. Haas was also instrumental in getting me in touch with Mary Anna C. Anderson.

The anonymous technical reviewers who provided excellent technical input are especially thanked for putting me on the trail of much interesting material for the ship *City of Beaumont*.

Kurt D. Voss, director of the Texas Seaport Museum at Galveston, generously provided of his time and knowledge in digging out files and pictures on the *City of Beaumont* and the "Hastings on the Hudson" era. He also put me on the trail of the panoramic picture of the shipyard, where most of the large Texas sailing ships were built.

Nathan R. Lipfert, library director at the Maine Maritime Museum in Bath, Maine, was very helpful in several areas, especially in resolving last-minute questions concerning draft versus depth of hold measurements.

Jane E. Ward, curator of manuscripts at the Peabody Essex Museum in Salem, Massachusetts, informed me of the holdings of the museum pertaining to *City of Beaumont* and provided a copy of the original Captain Butler letter.

My sons, Adam R. Bricker and Joseph D. Bricker, guided me in the selection of computer hardware. Adam made major contributions by installing the software, troubleshooting, and, most important, training a complete novice in computer use.

Finally, prior to submitting the manuscript, the grammar and punctuation was greatly improved by the last-minute editing of Mary Peterson.

Wooden
Ships
from Texas

Fourteen Fabulous Ships

On August 1, 1914, Germany declared war on Russia, soon involving most of Europe in World War I. As a result, a massive sailing ship construction program got under way at Orange, Texas, in 1916, well before the United States entered the war. An Italian-born lumber exporter from Gulfport, Mississippi, initiated the construction of fourteen sailing ships in Texas after the demise of sail as a major entity.

Henry Piaggio wanted sailing ships to haul Gulf Coast pine lumber to Italy, and nothing would stop him. No one else in the United States, including the traditional schooner yards of the New England States, started such an ambitious program. This resulted in Texas history's most fascinating shipbuilding era, more remarkable because it occurred after sail had almost died out.

Eleven of the vessels were magnificent five-masted barkentines built of East Texas pine. In this book I explore how Texans were able to build them, what instigated the program, and how the finished ships often found their own adventurous careers.

In another program, the United States Shipping Board wanted Gulf Coast shipyards to build wooden steamships in a bridge of ships to Europe. Texans from Sabine Pass to Rockport enthusiastically worked and made major contributions to this effort.

Texans had built various-sized vessels all along the Gulf Coast for nearly a hundred years before these major endeavors of 1916–19. A brief review of the Texas coastal heritage provides a foundation for this shining hour of Texas sailing ship construction.

SMALL BOATS ALONG THE TEXAS GULF COAST

The primary subject of this book is ships, loosely defined today as any large seagoing vessel. So, why discuss small boats? Knowledge of the

Texas experience with vessel construction and use will lead to the main theme of this book.

Pine, oak, and cypress were in plentiful supply as a source of material. Southeast Texas had massive stands of longleaf pine, an ideal wood for boat and ship construction. The early settlers learned carpentry skills necessary to survive the elements of the remote wilderness areas of Texas. Some of the immigrants brought boatbuilding skills with them from Mexico, Europe, or the East Coast.

Boats were very necessary along the coast, as the few roads available were impassable in bad weather. With few bridges, the overland distance was usually many times the overwater distance. A small boat could carry more cargo than the farm wagon, and there was no horse to feed or water. Furthermore, the sailboat is, by its nature, economical transportation. One person can operate a sloop more than 30 feet long, although an additional hand was usually along.

Fishing industries developed along the coast, resulting in the need for more boats. Live cattle and hides shipped to the east and to Central and South America for herd buildup, meat, and leather uses required a variety of vessels on the Texas Gulf Coast. From the early 1900s on, petroleum products were shipped on sailing vessels as well as steamships, a practice expanded during the extreme shipping deficit of World War I.

Eastern Texas had, and still has, massive stands of southern pine forests in a band up to a hundred miles wide and three hundred miles long. Shipping that lumber from East Texas required numerous vessels. Galveston, Houston, Beaumont, and Orange became leaders in the export trade as well as in the manufacture of lumber. As early as 1860, it was reported that 1 million board feet of sawed lumber, about 12 million shingles, and 97,000 staves were being exported from Sabine Pass within a year.

By 1880, shipyards were operating in Galveston Bay, Indianola, Matagorda, Sabine Pass, and Orange. Shipwrights constructed sloops, schooners, tugs, and steamboats, using the best longleaf pine timber available.[1]

The U.S. government required licensing of most vessels shortly after the Declaration of Independence. The issuance of official numbers did not start, however, until 1867.[2] This referenced letter based on an act of Congress, approved July 28, 1866, directed all custom collectors as to the location, size, and depth, if in wood, to make the markings (official number and tonnage) in the vessel.

The Director of the Bureau of Statistics was instructed to prepare an annual statement of vessels registered, enrolled, and licensed under the laws of the United States along with the class (propulsion), name, tonnage, place of registry, and other information that may be decided on. The result was that all vessels over five tons built after 1866 are included in the *List of Merchant Vessels of the United States*, an annual government publication. A modest sampling of small sailboats built along the Texas coast shows the variety of vessels built for various needs. Table 1 contains several Texas vessels found in a sampling of a few of the merchant vessel lists of the late 1800s. Some vessels built elsewhere and subsequently registered in Texas are also included, as they indicate how other needs were met.

The *Adelaida*, belonging to the Rio Grande Railroad Company, was a two-masted schooner built at Isabel, Texas, in 1895 and registered at Brownsville.[3] She had a length of 58 feet and measured 34 tons. (Gross and net tonnage figures, used throughout the book, relate to enclosed volume rather than weight.)

The term *ton* appears to have originated from *tun*, a cask of wine, and to have meant the number of such tuns that the ship could carry.[4] Each measurement ton is equal to 100 cubic feet of cargo space. The weight measurement used is deadweight tonnage.

The register length of a vessel is the length measured on top of the tonnage deck from the fore part of the outer planking or plating at the bow to the after part of the stern post of screw steamers and to the after part of the rudderpost of other vessels. The register breadth is the widest part of the vessel. The register depth of a vessel is the depth measured from the underside of the tonnage deck, amidships, to the bottom of the hold.[5] This is not the draft, which may be a lesser or larger number, depending on the vessel size and design.

The *Azalea*, built at Rockport in 1903 was a scow schooner and only 2.7 feet deep in the hold. She was registered in Corpus Christi with a length of 60 feet and capacity of 50 tons.[6]

Many boats built on the lower Texas coast were scow sloops and schooners, as described by Howard I. Chapelle:

On the western Gulf Coast, the scow had been used for both coastal and river work since the first settlement of the Texas coast by Americans. There was a very numerous type of scow sloop used in fishing at Port Isabel, Texas, that remained in use until quite recently. These sloops were from about 26 to 32 feet in length and 10 to 12 feet beam. They were decked and had a trunk aft, if used in fishing. As the boats did not have accommodation for the fishing gang, some boats were fitted with a removable trunk cabin forward and were used as camp-boats, to take care of the additional men. The sloops were often very smart sailers and,

TABLE I. TEXAS BOATS

Name/Owner	Rig, masts, number	L (ft.)	B (ft.)	D (ft.)	Net tons	Where built, year	Surrender and year
Alice / American Salt Co.	Sch., 2, 105990	109	27	7	272	Lynch burg, 1881	Abandoned, 1896
Ann Rebecca / Thomas Jackson	Sch., 2, 105774	42	15	3	17	Clear Lake, 1878	Abandoned, mouth of Turtle Bayou 1898
Elida / J. P. & E. O. Sjolander	Sch., ?, 136068	36	12	4	12	Beaumont, 1889	Total loss, Fishers Reef, Galveston Bay, 1900
Emily / G. E. Crosby	Sch., ?, 8318	42	15	3	17	Cincin- nati, Ohio, 1865	Sank several years prior to 1897 at Columbia
Lake Austin / H. Cross	Scow, 2, 14042	69	21	4.7	53	Matagorda, 1881	Total wreck, Corpus Christi, 1903
Lizzie / H. G. Schutte	Sch., 2, 15464	46	18	4	22	Greens Bayou, 1868	Abandoned, Galveston, 1890
Louis Gereau / William Roberts	Sch., 2, 14922	51	14	5	24	Rebuilt Aransas, 1877	Abandoned Corpus Christi, 1890
Maggie / Collins & Gebbs	Sch., 2, 91447	70	20	5	40	Lynch burg, 1882	Wrecked, Padre Island, 9 A.M., Mar. 10, 1890
Charlotte M. Allen / Thomas P. Converse	St. Scr., 127050	85	14	4	29	Clear Creek, 1894	Unknown but after 1912

Name/Owner	Rig, masts, number	L (ft.)	B (ft.)	D (ft.)	Net tons	Where built, year	Surrender and year
M. L. Weaver / Sam W. Hudgins	Sch., 2, 90767	51	17	4	18	Madison-ville, La., 1875	Abandoned, total loss, Velasco, 1910
Dauntless / Gulf Fisheries	Sch., 2, 157484	60	17	7.6	38	Essex, Mass., 1897	Abandoned, total loss, 1914
Cuba / Gulf Fisheries Co.	Sch., 2, 127684	72	19	8.6	44	Essex, Mass., 1902	Abandoned, 1924
Bonita / Gulf Fisheries Co.	Sch., 2, 3939	72	19	8.6	44	Essex, Mass., 1902	Lost w/all hands in hurricane of 1909
Try Again / W. O. Ilfrey	Sch., ?, 145154	42	14	4	14	Galveston, 1887	Unknown
Dolphin / T. C. Magee	Sch., 2, 157079	55	15	3.3	18	Red Bluff, 1882	Unknown after 1912
Hilda / Herman Platzer	Sloop, 95871	37	13	3	9	Clear Creek, 1885	Too old, abandoned as gas screw at Palacious, 1944
St. George	Sch., 2, 115669	42	16	3.3	14	Cedar Bayou, 1879	Abandoned, Beaumount, 1910
Hard Times / Peter Collins	Sch., 2, 11584	66	18	3.5	28	Galveston, 1867	Unknown after 1881
Mermaid / Specht & Collins	Sch., ?, 17861	31	11	3.5	7.8	Unknown	Wrecked & abandoned 1882
P. J. Willis / Rosamond & Milams	Sch., 3, 20429	82	23	3.5	45	Cedar Bayou, 1873	Anchored & abandoned 3 miles up Cedar Bayou, 1901

Name/Owner	Rig, masts, number	L (ft.)	B (ft.)	D (ft.)	Net tons	Where built, year	Surrender and year
Edward F. Williams / Gulf Fisheries Co.	Sch., 2, 7731	76	22	7	50	Brooklyn, N.Y., 1863	Stranded north jetty, 1913
Roseway / Lucher & Moore	Sch., 3, 212568	120	28	12	244	Shelborne, Nova Scotia 1907	Stranded at dock, Wolfville, Nova Scotia 1926

L= Length   B= Breadth   D= Depth of hold

though rough in build and finish, were not ugly craft as were some scow sloops in northern waters.

These craft sail very well and are often extraordinarily fast when light or partly loaded. They are cheap boats to build and can withstand very heavy going for they are very strongly built and are buoyant and lively in a sea. The crews of these scows were commonly of Mexican nationality or descent, and the boats were not always kept in a shipshape fashion, but they seem to have been well handled.[7]

A pair of scow sloops is shown in one of the color plates of this book. These boats fished the shallow Texas bays by towing a net between two of them while sailing downwind.

Scow schooners were larger versions of the scow sloops with a mast added. A centerboard, shallow draft, and flat bottom account for their good speed, and in heavy air some of these vessels were capable of planing. Chapelle went on to say that some of these small scows must be considered as among the forerunners of the very fast yacht racing scows and the more recent planing boats that are now engaging the sailing yachtsman's attention.[8]

Another scow schooner was the 69-foot-long *Lake Austin* built at Rockport in 1881.[9] She was issued a Certificate of Registry, which meant the vessel was licensed for foreign ports rather than coastal service.

The *Battlewhack*, built at Tres Palacios in 1898 and registered at Port

Lavaca, had a length of 31 feet and measure 5 tons.[10] The depth of hold for these boats did not usually exceed four feet, a design element required by the shallow bays and lack of dredged channels.

Galveston had many vessels for cargo and fishing use. Some of the vessels were built elsewhere, such as the *Edward F. Williams* built in Brooklyn, New York, in 1863. At 76 feet long and with a 7-foot depth of hold, her purchase by Gulf Fisheries was probably for fishing in the gulf. In New York she had belonged to the Sandy Hook Pilots Association.[11]

Also around the turn of the century, Gulf Fisheries of Galveston bought several fishing schooners designed by B. B. Crowninshield of Boston, Massachusetts. Crowninshield is famous as the designer of the *Thomas W. Lawson*, the only seven-masted schooner ever built. The vessels were built at Essex, Massachusetts, and fished for red snapper in the Gulf of Mexico.[12] The *Bonita* and *Cuba*, bought in 1902, had lengths of 72.5 feet and measured 44 tons.[13] Gulf Fisheries also bought the *Dauntless*, a slightly smaller schooner, in 1897 from the same source.[14] These are just a few examples of several schooners bought by Gulf Fisheries that fished into the 1920s. (figure 1.1)

The fishing schooners were more than seven feet deep in the hold. One schooner was reported to have made a return trip to Galveston of six hundred miles in sixty hours.[15] To average ten miles per hour for sixty hours is fast for this size vessel, although prevailing spring winds in the Gulf of Mexico provide very spirited sailing. These vessels were similar

fig. 1.1. Red
snapper fleet
drying out.
Courtesy
Rosenberg
Library,
Galveston, Tex.

*Wooden
Ships
from Texas*

*fig. 1.2. Galveston
Harbor.* Courtesy
Rosenberg
Library,
Galveston, Tex.

to the Georges and Grand Banks schooners and were fast and seaworthy. Fishing was from the schooner deck rather than from launched boats.

The schooner *Bonita* was lost with all hands in a hurricane in July of 1909. The surrender statement read: "Vessel lost at Sea in Hurricane of July 21, 1909. Locality unknown. Nothing heard from Vessel or Crew Since Sailing July 13, 1909."[16]

Figure 1.2 shows several three-masted schooners in Galveston Harbor in the early 1900s. These are cargo vessels of a type seen from Houston to the Port Arthur-Orange area. These ships were mostly from the East Coast, as very few, if any, vessels of this size and type were built in Texas, at least before 1916.

Besides the purchased boats, many small yards around Galveston Bay turned out vessels. The *Try Again*, a 42-foot schooner built at Galveston in 1877, hauled bricks from Cedar Bayou to Galveston.[17] Other brick-hauling schooners built at Galveston were the 31-foot *Mermaid*, built in 1882, and the 66-foot *Hard Times*, built in 1867.[18] These vessels all had a hold depth under 4 feet, necessary in the shallow waters of upper Galveston Bay and Cedar Bayou.

Other boats listed as brick haulers were the *Dolphin*, a 55-footer built at Red Bluff in 1882; the *St. George*, a 42-footer built at a Cedar Bayou yard; and the *Elida*, a 31-footer built at Beaumont in 1889.[19] E. O. and John Peter (J. P.) Sjolander, area pioneers, originally owned the *Elida*.

John Peter Sjolander was known as the "Sage of Cedar Bayou" and is recognized as one of Texas' important poets.[20]

These centerboard vessels were shallow draft but had sharp bows and slightly round bilges, unlike the hard-chinned scows. Figure 1.3 shows one of the schooners used for hauling brick down Cedar Bayou, usually to Galveston, as Houston had its own brickyards. Notice the small rowboat drifting alongside the stern, useful for getting ashore and as a small tug. This schooner, typical of the era, had a large sail area with at least two reef bands on the gaff sails and one on the jib. This provided many options of sail area, so the vessels had power in light air and could reduce sail in high winds.

Fourteen
Fabulous
Ships

Cedar Bayou had a towpath so a draft animal could pull the sailboats up and downstream. Brickmaking started along Cedar Bayou before the mid-1800s, and some of the brickyards were several miles up the bayou from Galveston Bay; hence the need for towpaths.[21]

One of the more interesting boats built at a Cedar Bayou yard was the *P. J. Willis*, a three-masted schooner built in 1872. "The marine news reporter usually said the *Willis* carried 25,000 bricks, apparently an astounding number, because he never mentioned a count for the others."[22]

fig. 1.3. Schooner ghosting along Cedar Bayou. Courtesy Bay Area Heritage Society, Baytown, Tex.

The permanent enrollment papers for this vessel give a good indication why this is so.[23] Her length was 82 feet, breadth 23 feet, and depth of hold 3.5 feet, a small number compared to the other dimensions. She measured 45.3 tons.

With a cargo volume of 4,530 cubic feet, and assuming a conservative 50 percent loading efficiency, she could be loaded with more than 50,000 bricks, so deadweight was the limiting factor. At an average weight of five pounds per brick, 25,000 bricks would weigh 62.5 tons, and deadweight tonnage (DWT) is usually empirically in the range of 1.5 times the net tonnage, or 67.5 DWT. In practice, the boat was simply loaded with bricks until the minimum safe freeboard was reached, and that important factor controlled the number of bricks carried.

The *P. J. Willis* was also the subject of an oil painting by Julius Stockfleth, a little known marine and landscape painter in Germany and Texas. According to James Patrick McGuire's *Julius Stockfleth: Gulf Coast Marine and Landscape Painter*, "Stockfleth was active in Galveston between 1885 and 1907, a period that saw the last of the commercial sailing ships and the predominance of steam-powered vessels in a port which was the only deepwater facility between New Orleans and Vera Cruz and the fifth most important in the United States."[24]

A painting in McGuire's book is titled *P. J. Willis in Snowstorm of January, 1886*. Several newspaper articles from the time give different versions of the source of this unusual title. In one telling, the schooner *Oranzoff* from Wallisville capsized with a load of lumber. The captain was presumed drowned. The *Galveston Daily News* also reported: "In another tragedy, a Captain Hutchings, along with two volunteers, rowed in gale force winds out to a sloop aground to check on the captain. They found the body of Captain Jefferson sitting on the forward part of the companionway with his arm over the main gaff. The body was covered with about six inches of ice and was of course dead. They broke the ice from the body with some difficulty and brought it ashore. All three of the rescue party were exhausted and nearly frozen."[25]

Upper Galveston Bay was also frozen for a distance of five miles from Morgan's point, according to a Captain Faulk, master of the steamer *Louise*. The two-inch-thick ice scraped all the paint off along the vessel's waterline, and the water was the lowest seen in the captain's thirty years on the bay. The lowest temperature reported was 7 degrees Fahrenheit.[26]

The *P. J. Ellis* was converted to a barge in 1893 and survived until September 6, 1901. Cause of surrender: "Vessel abandoned as unfit for use. Anchored in shallow water lake 3 miles from mouth of Cedar Bayou, out of way of navigation."[27]

The Platzer family immigrated to Galveston from Germany and settled in the Clear Lake area. Wilhelm Platzer and his four family members arrived in Galveston June 15, 1852, aboard the Bremen bark *Franziska*.[28] They had left Bremerhaven, Germany, forty-five days earlier for a distance of 6,100 miles (all distances are in statute miles), averaging 5.6 miles per hour (estimated speeds will be given when data is available to allow comparisons of various sailing vessels).[29] The distance sailed was considerably more than the straight-line distance, of course. Herman Platzer, born in 1852 became a carpenter and built and operated a sloop, the *Hilda*. Her length was 37 feet and she measured nine tons.[30] The boat was well built and lasted fifty-nine years. The License of Vessel Under Twenty Tons was issued in 1885, and the vessel documents were surrendered in 1944 at Palacios, Texas.[31] She had been converted to a gas screw for fishing. Herman Platzer eventually set up a boatyard in Kemah, a small settlement on Galveston Bay. He built a 35-foot-long sloop named *Gypsy Girl* in 1893 and took tourists out for sightseeing trips on her.[32]

Dan Platzer, brother of Herman, born in 1854, also went into shipbuilding, and his descendants have continued in that business. Boatyards were as important then as service stations are today, as most families on the bay had some kind of boat for transportation. Houses were built with widow's walks so the wife could watch from the roof using a spyglass to see if the boat was in and then send a wagon or buggy to the creek to pick up her husband.[33] E. W. Platzer, grandson of Dan, also set up a boatyard in the neighboring Seabrook area. Both yards built new boats, as well as repairing existing ones.

Many Platzer descendants continued in some business related to shipping or yachting. The Platzer Boat Works of Houston built tugs for the U.S. Army during World War II. Neal Platzer, son of E. W. Platzer had a yard that built steel barges until it was sold in the 1990s. He is now president of a maritime consulting group, Franziska Group, Incorporated.

The magnitude of shipping in the Houston area was indicated by the size of Commodore Charles Morgan's shipping line in the mid to late 1800s. According to Lee Vela and Mazine Edwards, in *Reaching for the Sea: The Story of the Port of Houston*, "At the peak of its service to Houston the Morgan line had a fleet of about 10 steamships, two steamboats, 32 schooners, 7 steam tugs, and 18 barges."[34]

A scene at Allen's landing at the foot of main street in Houston, circa 1912, is shown in the color plates. Here again a three-masted schooner is at the dock. The schooner was probably towed up Buffalo Bayou the 20 or so miles from Galveston Bay.

Moving up the coast to the East, the next important maritime area is the Port Arthur-Orange-Beaumont region. Port Arthur is closest to the Gulf of Mexico. As such, it was the first town in that area to get a ship channel and the status of subport of entry. Minor channel improvements, starting in 1901, resulted in the dredging of a 10.5-foot channel farther upriver, but Orange did not get an oceangoing ship channel until 1916. Until then, traffic was limited to small sailing craft, barges, and paddlewheel boats.

The largest lumber company in Orange, Lucher and Moore, had at least one three-masted schooner purchased by them in 1915 to haul lumber. She was 120 feet long, measured 244 net tons, had a crew of seven, and was built in Shelborne, Nova Scotia, in 1907.

The Certificate of Registry for the *Roseway* indicated she was only entitled to engage in foreign trade and could not engage in coastal trade, indicative of the widespread operations of the lumber company.[35] On November 14, 1916, the *Galveston Daily News* stated that the *Roseway* had just returned to Orange from Jamaica, a one-way trip of 1,725 miles (all distances are in statute miles).[36]

Of course, on a voyage of any significant distance, a sailing vessel almost never has favorable winds for the whole trip and upwind must travel 40 to 70 percent farther than the straight-line distance. Most of the older boats could not sail closer to the wind than 60 to 50 degrees at best. Even though steam engines were available in the 1800s and internal combustion engines were produced by the early 1900s, very few sailing vessels had auxiliary power installed. Cost and poor reliability were probably major factors. The *Roseway* left the Port Arthur registry in 1925 but did not survive long. All owners are required to turn in the vessel registration, when the ship goes out of service, for any reason, which must include an explanation of why the records are being surrendered. The surrender statement for the *Roseway*, at the Port of New York, read: "Vessel was a total loss by stranding at dock at Wolfville, NS on September 11, 1926, 6 persons on board, no life lost. Casualty report filed with collector at Boston, Mass. 2/17/27."[37] This location is at the upper end of the Bay of Fundy with a tidal range of 40 to 50 feet.

In many turn-of-the-century pictures taken at Port Arthur, Texas, numerous large schooners and square-rigged ships are seen, along with some steamships, but these were visiting ships, there to pick up lumber in enormous stacks, both on the docks and floating in the water. The seven-masted schooner *Thomas W. Lawson* called on Port Arthur during her short life, possibly for petroleum products, as both the Gulf and Texaco oil companies started there because of the Spindletop oil field.[38] She was also known to have hauled coal to Gulf coast ports.

No large, deep-draft schooners were built anywhere in Texas before

World War I, and it is obvious from table 1 that when Texans wanted offshore vessels, they obtained them elsewhere. Examples are the fishing schooners bought by Gulf Fisheries in Galveston: several were built at Essex, Massachusetts; the *Edward F. Williams* was built in Brooklyn, New York; and Lucher and Moore's *Roseway* was built in Nova Scotia.

With the exception of the *Alice*, at 109 feet long, all of the Texas-built vessels listed were less than 100 feet in length. A more extensive search of records from the 1870s and 1880s could turn up more large vessels, but the time scatter of vessels listed in table 1 indicates the general trend of Texas vessel construction. Additionally, the shallow channels precluded deep-draft vessels in most Texas ports prior to the 1900s.

This small sampling of the early Texas maritime industry shows the extensive involvement in construction, maintenance, and use of sailing vessels by Texans. Despite the smaller size of most Texas-built boats, Texans had enough experience, skills, and materials to build large wooden ships if the need arose. A listing of several Texas vessels with their dimensions is provided in table 1.

THE ITALIAN CONNECTION

The perpetrator of Texas' final affair with sail was not a native Texan, but an Italian-born, naturalized American from Gulfport, Mississippi. He was Henry Piaggio, owner of a lumber export business at Gulfport, with interests in Pensacola, Florida, and other locations. He was also president of the International Shipbuilding Company (ISC), the mother company for the construction of the last eleven of the fourteen sailing ships he had built at Orange, Texas.

Construction on the first ship started in mid-1916, and work on the remaining ships continued into 1919. Twelve of the fourteen ships were barkentines, meaning square-rigged on the foremast and schooner-rigged on the remaining masts. Piaggio's primary objective in building these vessels, at least initially, was to transport Gulf Coast pine lumber to Italy.

Why did Piaggio decide to build these vessels rather than use existing shipping? In *A Maritime History of Bath, Maine, and the Kennebec River Region*, William Avery Baker writes:

In 1914 American deep-sea merchant ships were carrying only about ten percent of the country's foreign commerce; the United States depended on the merchant marines of other nations for its foreign commerce, a situation it soon came to regret. After the outbreak of World War I the merchant ships of Germany were quickly driven from the seas while a considerable proportion of those of Great Britain, France, and their allies were employed in the support of military operations. To fill the gap there was a boom in steel shipbuilding in the United States.[39]

Also of significance were the local conditions existing along the upper Gulf coast, as Robert S. Maxwell and Robert D. Baker note in *Sawdust Empire:*

> The total production of lumber, which had declined to 1.5 billion board feet in 1914, rose to 1.75 billion board feet in 1915 and still higher in 1916. The Allies, who controlled the Atlantic sea-lanes, soon found that the war greatly increased their lumber and timber requirements, ranging from boxes and crates to temporary houses, army-camp structures, and timbers to shore up trenches and dug-outs. The prime source of lumber was the southern United States, particularly the Gulf Coast.

The authors went on to say that there was an acute shortage of shipping and anything that floated was in demand. This was caused in part by the efficiency of the German U-boat campaign. Old shipyards inactive for years were reactivated along the Texas and Louisiana coasts. The abundance of timber, plenty of skilled labor, and a good climate were cited as plus factors for these yards.

> In the effort to build as many ships as possible, many different types of construction were tried—steel, wooden, and even concrete ships. To those who contended that wooden ships would be ineffective and a waste of time and money, advocates replied that there were many good reasons for wooden-ship construction. They could be built much more quickly than steel ships, a great timber supply was at hand ready for use, and, indeed, they might prove able to withstand a submarine torpedo as well as or better than a steel ship. One enthusiast claimed, 'One torpedo, well-aimed, can sink a great steel ship of 10,000 tons—but as much effort and explosives are required to destroy the modest 3,000 ton wooden freighter.'

Major General George W. Goethals (of Panama Canal fame) thought that all priorities should go to steel ships, whereas Chairman of the U.S. Shipping Board William Denman was a strong supporter for wooden ships. Many of both varities were built along with a few concrete ships.[40]

The enthusiast contending that it took as much effort and explosives to destroy a wooden freighter as a much larger steel ship was not aware of the German naval doctrine. Small vessels were sunk with the deck gun or by time-charges placed in the hold of the ship. Only a few pounds of a well-placed charge were used to sink many ships. Between July 26 and August 20, 1916, a U-35 (German submarine) sank fifty-four ships totaling 91,150 tons, expending nine hundred shells and only four torpedoes in the process.[41]

By 1916, shipping costs were very high. Initiating a steel shipbuilding program by private enterprise would have been impossible during a major war, so Piaggio took the only viable alternative he had.

The location to build these fourteen vessels and the hailing port was Orange, Texas. By early 1916, Orange had a 26-foot deep channel to the Gulf of Mexico, necessary for ships as large as Piaggio planned. Orange has excellent protection from storms, being inland more than twenty-five miles from the Gulf of Mexico.

Orange had the raw materials, the required skilled labor from earlier boatbuilding years, and boat repair yards. An additional advantage was a moderate climate that allowed work throughout the year. In 1915, Henry Piaggio set up offices in Orange, Texas, to expedite lumber shipments from the Orange-Beaumont area. He also had the first ship laid down in the summer of 1916, and she went down the ways on November 20 of that year.

The first three ships constructed for Piaggio were built by F. H. Swails, who was listed on the Certificate of Registry as supplier of the master carpenter certificate. Each of the early ships belonged to a company in Gulfport, Mississippi, incorporated under the laws of Mississippi, and maintaining an office at Orange, Texas.

The first of the three ships built was a five-masted schooner, the *City of Orange*; the second was a four-masted barkentine, the *City of Houston*; and the third and smallest was a four-masted schooner, the *City of Pensacola*.

Approximately five hundred four-masted schooners worked the eastern seaboard and the Gulf of Mexico, so this size was fairly common. Far fewer five-masted schooners were built. Only a few six-masted schooners went down the ways, and only one seven-master was built, the infamous *Thomas W. Lawson*, almost 400 feet long. She ended up on the rocky shore of one of the Scilly Islands with thirteen of fifteen hands lost, plus an unlucky pilot who had boarded early. When schooners got above four or five masts at most, they became very difficult to tack, and on a lee shore this lack of maneuverability sometimes resulted in disaster.[42]

Whether this was a factor in Piaggio's decision making is not known;

however, the first seven ships had two Fairbanks-Morse Type "C-O" marine oil engines of 100 horsepower each. A subsequent change was made to two 200-horsepower engines for each of five ships. These engines could solve problems by eliminating the need for tugs and providing some continued movement in light-air conditions that might last for several days. The dependence on tugs could be a major delay for sailing vessels in some ports. The engines would also be useful for traversing straits and canals when the need arose.

Another important factor was the avoidance of very significant wear and tear on the sails and rigging under certain conditions. In weather with any wind above 5 knots, the sails are under forces that stabilize the sails and rigging. One component of the wind energy results in a force at right angles to the sail, and that holds the boom to leeward. The sail also has some lift on the lee side because it is an airfoil that adds to the leeward holding force. These forces also cause the vessel to heel leeward, holding the heavy boom on that side. In a sea with large swells and no wind, if there is no force on the sail and the vessel is rolling several degrees each way, the rigging is snapped back and forth, between several inches of slack to drum-tight. Further, the boom that may be 40 feet long and 15 inches in diameter, weighing 1,500 pounds or more, will swing back and forth across the deck until something fails. The slatting of the sails is also very wearing, and the only recourse is to drop them, which is time-consuming, especially since they will have to be raised again. Prevention tackle was sometimes used, but it was not always effective.

The auxiliary power would provide a speed of 5 or 6 knots, and the apparent wind resulting from this speed would again provide the holding force needed to prevent the swinging of the booms and slatting of the sails. Square-rigged ships had fewer problems in this respect because the yards holding the square sails were held from both ends by opposing tackle called braces.

The auxiliary power would also help the ship complete tacks and the sails would be engine-assisted when working off a lee shore. In extreme conditions, most or all of the sails could be furled while still maintaining steerageway with the engines. The lee shore problem is not always associated with high winds. Many sailing ships, while becalmed, have run aground due to adverse currents, and where conditions did not permit anchoring. The captain would have been very happy to have had a little mechanical propulsion in these helpless situations. Despite these theoretical advantages, less than 8 percent of the four-masted schooners built on the East Coast had engines.

A vessel is sometimes launched fitted-out and ready to sail. When only one ship was built without a committed follow-up, it was usually launched complete.[43] In the case of the fourteen ships built at Orange, speed was paramount, so when the hulls were completed, they were launched.

Launching pictures show the vessels without masts stepped; deckhouses were not finished, and even chocks for scaffolding were not usually removed until later. Final painting was deferred, all of this to expedite the construction—to get the next keel laid—because World War I was in progress, and shipping was in very short supply. For this reason, the issuing of the ship's documentation was several weeks after the launching.

What does one call a sailing vessel with small propulsion engines? The usual terminology is "auxiliary" sloop, schooner, or barkentine, as the case may be, placing the emphasis where it belongs: the vessel's primary motive force is sail, and the vessel is equipped with an engine, or engines, as an aid. Auxiliary power is usually far under the horsepower required to move the vessel at its theoretical hull speed and, with all of the wind resistance of masts, rigging, and deck structures, would not move the vessel to windward at all in high winds.

The application for official number for the twelve vessels with engines lists the horsepower for each of the first seven vessels at 200 horsepower total (two engines per ship) and 400 horsepower total for the next five ships. The same document lists the speed at 5 and 7 knots, respectively.

The ISC ships could exceed 10 knots with favorable winds, but winds are not consistent for long periods of time in most parts of the world. The several thousand square feet of sail area carried by these vessels provided potential propulsion forces far above that of a few hundred horsepower, so these ships were primarily sail-powered with auxiliary engines. Paul C. Morris noted in *Four Masted Schooners of the East Coast*, "Of the 520 U.S. four masters that worked our eastern seaboard 39 had within them auxiliary engines of one type or another on the day of their launching. A great many of these did not keep their engines very long, most of them proving uneconomical and taking up valuable cargo space."[44]

Having provided this general introduction to Texas wooden ships, I will now describe each vessel and its adventures in more detail. The real-life sagas of these magnificent ships range from the uneventful to the almost unbelievable.

The First Three Ships

The first three ships were constructed at the F. H. Swails shipyard at Orange, Texas. The shipyard was located on what is now Harbor Island in the Sabine River at Orange, and workers were transported to and from work by ferry.

The first ship, the *City of Orange*, was a five-masted schooner; the second, the *City of Houston*, was a four-masted barkentine; and the third and smallest, the *City of Pensacola*, was a four-masted schooner, more typical in size and number of masts. At least 458 four-masters were built on the East Coast with an average life span of 14.7 years.[1] (The previous number of 520 four-masted schooners working the eastern seaboard included ships built elsewhere.)

The schooner was a practical vessel for the coastal trades because of prevailing winds. The fore-and-aft-rigged vessel does best with the wind abeam, and it goes to windward better than a square-rigger. Along most coasts, winds usually blow onshore during the day and offshore at night, except when perturbed by weather systems.

THE *CITY OF ORANGE*

In the fall of 1916, as the time approached for the launching of the *City of Orange*, local anticipation mounted, and the *Galveston Daily News* carried the following article:

Orange, Texas, November 14,—Everything is in readiness tonight to receive the visitors coming here tomorrow for the launching of the five masted schooner City of Orange which is to take place a 12 o'clock noon. The boat was ready for launching at daybreak this morning, a crew of men having worked all night on her.

The sudden drop in temperature caused a change in program and the dance will take place in the armory hall in the Rein build-

ing instead of on the deck of the ship. The guests will be escorted
to the Frisco Wharf from the Holland hotel where boats will be
waiting to convey them to the launch. At 8 o'clock the visitors will
be tendered an automobile ride to the various places of interest in
the city. The visiting ladies will be the guests of Mrs. W. H. Stark
who will give a reception from 6 to 8 P.M.

The next day *Galveston Daily News* carried the following article under
the headline "Vessel to Carry Lumber" and a subheading, "Schooner
City of Orange Built Entirely of Texas Yellow Pine Will Engage in Foreign Trade":

Orange, Texas, Nov. 15. High winds made it necessary to postpone
the launching of the five-masted schooner City of Orange here
today. Elaborate preparations had been made for the launching,
and many persons from Texas and Mississippi and as far away as
Florida were here as guests for the ceremony. Though the launching could not be carried out, the remainder of the program
arranged by the local committee was followed to the letter, and the
guests were made to feel the warmth of Orange hospitality. Henry
Piaggio of Gulfport, Miss. and Orange, owner of the schooner,
was here and had with him fifty-three guests who came in a special coach.

The account went on to describe transportation to the shipyard, which
was on Harbor Island and accessible only by water transportation. The
U.S. Coast Guard Cutter *Comanche* and the yachts *Swift Sure* and *Capi-
tan* carried hundreds of visitors down the Sabine River to inspect the
City of Orange and the other sailing ships being constructed. Some
guests were taken by automobile for a sightseeing trip in the city and
surrounding countryside. The women were given a reception in the
evening by Mrs. W. H. Stark and the men attended a banquet at the
hotel with F. H. Farwell serving as toastmaster. Several members of the
Texas Legislature attended, headed by James T. Denton of the Fourteenth Legislative District.

Other dignitaries attending were W. B. Scott, president of the Southern Pacific Railroad; J. W. Link formerly of Orange, but now a leading
businessman of Houston; A. L. Staples, vice president of the bank of
Mobile in Mobile, Alabama; and Mr. Akin of Akin Loading Company in
Pensacola, Florida.

The total coast of the constructing and outfitting of the schooner
was stated to be about $100,000. She was built throughout with yellow

pine lumber (a generic term for at least four species of southern pine). The ship was reported to have two 100-horsepower gasoline engines that will operate twin screws and a capacity for 32,000 gallons of crude oil. The ship was designed to carry about a million-and-a-half feet of lumber and was expected to be ready in about three weeks.[2]

Obviously, this was not a back-lot operation and Piaggio had some powerful friends or perhaps fellow investors. The hometowns of these industrialists and financiers also provide a clue as to how at least five of the ships' names might have originated. One obvious error in the article is the statement that the vessel had two 100-horsepower gasoline engines. These were pre-diesel, oil-burning engines, and, as noted in the article, the ship carried fuel oil. The newspaper also carried two pictures of the partially completed vessel with the caption, "Views of the First Ocean Vessel to Be Built Entirely in Texas yard of Texas Material."

Additional problems occurred, as the launching did not take place until November 20, 1916. Work remaining after launching included stepping masts, installing rigging, bedding engines, completing deckhouses, and painting. As a result, the anticipated date that the vessel would be ready for service was about fourteen weeks short, as the official number application was not submitted until March 17, 1917, by the collector of customs, R. E. Latimer, Port Arthur, Texas.[3]

The Certificate of Registry issued by the Bureau of Navigation was dated April 23, 1917, and listed J. W. Billingsley of New Orleans, Louisiana, as the official of the Ship Ownery Company, which was incorporated under the laws of the state of Mississippi, with an office and place of business at Orange, Texas. The Ship Ownery Company was listed as the only owner of the *City of Orange*.[4] Rupert Wry, a citizen of the United States was listed as master. F. H. Swails, master carpenter, and J. F. Raden, acting admeasurer, certified that said vessel was a motor schooner, with two decks, five masts, a sharp head, and a square stern, that her length was 226.2 feet, her breadth 43 feet, and her depth 22.5 feet. Gross tonnage was 1,632.52 and net tonnage was 1,360. Tonnage figures were: crew space 45.26, master cabin 24.95, chain locker 6.12, storage of sails and poop 97.18, and propelling power 98.43. These latter numbers add up to 271.94, and this subtracted from the gross tonnage of 1,632.52 equals the net tonnage of 1,360, which is the usable cargo volume.

As discussed in chapter 1, these tonnage figures are a measure of the internal cubic capacity of a vessel in tons of 100 cubic feet each. We know how much volume the captain had, how much the crew had, how much was allotted to propulsion, and most important, the cargo capacity. The numbers are only indirectly related to weight. The maximum weight

TABLE 2. COMPARISON OF SCHOONER AND CLIPPER SHIP

Ship	Rig	L (ft.)	B (ft.)	D (ft.)	G.T.	N.T.
City of Orange	Sch. 5	226.2	43	22.5	1632	1360
Flying Cloud	Clipr	225	40.7	21.5	1793	Ukn.

L= Length   B= Breadth   D= Depth of Hold   G.T.= Gross tonnage   N.T.= Net tonnage

that a vessel can carry is called the deadweight tonnage, and for the *City of Orange* it was around 2,250 tons, controlled by the Plimsol mark or load line on the sides of a ship.

The load-limiting factor could be net tonnage or deadweight tonnage, depending on the cargo density. The number of crew listed was fifteen, not including the master. A donkey engine and boiler was listed as having been omitted from measurement spaces. Steam or internal combustion donkeys were almost universal on large schooners and a real labor saver for hoisting anchor, raising sails, and pumping out water leaking into the vessel.

A comparison of the *City of Orange* to one of the American clipper ships, *Flying Cloud*, is given in table 2, as they were close to the same size, but totally different in rig and use. Measurement formulas changed after *Flying Cloud* was built in 1851, so the tonnage numbers are not directly comparable. With its much sharper bow and dimensions slightly less on all points, *Flying Cloud* would not come close to the cargo capacity of the *City of Orange*.

Flying Cloud could exceed 18 knots and had some daily runs over four hundred miles, but it could do this only in near gale-force winds, with much wear and tear on sails, rigging, and crew. The *Flying Cloud* averaged 7.1 mph for the ninety-day trip from New York to San Francisco (15,268 miles) and although this sounds low, it was quite good for such a lengthy voyage. She also required a much larger crew than a comparable size schooner and was much more expensive to build. These are some of the reasons such vessels were no longer even considered when the *City of Orange* was built.

A few entries made by Captain Joseph P. Cressy in the first voyage log out of New York indicate problems resulting from pushing sailing vessels to attain higher speeds. The entry for June 6, 1851, stated: "Lost main topsail yard, and main and mizzen top-gallant masts."

This was only three days after leaving New York, and Cressy kept right on, desperately forcing the vessel. He wrote on June 11:

> Very severe thunder and lightening. Double-reefed topsails. Latter part, blowing a hard gale, close-reefed topsails, split fore and main-topmast staysails.
>
> At 1 p.m. discovered mainmast had sprung. Sent down royal and topgallant yards and studding sail booms off lower and topsail yards to relieve the mast.

Then on June 14: "Discovered mainmast badly sprung about a foot from the hounds and fished it."[5]

These are not Cape Horn entries but occurred during the first eleven days out of New York, demonstrating the high cost of speed under sail, even on ships designed for such conditions. Very few seamen capable of crewing such demanding ships were around in the World War I era. Paul C. Morris wrote:

> In the old days deep water square rig sailors had a tendency to look down their noses at coasting sailors. Generally speaking the deep watermen had to know more about rigging, marlin spike seamanship, etc., in case of dismasting or other misfortune overtaking them far from home and the aid of tugs or salvage vessels.
>
> Toward the end of the era schooners were the only place many of the square rigger men could find employment. Many of those comprising the crews of the later day schooners were not native Americans, but were what was termed "White-Washed" Americans hailing from Germany, Scandinavian countries and any where and every where. The officers, however, remained basically United States citizens through-out.[6]

The number of crew on the *City of Orange* was somewhat higher than for other five-masters, a result of the engines and some extra luxuries such as stewards, mess boys, and three mates. The East Coast general rule of thumb was one man per mast, a captain, one mate, and a cook. Another rule said two men per mast and a captain.[7] The first rule allowed a crew of eight with the captain, the second allowed eleven with the captain, both fewer than the sixteen including the captain on the *City of Orange*.

The rig selection and design merits of the vessel are of interest since it was intended for transoceanic voyages. First, at the time the *City of Orange* was built, four- and five-masted schooners had been around for a long time. The *Bath (Maine) Independent* for November 27, 1883, compares the merits of the square-rigger and the schooner:

> The schooner is a very economical vessel. She costs less to build, because there are no yards to make and rig. The masts cost less. A smaller crew can handle her with equal safety. Did you ever watch a ship go about from one tack to another? What with rising tacks and sheets and bracing around the yards and getting everything snug again, it is a job that is performed when the watch is called, so that all hands can have a chance at the sport. Besides that, the ship while in stays often loses her headway and drifts astern part of the time.
>
> But when a schooner is beating to the windward the helm is put down by the man at the wheel. She comes up with her canvas shaking fore and aft. A man shifts the topsail tacks, and the booms swing over. The mate looks on with his hands in his pockets. Two men only are on deck. She never loses headway for an instant, but gains several lengths every time she tacks. Once around she will run from one to two points nearer to the wind than the ship [a point is 11.25 degrees]. For the coastwise and Gulf trades schooners are unequaled. The most profitable size for the coast trade is one that will carry 800 or 900 tons of coal. For the West India trade large ones are built, with great success. The whole question of rigging a ship is to get the necessary spread of canvas in the most convenient shape.[8]

The suitability of schooners for long voyages was also a subject for debate:

> It is said that men who have taken schooners to the East Indies once cannot be persuaded to do so again. After a gale of wind it is impossible to spread canvas to steady the vessel. In a schooner there are no braces to steady the gaffs, as there are on square-rigged ships to steady the yards. When a schooner is rolling around with no wind the sails sway and surge across the deck with a report like that of a cannon. The sails have to be lowered to keep from slatting out, and there the vessel lies wallowing in the swells like a porpoise. That is an experience to make any man sick. On a square-rigged vessel the lower topsails could be set.[9]

In any event, at least two schooners have circumnavigated the globe, although not without problems, and numerous schooners made transatlantic voyages, especially during World War I. Many schooners traveled to and from New England, South American, and West Indies ports in various trades. Captain Frank W. Peterson's comment about the *Alicia Crosby* includes a reference to potential schooner speeds: "She'd run in anything that ever blew, and I never had to heave her to . . . Her best passage of any length while I had her was from Fire Island to Cape Henry with an average of fourteen and a half knots. . . . In the Crosby we carried mostly coal and ice."[10] The ships built by ISC had the potential to make these speeds.

The *City of Orange* was built of southern yellow pine with live oak for the bow stem and stern and Oregon fir for spars (masts, booms, and gaffs). More than one million board feet of choice longleaf pine were worked into the ship.[11]

These vessels were of relatively deep draft, which results in a stronger structure, more resistant to hogging or longitudinal bending. The longleaf pine is somewhat stronger than loblolly or shortleaf pine and is, in fact, one of the strongest American woods.[12]

The fir picked for the spars was excellent because of its high strength-to-weight ratio, reducing weight aloft. The selection of five masts for this length schooner was on the conservative side, as many schooners this length and longer had only four masts. An additional mast in the same length vessel results in proportionally smaller sails, which reduces boom lengths, weights, and structural loads on each mast and the shrouds and stays. The gaff and topsails were attached to the masts with mast hoops, the usual technique in that era. The masts were more than two feet in diameter, and the booms and gaffs were approximately thirty-five feet long with a much longer spanker boom. The booms were twelve to fourteen inches in diameter and weighed as much as 1,100 pounds and more, with all the iron fittings. The gaffs were slightly smaller in diameter.

Fairbanks-Morse of Three Rivers, Michigan, built the auxiliary engines. FM entered the internal combustion engine field in 1893 and has been in the engine business ever since. The marine oil engines used on the *City of Orange* were four cylinders each with a 10.5-inch diameter bore and a 12-inch stroke, rated at 25 horsepower per cylinder, or 100 horsepower per engine at 340 rpm. The engines had a hot bulb in the head (initially heated with electric glow plugs or kerosene burners) into which the fuel was injected. Compressed air was used for engine starting.

The engines burned fuel oil but were not called diesel because the compression pressure was only 150 psi. These were two-cycle engines that used crankcase scavenging with intake and exhaust through cylinder wall ports. There was a bulkhead in the crankcase between each cylinder, so on the downstroke, the air was compressed sequentially for each cylinder.

Two compressed air storage tanks came with the engine, one for engine starting, and one to supply a ship's horn. Storage pressure relief was at 175 PSI, and air was supplied from an engine shaft compressor. An auxiliary system was recommended for the initial start and in case the tank volume was used up or lost.[13]

The *City of Orange* carried 32,000 gallons of fuel oil in tanks on deck and elsewhere. The fuel consumption for these engines was 400 gallons per day for both engines. This quantity of fuel combined with consumption resulted in 80 days' running time or, at 5 knots, 11,040 miles (all distances are in statute miles). Put another way, it was almost enough to get to Italy and back to Orange.

Normally, sailboat auxiliaries are not used continuously, as they are not needed if the winds are favorable. These engines required a lot of attention, as the forced nonrecirculating lubrication system was controlled by eight adjustable drip rates that differed, depending on the bearing. These would have to be readjusted frequently because of viscosity changes in the oil as the engines warmed up and as ambient temperatures changed.

There was a clutch to disconnect the screw from the engine gearbox. The function of the gear box was to allow reversing the rotational direction of the screw. The screw was approximately 2.5 feet in diameter, and the drag of two of these screws would be significant. The engines could be used to pick up speed before tacking in adverse conditions, and one engine could be reversed to provide some differential thrust in really bad conditions.

The subject of engine running was mentioned in a letter from the International Shipbuilding Company to Captain Wry with the following first sentence: "Please be advised that we have a clause in our Insurance Policies requiring a continuous running of your Motor Engines from the time you leave Port until you arrive at your destination."[14] This letter was not written until March 9, 1918, so what instructions, verbal or otherwise, were provided earlier to the masters is unknown. Aside from the insurance company requirements, running the engines may have been a way to negate some of the screw resistance. On the other hand, some captains might decide for themselves when to run the engines.

While the *City of Orange* was being constructed, more ships were started on adjacent ways. The next two to be completed were the *City of Houston* and the *City of Pensacola*. Piaggio's letterhead for his timber export business showed a branch office at Pensacola, Florida. Also, an Akin of Akin Loading Company of Pensacola attended the launching of the *City of Orange*, so perhaps business connections contributed to *City of Pensacola*'s name. The only visible Houston, Texas, connection was a

fig. 2.1. The City
of Orange
ready to sail.
Courtesy Dr.
Howard C.
Williams
Collection

J. W. Linkl "formerly of Orange, but now a leading business man of Houston," according to the newspaper article covering the launching of the *City of Orange*, cited earlier in this chapter. Later, the letterhead for the International Shipbuilding Company, builder of subsequent ships for Piaggio, showed a Marine Iron Works of Houston, Texas.

The *City of Houston* can be seen in the background on the ways behind the *City of Orange* in figure 2.1. This picture came from a postcard that had been modified. The ship name on the bow is much too large, and it appears that the modifier also added two yards to the foremast. This ship was not a barkentine, and the yards seemed to be in the wrong places vertically for a topsail schooner, however, the possibility cannot be totally ruled out. Since various masts are mentioned throughout the book, figure 2.1 is a good reference for mast names, which were not as consistent as most people believe. From the bow aft the mast names usually are fore, main, mizzen, jigger, and spanker.[15]

The ship in this photograph, sitting low in the water, is loaded with lumber in the holds and on deck and is ready for her maiden voyage. It also appears that two large fuel tanks run across deck just forward of the mainmast, eliminating deck storage of lumber in this region.

THE *CITY OF HOUSTON*

The Certificate of Registry for the *City of Houston* was issued July 28, 1917, at Port Arthur, Texas, listing the only owner as the City of Houston Ship Company of Gulfport, Mississippi.[16] The documentation

TABLE 3. COMPARISONS OF FIRST THREE SHIPS

Ship	Rig, masts	L (ft.)	B (ft.)	D (ft.)	G.T.	N.T.	DWT	Crew	Registration Date
City of Orange	Sch., 5	226.2	43	22.5	1632	1360	2450	15	Apr. 23, 1917
City of Houston	Bkt., 4	227.6	43.8	22.7	1519	1335	2280	16	July 28, 1917
City of Pensacola	Sch., 4	171.2	37	15.3	705	602	1060	10	Sept. 6, 1917

L= Length B= Breadth D= Depth of hold G.T.= Gross tonnage N.T.= Net tonnage

listed four masts, a billet head, and an elliptic stern, with a register length of 227.6 feet.

Each of the first three ships differed either in rig or size, as can be seen in table 3. The first two were similar in size, but, as mentioned earlier, the *City of Orange* was a five-masted schooner and the *City of Houston* was a four-masted barkentine. F. H. Swails was also listed as the builder for this ship on the Master Carpenter's Certificate.

fig. 2.2. The City
of Houston
with sails up.
Courtesy
Dr. Howard
C. Williams
Collection

The *City of Houston* was photographed with all of her sails up, a rarity, and the only such picture found of the fourteen ships built. She was docked as opposed to sailing, but her sail plan is defined very well in figure 2.2. As can be seen in the photograph, the *City of Houston* had four headsails and five square sails on the foremast. She had a spike bowsprit approximately thirty-five feet long, but no jibboom, which is a conservative design choice that keeps the enormous forestay and headsail loads closer to the bow. The ship had two and possibly three staysails between the foremast and mainmast. The spars were in the same size range as those on the *City of Orange*.

The aft end of the ship is significantly different from other, similar size sailing ships. Notice the raised poop from abaft the mizzen mast toward but not to the stern, leaving a protected area for the wheel and helmsman. It is well-protected forward, but exposed to following weather. This dropped poop was used on some of the subsequent five-masted barkentines also. Tonnage listed for the poop was 83.41, or 8,341 cubic feet, and utilization of this space probably included the officers' quarters, sail stowage, and fuel tanks. Crew quarters, the donkey engine, and the galley were forward.

THE *CITY OF PENSACOLA*

The *City of Pensacola* was the smallest of the fourteen vessels built and was closer in size to the more than four hundred four-masted schooners built along the East Coast and in the Gulf of Mexico. Her Certificate of Registry was issued September 6, 1917, at Port Arthur to the only owner, the City of Pensacola Ship Company, incorporated under the laws of the state of Mississippi.[17] Her length was 45 feet less than the two preceding ships, and she had a smaller crew of nine. She also had two of the 100-horsepower Fairbanks-Morse marine oil engines, and her net tonnage was less than half of the first two ships at 602 tons. A rather poor picture of the ship indicated she had the schooner's typically long bowsprit with jibboom and martingale.[18]

Each of these three ships had either tragic or exciting careers, depending on the vessel and one's perspective. To the owners, tragic; to the participants, exciting and, in some cases, painful; and to the reader, an epic stranger than most fiction.

Eleven Barkentines

The next eleven ships were unique, and an introduction to barkentines is in order. Although not used extensively, the barkentine rig had been around for a long time. The original definition of a barkentine was a vessel having three masts, the foremast square-rigged like the bark, but the main and mizzen fore-and-aft rigged.[1]

The definition eventually was applied to all vessels square-rigged on the foremast with any number of after masts (except one, which is a brigantine) fore-and-aft rigged. At least one six-masted barkentine was built, the *Everett C. Griggs*, renamed the *E. R. Sterling*.[2] The *David Dows*, built in 1881 at Toledo, Ohio, was called a five-masted schooner but was a barkentine.[3]

Unlike the East Coast, the Gulf Coast did not have a history of building large sailing ships. Agricultural products were the same along the coast, so there was little demand for large cargo carriers. Big schooners were built in the Northeast to go south along the eastern seaboard and haul southern pine lumber from Georgia, the Carolinas, and Virginia back up north for building more ships. They also carried pilings, poles, railroad ties, and other construction materials.

Another major cargo going north and south was coal, which was transported regularly from Newport News and other coal ports. Coal was used in enormous quantities by northern cities and to a lesser extent in the South, directly by industry and for domestic uses. Manufactured gas producers were another major consumer, prior to the availability of natural gas. In earlier days, ice was sometimes carried, but with the advent of mechanical refrigeration, ships frequently went south in ballast (soil or other material to help stabilize the ship). Occasionally they might carry quarry products, but most of their trade was in southern forestry, coal, agriculture products, and phosphate rock from Florida. The population density was also much lower on the Gulf Coast than on the eastern seaboard.

A limiting factor along the Texas Gulf Coast, except for Galveston and Port Arthur, was the lack of deepwater ports and channels until the mid-teens of the twentieth century. The major rivers all had relatively shallow bars at the entrance, limiting vessel draft, and the rivers and bays themselves were not much deeper. These restrictions were very much evidenced in the Texas-designed and built vessels of chapter 1.

BARKENTINES

Maritime experts thought highly of the barkentine, and the topmost authorities in the United States were prepared to stand behind their convictions in 1905. The Sewalls of Bath, Maine, built and operated deepwater windjammers for eighty years; their last ten sailing ships were steel and, except for two, were all more than 300 feet long. These ten ships were built between 1894 and 1902 and were the only fleet of steel deepwater ships sent overboard from an American shipyard. Six were managed by the Sewalls, three were built for Standard Oil Company of New York, and one was built for Pacific Coast interests.[4] All were square-riggers except for one five-masted schooner that circumnavigated the globe with some considerable difficulties. None of these ships had any mechanical propulsion and only one was lost by natural causes—and that one without a trace.

One of these ships sailed out of Port Arthur, Texas, from 1916 to 1922. The *Edward Sewall* was purchased by Texaco in 1916 because of the wartime shortage of shipping. At the same time, a subsidiary of Texaco was building steel ships for the United States Shipping Board at the old Sewall and New England yards in Bath, Maine.[5]

In 1903, after all of the steel ships were in operation, the Sewall yard closed down. Two years later, Hawaiian sugar interests proposed that they build a five-masted, fully rigged ship with a deadweight capacity of 8,000 tons for the sugar trade, similar to the large German nitrate ships. Samuel S. and William D. Sewall were managing the company at that time, and, though they were very interested in building more ships, voiced their objections to what they considered a somewhat risky venture. These objections were based on several factors, such as being unable to enter some ports—including Philadelphia, the main sugar receiving port—under low-water conditions because of the ship's draft, insurance costs, the difficulty of finding consignees for other cargoes, and the probability of having to sail to Hawaii in ballast.

Mark W. Hennessy wrote in *The Sewall Ships of Steel:*

One of the most serious objections, however, would be the ability of properly manning such a vessel with competent seamen. Owing to the decay of our mercantile marine, masters and officers have been growing less available for the past fifteen or twenty years, and we hardly have what can be called, truthfully, an American seaman, the most of crews being composed of men of foreign nationalities and a mixture of these in every crew. In shipping at any of our United States ports of a crew of say twenty-four so called able seamen, about one-third of these are really able seamen, possibly one-third ordinary seamen, and very ordinary at that, and the remaining third composed of men who have hardly acquired the sea habit and no seamanship at all. . . .

As an alternative, A. Sewall & Co. proposed construction of a 5-masted steel barkentine. Their appraisal of her prospects as a money-maker—and after all, vessels are built to make money—stand in emphatic contrast to the lack of prospects that, in their judgment, killed the 8,000-ton ship proposition as a practical venture. In a letter to their Honolulu friends and prospective associates, they referred to plans run off for them by B. B. Crowninshield of Boston, designer of the ill-fated 7-masted steel schooner *Thomas W. Lawson* that Fore River launched in 1902.

The Sewalls' letter indicated that the plans showed a steel five-masted barkentine, 332 feet long, with fine lines, large sail power, and a cargo capacity for 6000 tons of sugar. The ship would be equipped with 2100 tons of water ballast, saving considerable time and expense in ballast handling. A crew of twenty-four including four boys or apprentices would man the ship. The Sewalls thought this vessel would be as fast or faster than a square-rigged ship with only two-thirds the crew.

The company went on to estimate that the ship would return about 13.5 percent on its cost annually. The ship was never built, but these comments are expert opinions that possibly contributed to ISC's decision to build all barkentines after the first three ships. Regardless of why the decision was made, it appears well founded.[6]

Some disadvantages come with barkentines, including the need for a few higher qualified sailors and officers for the square sails, even if only on one mast. The ship may also be harder to tack, especially in heavy air, for the square sails will be laid aback in those conditions, as the ship comes up head to wind. The resistance to tacking is not as strong for a barkentine as for a three-or-four-masted square-rigger but is still present. In this situation the two engines could be used to pick up speed before the tack and to provide some differential thrust during the tack by reversing one engine. Even though the engines are of low power, with two screws separated by several feet, a strong turning moment exists in this mode of operation. Whether the ship was going forward, standing still, or even going backwards temporarily, the differential thrust would turn the ship unless the winds were very high. In that case the square sails would probably already have been furled. The other option was to wear ship, which was a downwind maneuver that generally lost considerable up wind distance, analogous to a controlled jibe in a smaller vessel. On long ocean voyages, changing tacks usually would not be required frequently.

THE MASTER CARPENTER FOR THE BARKENTINES

A northern marine historian and author, Paul C. Morris, wrote: "Except for the shipbuilders in New Jersey, Delaware and Maryland, most of the companies which launched four masted schooners south of New England were 'Johnnie-come-latelies' who tried to profit by decreasing the shortage of vessels caused by World War One. The vast majority of these companies had little or no experience in building sailing vessels of this size and much of their knowledge had to be imported from states to the north or west."[7]

Texans had been building both work and racing boats for years, including many two- and three-masted schooners, and, though generally not as large as ships built elsewhere, the skilled men and experience were available in Texas.

ISC fit in the category of "latelies," but they did not need to import Yankee builders. In fact, they did not stop at four masts but went on to five, with square sails on the foremast at that. No other yard in the country came close to building this many five-masted ships in the time frame that ISC did, let alone barkentines. The man responsible for this was not a northerner but a native saltwater Texan by the name of John Leonard Bludworth.

His father, Bernard Leonard Bludworth, moved to Texas and worked on Matagorda Island at the Joe Haas Ranch. John Leonard Bludworth was born there in 1867. Later, the family moved to Cape Carlas, where the father had obtained land. This was a very isolated area surrounded by water and was not much above sea level. The area is now Bludworth Island and is shown on maps and charts as such, a few miles northeast of Rockport, Texas. The family moved to Rockport where the father started a sheet metal and plumbing shop. Two of his sons, just barely in their twenties, started a boatyard at Rockport for boat repair and construction. They were also seriously involved in building fast boats as well as racing.

Rockport and other coastal cities held sailboat races frequently, and these regattas attracted large crowds. Excerpts from a Rockport newspaper in 1893 are enlightening. The yacht races drew immense crowds, including a load of excursionists aboard the steamcraft *Hoyt* from Ropersville.

Novice, a Rockport boat built and owned by the Bludworth brothers, was 32 feet long, with a beam of 13 feet and a draft of 3 feet, 10 inches. She carried a main sail and standing jib of 200 square yards (1,800 square feet) besides a spinnaker sail and balloon jib. This is a substantial sail plan compared to contemporary boats; however, the wider beam and heavier wood construction allowed large sail areas. These boats also had several reef options. Serious racing sailors tend to carry as much sail area as prudence allows or, in today's world, as the rules permit.

The *Novice* carried off all honors in every race she entered. Another competitor, the *Viola Vaughn*, after winning many races at Galveston, came to Rockport to defend the Texas cup against the *Alice*. Following defeat in the three-day regatta, the *Viola Vaughn* made Corpus Christi her home.

The *Wasp* of Galveston, which came up for the express purpose of taking the wind out of the *Novice*'s sails and placing it in the class of a back number, was a northern-built craft, or, in the words of the Rockport people, "a Yankee boat." A sailboat-racing handicap system existed, as some variations in dimensions were present, and the *Novice* had to give the *Wasp* seven minutes in each race. This caused the betting odds on the first day to be even. The windward leg of five miles went to the *Novice*, more than eight minutes ahead of the *Wasp*.

The *Novice* won both races handily, along with $150. The odds changed from being even the first day of racing to 10 to 1 in favor of *Novice* on the second day's racing, which she again won. An article in the *Rockport Pilot* reported, "The lady visitors exchanged a great deal of money on the races yesterday and today. The Rockport people say the boat that beats the *Novice* is yet to be made."[8] Figure 3.1 shows the *Novice* crossing the finish line. John L. Bludworth is at the helm and his brother Jim is out at the end of that very long bowsprit. Though it sounds like a contradiction in terms, "Cat sloop" was the correct terminology for this type boat.

In September of 1894, John L. Bludworth with the cat sloop *Novice*, won the Texas State Challenge Cup presented by the Aransas Pass Yacht Club. Tiffany and Company of New York made the sterling silver cup.[9] It was a very expensive and prestigious trophy and an indication of the importance Texans placed on sailboat racing in the late nineteenth century. The cup is currently on loan by the Bludworth family to the Museum of Fine Arts in Houston, Texas.

fig. 3.1. The cat sloop Novice. Courtesy Texas Maritime Museum

Eventually, J. L. Bludworth migrated up the coast to Galveston. He and his brothers had a boatyard there, and one of the many vessels built by him was the *Galvez*, an excursion boat. This vessel was an oil screw, eighty-nine feet long, built in 1914.[10] It foundered forty-two years later in Bayou Bienvenue, St. Bernard Parish, Louisiana, on October 31, 1956.[11] Bludworth built many other wooden vessels, along with overhauling and repairing boats. It is said that the best way to learn to build boats is to repair older ones, as that is usually more difficult than starting from the keel up. Bludworth went to work for ISC sometime in 1917 as the master carpenter for the eleven barkentines, and he carved the half model for the *Monfalcone*, a tribute to his expertise.

THE INTERNATIONAL SHIPBUILDING COMPANY YARD

The next eleven ships built by the ISC in Orange, Texas, were a continuation of the previous operation. The yard had the necessary large woodworking equipment for this construction. These tools included the cut-off saws, band saws, shapers, planers, and drill presses for fabricating the complex shapes of stems and stern posts, frames, deck beams, ceilings, hull planking and decking, and all of the other components necessary to build ships.

Large logs were squared into timbers (20 inches by 24 inches and larger) before delivery to the yard, where they were kept in a penned-up area of the river to prevent drying out and splitting. Electric motor-driven cranes (with tongs similar to ice tongs) on overhead monorails were used to carry the timbers from the river to work areas at the head of the ways, as shown in figure 3.2.

Figure 3.3 shows the timbers being moved to the woodworking tools with the aid of chain hoists on overhead tracks and side and longitudinal roller systems to facilitate movement. Other pictures from the period show numerous outside covered shops and at least one well-equipped inside shop, as shown in figure 3.4. A boat in frame about 25 feet long is visible in the back of the shop.

The ways were straddled by gantry cranes that were used to move construction elements from the woodworking areas at the head of the ways to the proper place along the keel. After being cut, the frames

*fig. 3.2. Monorail
for timber handling.*
Courtesy
Bludworth
Collection

were assembled on a framing stage at the head of the ways and then erected and squared with both the centerline of the ship and the top of the keel.

Figure 3.5, in a view looking forward, shows a gantry crane lowering a beam into one of the hulls. This demonstrates one of the many advantages of this type of crane, in this case the proximity of the crane operator to the positioning of the load.

The next several figures show hulls ready for launching or being launched. (Ships are not shown in the order constructed.)

A narrow gage rail system was used for moving materials and equipment to and from the various facilities. The yard was very well engineered for the job at hand. One of the ships with a gantry crane astride, and one on the adjacent ways is shown in figure 3.6. The ship's size can be discerned by noting the workers at the bottom of the vessel. This ship is almost ready for launching, as the christening platform is in place. The gantry cranes, though not absolutely required, expedited construction, and the several that are in place indicate the desire that ISC had for speed in building their ships.

fig. 3.3. Timber movement to woodworking equipment. Courtesy Bludworth Collection

A panoramic view (see figure 3.7) of the shipyard, taken in 1918, shows, in part, the magnitude of the ISC operation. At least six ships are under construction prior to launching, and two five-masted barkentines are in the water being fitted out. ISC was not a participant in the wooden steamship-building program of World War I and these vessels were all five-masted barkentines. These numbers were determined by a count that two current shipbuilders and I made from the original picture, which is forty inches wide. Four gantry cranes can be seen in the picture. A sawdust collection system also traverses the scene. The site of the yard is approximately 4,500 feet long and is from 500 to 1,500 feet wide, thus allowing room for at least six ways in addition to the other facilities. By getting an early start, Piaggio was able to get this elaborate facility built before inevitable wartime shortages occurred, which would have made such a program impossible.

None of the Texas yards building wooden steamships for World War I had gantry cranes; they used gin poles and stationary cranes instead. Nathan R. Lipfert, of the Maine Maritime Museum and very knowledgeable in maritime construction techniques, stated: "I have never seen gantry cranes used in that fashion in any other shipyard, either for

fig. 3.4. Woodworking shop with overhead belt drive. Courtesy Bludworth Collection

*fig. 3.5. View
forward in
hull with gantry
crane in use.*
Courtesy
Bludworth
Collection

wood or steel construction, I suppose because of the problem of using it after the superstructure is erected, or the rig installed."[12]

As previously mentioned, the ISC ships were launched as early as possible to get another ship started, and deckhouses, masts, and rigging were built up and installed after the vessel was in the water. The gantry cranes were an efficient method of moving large structural timbers to the exact location needed, and the crane operator was in an excellent spot to control the operation. This is especially true when compared to the traditional gin pole and shear leg operations. Gantry cranes are still seen in trade magazines astride big ships in some of the larger shipyards. Local shipbuilders indicated the gantry crane is the best way to go for ship construction from both operational and safety considerations. It is probable that any yard in the country, getting the obvious financial support that ISC had, would have set up a similar operation, unless they allowed tradition and conservatism to get in the way of progress.

Figure 3.8 shows the *Macerata* framed and the gantry crane providing a timber. Here, three gantry cranes are seen, along with the track for one and the enclosed house for the crane operator.

ISC also had their own sail loft, as seen in figure 3.9. The loft had the large, polished wooden-floor area needed for efficient and clean sailmaking. Sewing machines are along the left side, and bolt rope materials are also visible. An overhead cable and pulley is installed to facilitate handling of the very heavy and cumbersome sails (some of the spanker sails were about 55 by 50 feet and the forecourse larger). In the center right are storage bins for finished sails.

Each of the eleven barkentines had four headsails, five square sails on the foremast, and three staysails between the foremast and mainmast. In addition, each ship had four gaffsails and four topsails, for a total of twenty sails plus spares. A minimum total for the eleven barkentines is 220 sails without spares, which, of course, were necessary. The first three ships add another forty-four sails for a total of 264 sails, plus a substantial number of spares. Even though the making of sails was spread out over a period of three years, it still was a massive task, considering the size of most of the sails.

As the various ships returned to Orange, repairs and sail replacement would also be required. Sail covers are seen on the gaff sails in several pictures, and making them was another job for the sailmaker.

A broadside view of the *City of Orleans*, which is one of the ships having lengths in the 280-foot range, permitted scaling some dimensions to

fig. 3.6. Macerata *ready to launch.* Courtesy Bludworth Collection

approximate spar lengths and sail areas. The total mast heights, from the bulwarks to the top, were about 112 feet. Lower masts were 70 feet above the bulwarks and topmasts (main aft) 52 feet long with about 10 feet of doublings. Booms were in the range of 42 feet long with a spanker boom about 60 feet long. A conservative estimate of the sail area is 20,000 square feet based on calculations using scaled dimensions.

Like the *City of Orange*, mast heights were on the conservative side; boom lengths, however, were as long as those on schooners of similar size.

One point of interest concerns the *City of Lafayette*. A picture at the Texas Maritime Museum shows a barkentine being launched with the *City of Shreveport* painted on the transom, but the picture was labeled *City of Lafayette*. No records were to be found for a *City of Shreveport*. Why the name was changed is a mystery, although owners are not committed to a name until submission of the Application of Owner or Master for Official Number is made.

Another picture (figure 3.10) of one of the later built barkentines shows more interesting details. It shows the aft deckhouse and a wheelhouse on top of the poop deck instead of the exposed wheel in the open. All sails appear to be on (furled), including the gaff topsails. With magnification, twelve topsail mast hoops can be counted, typical for this size vessel. One can also see steamship-type deck ventilators to provide air to the engine room and quarters.

A port bow view of the *City of Galveston* at her launching is shown in figure 3.11. The tug *John Sealy* is toward the stern, a floating timber pen is seen to the right side, and four mast doublings are in the foreground. Downtown Orange is in the background, with the Holland Hotel at the right. Scaffolding chocks are still on the hull, and much work remains to be done before the ship is ready to sail; this explains the several weeks' interval between launching and issuance of the Certificate of Registry.

All of the barkentines were listed as having a billet head and an el-

fig. 3.7. Panoramic view of ISC shipyard. Courtesy Johnny Bludworth

liptic stern. The early barkentines had an exposed wheel in a dropped deck behind the poop, similar to the *City of Houston* in figure 2.2.

Later ships had a raised poop going all the way to the transom with a fairly large enclosed wheelhouse on the poop deck. This design did not start until after the *City of Dallas*, the fourth five-masted barkentine. The poop deck area was surrounded by a rather ornamental balustrade (taff rail) in both designs, which was typical at the time. The full poop deck and balustrade are seen quite well in a photograph of the *City of Galveston* (figure 3.12).

This is the outfitting dock where the masts are stepped, rigging attached, and the booms, gaffs, and yards, are installed. The husky sheer leg structure (A-frame) is used for these operations along with putting aboard engines, fuel and water tanks, and all of the other heavy items. The long spanker boom can be seen extending out over the ship's stern, and davits for one of the ship's boats are also on the stern. A lifeboat on davits is located forward on the port bow, and other pictures showed a lifeboat on the starboard side. Each of the ships had three lifeboats located similarly.

When the gaff is raised, two halyards are used, the gaff peak halyard and throat halyard. The gaff peak halyards had three single blocks per gaff, and the gaff throat halyard usually had treble blocks. Since a donkey engine was aboard for this task, the heavy gaffs and sails could be easily raised.

Another cosmetic difference between the two ships is that the recessed band at bulwarks level, from the stern to the bow, becomes narrower at the bow on the *City of Galveston* and is of constant height on most of the other ships. This is much more visible in figure 3.11.

Ladies awaiting the *Monfalcone* launch are shown in figure 3.13. Master carpenter John Bludworth's daughter Bernice Bludworth is in the middle of the front row and his niece Marybell Bludworth is behind her. Bludworth carved the half model for this ship, which may be why his relatives were present for the launch.

Another photograph (figure 3.14) shows the *Macerata* as it is starting to be snubbed by the cable coming out of the hawse pipe. Drag chains on the right side of the picture slow and stabilize the ship during the launch. Other pictures indicate there were two or three sets of these chains on both sides of the ship to slow the hull down and maintain control. Two wooden steamships are seen on the left side of the picture.

All of the ISC ships with engines had tankage for fuel oil and, where listed, the quantity was from 25,000 to 32,000 gallons. This information appears only on the back of the Application for Official Number, and that page could not be found for the first four ships. Documentation for the next three ships—the *City of Mobile*, the *City of Beaumont*, and the *City of Dallas*—showed that they carried 1,250 to 1,350 gallons of gasoline with a consumption rate of three, ten, and two gallons per 24-hour period, respectively, which indicated that the answer was not really known with any degree of accuracy. Later vessels did not list any gasoline; however, that side of the form was never filled out very accurately, and the answers were inconsistent, if answered at all.

The first four ships probably had gasoline; however, the documents that might corroborate this information were not found. Some, and possibly all, of the ships had at least one lifeboat that was gasoline-engine-powered. Motor generator sets, though crude compared to current technology, were available, and Fairbanks-Morse, the propulsion engine supplier, had such systems in both gasoline and oil. It is also possible that the later ships had gasoline or fuel oil donkeys.

Paralleling the massive operation at Orange, Texas, two ship hulls were built at a yard in Beaumont, Texas, approximately twenty-five miles to the west. These were the *City of Beaumont* and the *City of Dallas*. A prelaunch photograph of the *City of Beaumont* shows, from left to right, Frank Alvey, official, First National Bank at Beaumont; John L. Bludworth, master carpenter; Mary Anna Crary, sponsor; Robert Parker, her escort; Mrs. Nathan N. Crary; Mrs. Will Alvey, sister-in-law of Frank Alvey; Una Washington, Mrs. Crary's niece from Houston; Una's "date," name unknown; and Nathan N. Crary, yard superintendent (figure 3.15).

Mary Anna (Crary) Anderson provided the names of the individuals

45

Eleven Barkentines

fig. 3.9. ISC sail loft. Courtesy Bludworth Collection

*fig. 3.10.
Completed
barkentine at the
ISC dock.*
Courtesy
National
Archives

in this photograph and pointed out that this listing shows that these launches were not big, civic-leader-attended events and were fairly routine. With the large number of ships being launched in the Orange-Beaumont area, it's little wonder that they were no longer looked upon as exceptional events.

The picture shows two rather significant additions at the bow compared to the other ships ISC built at Orange. One is the lumber ports on each side of the hull just above the bobstays and close to the bow stem. On the East Coast, schooners for the lumber trade were outfitted with lumber ports to permit the loading and unloading of long timbers directly into and out of the holds. These hatches had to be carefully re-placed after use and securely fastened and caulked before the ship went to sea. Another difference at the bow not on the other ISC ships was four bobstays instead of three. This was not a major difference but indicates that other design ideas were imposed on these two ships.

The photograph also shows where thicker planking on the hull starts (the white diagonal line running to the lumber hatch), and similar thicker planking can be seen on other ships, including the wooden steamships. Numbers indicating the depth of water the ship is drawing can be seen along the bow stem. This ship drew twenty-five feet loaded and seventeen feet in ballast, according to her Application for Official Number.[13] The bobstays would all be under water when the ship was loaded.

The arrangements for billeting and machinery were not described but probably followed traditional locations. The captain and other ship's officers lived aft, and the crew slept forward. The galley was forward, and the donkey engine was usually located on the starboard side of the forward house with the crew in the port side.

fig. 3.11. City of Galveston *launching.* Courtesy Bludworth Collection

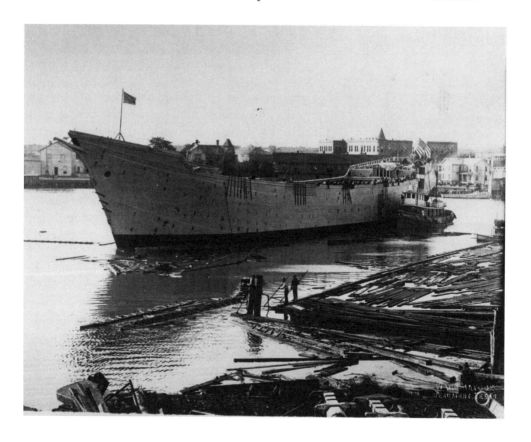

The propulsion engines would be aft and below deck, and the exhaust would be vertical with an elbow directing the exhaust away from any nearby sails. Fairbanks-Morse recommended that the two engine exhausts impinge downward into a common larger pipe with water circulating though the bottom to extinguish any exhaust sparks. The 100 horsepower engines required six-to-eight-inch exhausts, and the 200 horsepower engines called for eight-to-ten-inch exhausts. The 100 horsepower engines had a clutch and reverse gear for going astern, whereas the 200 horsepower engines had a clutch, but were direct reversible.[14]

Scaffolding on the ways to the far left surrounds another ship, the *City of Dallas.* After the ships were launched they were towed to Orange for fitting out.

Mary Anna C. Anderson, daughter of the Beaumont yard superintendent and the sponsor for the *City of Beaumont* launching, graciously provided information concerning her father and the launching:

Nathan N. (Nate) Crary was the secretary of the Texas Tram and Lumber Company and later owner of the Texas Arm and Pin

*fig. 3.13. Ladies
before launching of*
Monfalcone.
Courtesy
Bludworth
Collection

Company, manufacturers of arms and pins for telephone poles. In
his timber lexicon, longleaf yellow pine was treasure and loblolly
was a dirty word. I imagine his business experience and knowledge
of timber was the reason for his position as superintendent of
Piaggio's Beaumont Shipyard. I wonder what my father would say
if he knew how much the family heirs received recently for a stand
of loblolly?

I don't remember who coached me about breaking the bottle of
champagne, but it was demonstrated how to pinch the bottle gen-
tly and swing it gracefully by its three satin streamers, red, white,
and blue. When the whistle for the moment blew I grabbed the
bottle by its neck and bashed it on the bar of iron pipe suspended
from the ship by ribbons. The ship got a good bath of foam at the
words, "I christen thee . . ." She slid silently, stern first. This is always a sacred, heart-gripping moment of a launching. I once knew
a minister who objected to this kind of talk, especially the use of
the word "christening." Perhaps he was never on a ship at sea, and
certainly never a sailor.

The *City of Dallas* sponsor was an older girl, about eighteen,
and she followed the orders to be dainty. The bottle hanging from
the prow didn't break, so some men on the ship pulled it by its ribbons and broke it on the ship as it was sliding down the ways. So
much for sailors' superstitions—poor *City of Dallas!*

The Beaumont yard was not called International Shipbuilding, it was called Piaggio Shipyard. It was located on a point of land where the Neches River made a sharp turn to circumvent an island. This is part of the Port of Beaumont now.

Anderson described the end of the launch, relating that the *City of Beaumont* poked her stern into the island. She considers a launch photograph a prophetic scene because the *City of Beaumont* was built too late in time. To quote the late Frank Karppi, "Despite the beauty of sail, the challenge to seamanship and all the things that make sailing ships appealing—their time was passing, if not past in 1918. The steamship was beginning to replace, entirely, the sailer." The picture referred to is prophetic because in it the *City of Beaumont*, just launched, so clean and new and lovely, is dwarfed by a big black steamship, emitting black smoke, passing within a few feet.

Anderson received a gift from Piaggio: "The card that accompanied the gift to me as sponsor bore in ink the name of Henry Piaggio; on reverse,

City of Beaumont, March 16, 1918. The gift was a lavaliere hung from a gold chain by a short length of pearls and was a diamond in a triangle of three oblong sapphires. Though it sounds lavish it was not a large piece, appropriate for a little girl."[15]

Another interesting fact reported by Anderson was that cabinetwork on the ship was performed by Ole Didriksen, an accomplished and proud craftsman and foreman at the Piaggio shipyard. He was the father of Babe Didrikson Zaharias (an "o" was substituted for the "e" in Didrikson after the 1932 Olympics), the famous woman athlete who excelled at several sports from the 1930s through the 1950s.

Except for a ride on the ship as she was towed from Beaumont to Orange, Anderson never saw the *City of Beaumont* again. But she has always maintained a strong and dedicated interest in any news pertaining to the ship.

Another view of the ship in the water is shown in figure 3.16. Here the head knees terminating in the billet head can be readily seen. This picture gives the best view of the poop area. A skylight is in the center

fig. 3.15. City of Beaumont *launching.* Courtesy Bludworth Collection

forward area of the poop deck and a stairwell (ladder) housing is to the right.

Table 4 gives the completion dates and the more significant dimensions and capacities for each of the eleven ships, along with the engine configuration. The first four ships were close in size and capacity, while the following seven ships were increased in length by approximately 30 feet. This increased the net and deadweight tonnage substantially. With the length increases, the two auxiliary engines were increased from 100 horsepower each to 200 horsepower each.

Notice that the depth of hold dimensions are less than the draft dimensions which might appear to be a reversal of what would be expected. Since these same numbers are repeated for all of the barkentines and on more than one document, a reversal is not the answer. The draft measurement encompasses several significant dimensions not included in the inside measurement for the depth of hold. These are the keel projecting below the hull a foot or so; the hull planking several inches thick; the frames at least a foot and probably more; and the floor ceiling several inches thick. Although the barkentines were single decked they had cross timbers a few feet below the deck and it is possible that

fig. 3.16. The City
of Beaumont in
the Neches River.
Courtesy
Bludworth
Collection

TABLE 4. DATA ON ELEVEN BARKENTINES

Ship	L (ft.)	B (ft.)	D (ft.)	Net tons	DWT	Draft Loaded (ft.)
City of Gulfport	251.3	45.1	22.0	1672	3000	24
City of Mobile	250.2	45.2	22.4	1777.96	3000	24
City of Beaumont	254.2	45.6	22.4	1802	3000	25
City of Dallas	255.2	45.3	22.1	1760	3000	24
City of Austin	281.8	45.5	23.2	2032	3600	25
City of Galveston	282.0	45.9	22.0	2060	3600	25
City of Orleans	283.0	45.9	22.4	2137	3600	24
City of Lafayette	285.7	45.7	22.7	2227	3600	24
City of Waco	NA	NA	NA	NA	NA	NA
Macerata	282.0	45.2	22.4	2190	NA	NA
Monfalcone	282.4	45.8	23.0	2270	NA	NA

Data for *City of Waco* was reportedly very similar to the other larger barkentines.

the depth of hold measurement was made to the bottom of these structures again reducing the depth of hold measurement significantly.

The four-cylinder, 200 horsepower engines had a bore of 14 inches and a stroke of 18 inches. These engines did not require a gearbox as they were direct reversing.[16] The increased horsepower and lower speed of only 250 RPM resulted in a screw almost four feet in diameter.

The last two barkentines did not have engines installed. All of the ships were of the same breadth at 45 feet, with a register depth of 22 feet with some minor variations, the most being plus 1.0 feet.

Two marine historians, in a of recent book, stated in reference to shipbuilding in Maine: "The *Bertha L. Downs* and her sisters the big American multi-masted schooners were the only large, wooden mer-

TABLE 5. ISC SHIPS AND TONNAGE BUILT BY YEAR

Year	Ships Built	Net Tonnage	Deadweight Tonnage
1917	3	3,297	5,790
1918	4	7,012	12,000
1919	7	15,116	25,200
Totals	14	25,425	42,990

chant sailing ships in history built in relatively highly capitalized, well-equipped and well-organized big yards equipped with a great deal of machinery."[17]

For just a time, the most highly capitalized and well-organized big yard equipped with a great deal of advanced electrical machinery was in Orange, Texas, and not in New England. The yard not only existed but successfully built fourteen large multi-masted sailing ships in a little over three years. Table 5 summarizes the ship construction completed.

Being able to construct a yard of this magnitude was a major engineering feat in itself. Because Piaggio was working to the Italian war calendar, he got started in 1915, before steel and all of the other materials and equipment required became scarce, as they inevitably do in wartime.

Never before or since has this number and size of sailing ships been built as one enterprise at one yard (two hulls built at Beaumont) anywhere in the world. The Texas builders applied advanced multiple hull production techniques to a relatively obsolete form of transportation and turned out five-masted barkentines at an unprecedented rate.

The Maiden Voyage
of the City of Orange

The fourteen ships were initially built to haul pine timber to Italy, and that was the cargo for the maiden voyage of the *City of Orange*. But even before sailing, minor problems arose with the government.

A DOSE OF BUREAUCRACY

The United States declared war on Germany on April 6, 1917; however, Piaggio was already committed to supplying Italy with Gulf Coast pine lumber long before that date. Italy entered the war on May 23, 1915, and Piaggio got his shipbuilding operations under way in early 1916 with the *City of Orange*.

The Application for Official Number was submitted March 17, 1917, and the owners were in a rush to load, for on March 20, a customs collector at Port Arthur and official of the Department of Commerce by the name of R. E. Latimer sent a telegram to the Commissioner of Navigation, Washington, D.C.: "Have mailed application for official number catalog number thirteen twenty for schooner City of Orange on receipt of same please wire me number allotted as owners desire to carve same in hatches before putting on deck load answer collect."[1] The ship was to have a deck load, which was customary for lumber ships.

The International Shipbuilding Company was surprised to learn that the government applied steamship rules to any vessel having propulsion engines of any type. This required three licensed steamship mates and two licensed engineers in addition to a master holding steamship papers. Now the ship had operating engineers and three mates, which made for a larger crew than most five-masted schooners would have; however, only the captain, one mate, and one engineer met the steam license requirements. A sailing ship without engines only required a qualified captain and a licensed operating engineer if they had a steam donkey engine; however, the propulsion engines and not the donkey engine caused this problem.

Piaggio had a friend in Congress, the Honorable J. P. Harrison, and on April 12, 1917, a telegram was sent to him by Roy McInnis, an official of ISC. He objected to the application of the steam requirements to an auxiliary sailing vessel, indicated the company had made extensive searches for qualified officers, and asked whether the congressman could suggest any solution. He also pointed out the importance of keeping vessels on the move and emphasized the seriousness of the matter.

The next communication on this issue was a letter dated April 13, 1917, from E. F. Sweet, the assistant secretary for the Bureau of Navigation, to Congressman Harrison. Referring to the telegram, Sweet indicated he had instructed the collector of customs at Port Arthur, Texas, that if the vessel cleared without the full complement of licensed officers, the department would give full consideration to mitigating circumstances, provided the collector was satisfied that such licensed officers were not available.

The next letter on Piaggio's lumber company letterhead at Gulfport, dated May 21, 1917, was to the secretary of commerce and contained a sworn statement signed by an official of the Ship Ownery Company. In it, he indicated he had received a letter from the collector of customs at Port Arthur referring to the *City of Orange* as having sailed on April 24, 1917, without the required officers, and he again reiterated the previous excuses.

The collector of customs disregarded the instructions received from the Bureau of Navigation and imposed a $500 fine on the ship's owners. The collector of customs transmitted the sworn statement to the secretary of commerce. Comments in his cover letter are of interest. The collector, R. E. Latimer indicated that the *City of Orange* sailed from Orange "on or about 24th, ultimo, for Genoa, Italy without having on board and in its service any licensed mates." Latimer went on to say that apparently efforts were made to secure licensed mates at Gulf ports, but none would go to the war zone. His complaint was that efforts were not made at other than Gulf ports and especially "that the owners endeavored, by the influence of a congressman, to secure special privileges or exemptions. For this I would recommend that a penalty be imposed." On May 31, 1917, after papers referring to the steamer *City of Orange* had been reviewed by the acting supervising inspector general, he recommended to the commissioner of navigation that the full penalty be imposed.

It seems the American way prevailed, and on June 6, 1917, the assistant secretary for navigation, E. F. Sweet, sent a letter to the collector of customs at Port Arthur, informing him that the penalty had been remitted. On the same day, he took pleasure informing Congressman Harrison that the department had remitted the penalty. At least nine separate communications were required to settle this matter.[2]

Would it have been a great help to have met these somewhat arbitrary requirements? A review of the operating instructions for the engines indicates that the operating engineers needed to be well-trained in the requirements of these specific engines, but having officers qualified in steam would not provide much knowledge applicable to internal combustion engines.

The Ship Ownery Company letter and Latimer's cover letter indicated that the *City of Orange* got under way for Genoa, Italy, 6,500 miles away on or about April 24, 1917.[3]

CAPTAIN RUPERT WRY

The master for the maiden voyage was Rupert Wry, and none of the records reviewed indicated where he originated. Most of the masters of that period, especially for large schooners, came from the northeastern states, the Canadian Maritime Provinces, or the West Coast. He may have come from steamships, as he was qualified in steam. Actions by ISC seem to indicate that he was well thought of by them for a time.

Sometime during the day, on or about April 24, 1917, the *City of Orange* got under way with her holds and deck loaded with pine lumber. The *Galveston News* article covering the launching in chapter 2 indicated the ship was designed to carry 1.5 million board feet of lumber, and a few simple calculations, using the cargo capacity of 1,360 net tons and dimensions of the deck load, indicate the newspaper number to be valid.

Photographs or paintings of the vessel under sail seem to be nonexistent, but a painting of the ship as she was passing Sabine Light appears in the insert of color plates in this book. The painting shows the rigging and all sails up as they would appear when the ship was under way with a fair breeze. Missing is a towboat, because the ship had her two auxiliary engines to maintain way and stay out of trouble if the wind died.

Before getting into the maiden voyage, a description of the feel under sail is in order. Let us imagine the *City of Orange* with a stiff breeze, building up to 20 knots on her quarter, called a broad reach. The ship would accelerate to perhaps 14 knots, for this wind direction would produce her best speed. Even veteran sailors thrilled to this feel of power and the knowledge that they and the ship were blasting through the waves at what would have seemed like breakneck speed, without engines.

The apparent wind that one would actually feel on the ship and the wind the sails would be set for would be coming from abeam or forward of the beam rather than from the quarter. The apparent wind is the component resulting from the true wind, and the boat speed is analogous to that of the automobile, except, in the car, the forward speed is the predominant factor. Going to windward, the apparent wind will also be at a higher velocity than either the true wind speed or the vessel speed. Usually the slowest (and hottest in summer) direction of sailing is straight downwind, for in this case the boat speed is subtracted from the true wind to get the apparent wind.

Another significant difference between sailing ships and those with engines only are the wave effects. A steamship or motor vessel will roll uncomfortably from side to side in a beam sea. The sailing vessel is quite comfortable by comparison, for the powerful side thrust of the wind on the sails provides a strong stabilizing effect. The ship will be heeling some to the lee side and does not roll back against the strong force of the wind.

Some of the early powerboats had a small sail to provide this stabilizing effect in a beam sea, and many contemporary classic designs of trawlers and other workboat copies have a mast and boom with a staysail. If the wind is dead astern, the ride is less comfortable and the vessel will roll more, will be more difficult to steer, and will not travel as fast. Straight downwind, the schooners sometimes sailed wing-and-wing, which meant they put the booms out on alternate sides.[4] Preventer tackle was put out on the backside of the boom to prevent a disastrous accidental jibe. Most of the time, the ship will be going to windward or have the wind abeam, and these conditions provide the stabilizing effect, which is much more comfortable both physically and mentally.

CAPTAIN WRY AND THE BOOMS

Because the *City of Orange* had a deck load, a description of the usual way they are made up is of interest:

> After the hold was completely full the hatches would be battened down after having been covered with hatch covers and tarpaulins. If a deck load was to be carried the hatches would be additionally protected by having strongbacks fastened across their tops. Then heavy timbers would be fastened on end inside the rail which in effect would create a higher barrier to contain the deck load. The

lumber then would be piled on deck to a depth of six or eight feet and then securely fastened with turnbuckles and chains that ran across the top, from side to side and fastened to bolts in the waterways. All the lower running rigging had to be raised to accommodate the higher deck load. The lower sheet blocks were raised on chains and the sheets made fast to cleats that were on "sheet planks" that were made fast to the top of the deck load. Halyards and clewlines were led to pins in pin rails that had been made fast higher in the shrouds and backstays. The sails would have been shortened by having been reefed at the lowest set of reef points, which incidentally was often called the "lumber reef."[5]

Shortly after leaving Orange and approximately fifty miles out in the Gulf of Mexico, Captain Wry allegedly ordered some members of the crew to start throwing three tiers of the deck-loaded lumber overboard. This incident was brought to the attention of the authorities several days after the ship reached Genoa, Italy. On August 2, 1917, the third engineer and three seamen appeared before David F. Wilber, the consul general of the United States, and made a sworn deposition on this matter.

The statement indicated that the deponents were ordered by Captain Wry to throw three tiers of the deck load overboard on or about April 28 or 29. This constituted a length of 117 feet and a width of 41 feet, approximating the full length of the deck load, from the mainmast to the spankermast. The timbers were 20 to 40 feet long and 10 to 15 inches in diameter. This occurred about fifty miles out of Port Arthur in perfectly calm conditions.

The estimated value of the lumber thrown overboard was $18,000, and the jettisoning took four or five days. When Captain Wry was reminded by deponents that this might be against the insurance laws, he remarked: "To hell with the insurance, they'll pay for it." When deponents also suggested to Captain Wry that the deck load ought to be lashed (presumably after the jettisoning), he only remarked: "Oh, if it washes overboard, the insurance company will pay for it."

The deponents also stated that the captain, in explaining the missing timber, made an entry in the log book after arriving at Genoa that the missing timber was jettisoned off the Azores in a severe storm, for the safety of life, limb, and vessel, when, in fact, there was no bad weather at any time on the trip.

According to crewmen, the reason the captain gave for jettisoning the deck cargo was that the two booms were scraping the deck load, but the lower sails could have been reefed to prevent scraping, as was actually done after leaving Key West. While at Key West, some of the lower sails were cut off. It is unclear as to why these measures were necessary after the lumber jettisoning, but the fact that the proper measures were not taken before sailing from Orange suggests inexperience with deck loads.

The men went on to say that, as far as they knew, the captain did not appear before the American Consul at Genoa after arrival to make an extended protest and explain the jettisoning of the deck load in the Gulf of Mexico. The deposition was signed by L. O. Goodwin, 3rd engineer, age thirty-eight, of Kansas City, Missouri; W. P. Hurlston, sailor, age twenty-one, British citizen, of Grand Cayman, British West Indies; Jim Smith, sailor, age twenty-two, Panama citizen, of Mobile, Alabama; and Charles Simmons, sailor, age twenty-one, Panama citizen, of San Blas, Panama. The deposition was subscribed and sworn to on August 2, 1917, before David F. Wilber, consul general of the United States. (The names, ages, nationalities, and home addresses of individuals mentioned in the documentation will be given where possible to provide a cross section of seamen manning the ISC ships.) The American Consulate letterhead address used for the deposition is somewhat interesting. It was Kingdom of Italy, City and Province of Genoa, Consulate General of the United States of America.[6]

If the estimated cost of $18,000 for the jettisoned lumber was valid, some indications of the total cargo value can be made. Based on the dimensions given, calculations indicate that the lumber was going to bring at least $100 per thousand board feet in Genoa, Italy. In 1917, the average price of pine lumber in the Orange area had risen to $26 per thousand board feet at the mill, and big timbers were somewhat higher.[7] The shipload of lumber would have cost $39,000 at Orange and sold for more than $150,000 at Genoa, based on the numbers from the affidavit.

Before one assumes war profiteering, a look at expenses is in order. First, the ship would have to return to Orange in ballast, a distance of 6,500 miles. The round-trip would take several months. The crew pay, though not extravagant, was topped with a bonus for going into the war zone, and apparently ISC had insurance on the ships and cargo.

Another deposition on this same matter was made by Orsi Gonzalez, seaman, age twenty-one, from Arecibo, Puerto Rico, temporary address of Mobile, Alabama. His statement varied somewhat, and he recalled the starting date as May 4 or 5, or two days after leaving Port Arthur. He had the quantity thrown overboard at a length of 80 feet, and the timbers 12 inches by 12 inches.

The scaled length judging from the picture of the *City of Orange* is about 110 feet, or closer to the number in the first affidavit. Gonzalez agreed on the four to five days, the calm seas, and that three tiers were thrown overboard.[8] The first affidavit described the timbers as being

round, and it is possible that pilings or poles were being provided. The
task would have been pretty big, considering the timber sizes that were
no doubt loaded by crane. A 20-foot-long, 12-by-12-inch timber will
weigh 700 pounds and longer ones more (35 to 40 pounds per linear
foot). The number thrown overboard would be more than 600 pieces,
with a lesser number if some were forty feet long, and that would have
taken considerable time.

The American consul general transmitted the two affidavits, along
with his comments, to the secretary of state in a letter dated August 8,
1917. David F. Wilber's letter summarized the affidavits and added that
Captain Wry entered a note of protest when he delivered his papers to
the consulate office on July 5. He also indicated to Consular Assistant
Yost that he intended to extend the protest (a sworn statement concerning possible damage caused during a voyage)[9] before leaving Genoa,
which he failed to do. Captain Wry did not even mention the fact of having jettisoned the cargo, its coming to the knowledge of the consul general several days after Captain Wry's departure for the United States on
July 9. Mate W. W. Lamb was then in charge of the vessel. Captain Wry
may have been directed by his superiors to return to Orange promptly
for another ship, as the captain did go out on other ISC ships.

On August 3, William Imke, former master of the schooner *Glynn*,
now in this port (Genoa, Italy), was appointed master of the *City of Orange*. The consul closed by stating that the information was being forwarded as cumulative evidence for the possible information of the
secretary of commerce and for the owners of the *City of Orange*.[10]

The secretary of state did not have jurisdiction over shipping, so he
transmitted the letter and affidavits to the secretary of commerce. This
letter, dated September 1, 1917, read: "The Secretary of State presents his
compliments to the Honorable the Secretary of Commerce and has the
honor to transmit the enclosed communication for consideration and
such action as may be required."[11] Regardless of how dismal the information was, this was the usual wording for those letters of transmittal.

The documents filtered down to the Bureau of Navigation on September 4, 1917, and, at least officially, that was the end of the story. Since
these materials were war goods for an ally, one would expect more re-
action from both the government and the owners, but the owners' and
recipients' reactions to the missing lumber is undocumented.

SHANGHAIING STILL IN VOGUE

The ship was delayed at Key West, Florida, for several days because of
engine trouble and a damaged windlass. This was probably not because

of unqualified mates in steam but rather because of inadequate training of the engineers on these specific engines or other problems.

As the ship was preparing to leave, Captain Wry allegedly went recruiting. The victim, the first and second mates, and five other crewmen made sworn affidavits that a shanghaiing took place before the U.S. Consulate General at Genoa, Italy. The dates of these affidavits were a few days before the lumber jettisoning statements but after Captain Wry had left the ship.

The alleged victim was D. W. Patterson, age thirty-three, an American citizen, from Atlanta, Georgia, presently a sailor on board the *City of Orange*. He stated that, on or about May 19 or 20, 1917, while the deponent was in a drunken condition in a saloon in Key West, he was seized and taken down to the docks, placed in a rowboat and taken out to the *City of Orange*, forcibly hauled on board, and placed in a bunk in the forecastle to sober up as he was told.

When he had partially recovered from his drunkenness, he tried to regain the shore by climbing overboard into a water lighter alongside and was helped by William Hurlston. The first mate, W. W. Lamb, urged him back, however, with "What you want is more whiskey, you don't want to go ashore." Patterson was taken down into the cabin where Lamb gave him a half tumbler of whiskey. Afterward, on several occasions, he was given more whiskey to keep him drunk and prevent his going ashore. While in this state, he was induced to sign on for a voyage to Genoa, Italy, and return.

The shipping commissioner at Key West was on board at the time and protested to the mate that the deponent was drunk and that no more whiskey should be given to him. To this Lamb replied, "That is all right, we will fix him up when we get him out to sea. All he needs is a little more whiskey. He is a sailor all right." Patterson stated that, in fact, he was a ship painter and had never served at the wheel. He further stated that when he signed the articles, he did not know what he was doing.

He was allowed to remain in bed the first night to recover from his drunken stupor. After two days or so, he was put to work at painting and other deck work, arriving at Genoa, Italy, on July 4. "Deponent now prays the Consul General of the United States at that port to report these occurrences to the competent authorities in the United States with the view of obtaining the reparation proper in the case." Date of deposition was August 1, 1917, which was twenty-six days after the ship arrived at Genoa.[12]

The articles referred to in Patterson's affidavit were a government requirement and had to be signed by the seaman before a United States Shipping Commissioner. This only applied if the vessel were going to a

TABLE 6. CREWMAN MAKING AFFIDAVITS
CONCERNING ALLEGED SHANGHAIING

Name	Job	Age	Nationality	Address
L. O. Goodwin	3rd engineer	32	American	Kansas City, Mo.
Alford Tusley	2nd steward	27	American	New Orleans, La.
George Smith	2nd mate	29	American	Cleveland, Ohio
W. W. Lamb	1st mate	39	American	Mobile, Ala.
Orsi Gonzalez	seaman	21	Arecibo, Puerto Rico	Mobile, Ala.
T. A. Jackson	donkey engineer	34	British	Grand Cayman, B.W.I.
W. P. Hurlston	sailor	21	British	Grand Cayman, B.W.I.

port outside the United States. These articles mentioned the men's names, ratings, wages, and probable length of time of the voyage.[13] Since there were seven affiants in addition to that of the alleged victim, their personal data have been condensed in table 6.

L. O. Goodwin stated that for five or six days, Patterson was sick and wholly useless. He also stated that Patterson did not know the first principles of sailing and was incapable of taking the wheel. Goodwin further stated that he heard Captain Rupert Wry, master of the *City of Orange*, remark while at Key West that he would get another sailor even if he had to shanghai one before Patterson was brought on board. On the same day, Captain Wry told Goodwin, after Goodwin had declined to go with the ship, that he would take him along as a donkeyman even if he had to handcuff him.

Alford Tusely's affidavit essentially duplicated the other statements; however, his last paragraph is of interest. In it, he stated that when he and the rest of the crew applied for a bonus at Key West, the master of the *City of Orange*, Rupert Wry, picked up a big revolver and said, "If anybody else wants anything more out of this, I'll give it to him right now."[14]

Most captains had one or more weapons on board, but they were only brought out in the event of mutiny or other serious problems. Second Mate George Smith reiterated the other statements, stating that

Patterson was not a seaman, had no experience on a sailing vessel, and for the first few days was useless, apparently from his dissipation. He further stated that on the voyage from Key West to Genoa, Italy, Patterson did some painting and other work on deck and stood watch as a lookout every night for four hours at a time.

Of significance here is that after his forced detoxification, and despite his inexperience, Patterson did do some useful work. A painter is always of value on ships and probably even more so on a wooden one. Additionally standing the four-hour lookout watch was an important duty especially before the advent of radar.

Surprisingly, First Mate Lamb also made a sworn statement August 3, 1917, and, although it is not clear why, he directly implicated the captain. He stated that, while the captain of the *City of Orange* was on shore at Key West on or about May 19, the captain engaged a man named Patterson as a sailor to work on board the ship; that Patterson was then in a saloon at Key West and was called out by a policeman who asked whether he wanted a job. Patterson was then brought out to the ship in a boat belonging to a ship chandler.

He then tried to escape, but Lamb would not let him because the vessel was in need of more men. Lamb further stated that he took Patterson down into the cabin where the shipping commissioner was and that he, Lamb, gave Patterson a drink of whiskey to brace him up and prevent his getting the delirium tremens. When Patterson was asked to sign on the articles he remarked: "I don't know what I'm signing." The commissioner then said, "Get out of here."

After sitting there a while, Patterson did sign the articles, the commissioner making no further protest. Lamb went on to state that a great many seamen were signed on when drunk. Interestingly, it appears that the captain's effort was aided by a policeman. Was the policeman just trying to help Patterson get a job or, more likely, was he hoping to get rid of a problem? Was Captain Wry then instrumental in having Patterson taken back to the ship? He probably would not have gotten there on his own, considering the repeated descriptions concerning his condition and apparent reluctance on his part. Or, was he initially enthusiastic with alcoholic bravado and then changed his mind? In any event, Lamb was instrumental in seeing that he stayed, and it did not appear that Lamb was even slightly concerned with self-incrimination; the ship needed men, and this was the time-honored way of getting them.

The statements of Orsi Gonzalez and T. A. Jackson repeated the other statements and were made August 1, 1917. The statement of W. P. Hurlston indicated that their reason for being at Key West was engine trouble and a damaged windlass. He went on to state that when

Patterson was on the lighter, Lamb tried to coerce him back and Patterson replied, "No, I'm not coming. I've got to go ashore on this boat. I wouldn't come aboard the damned thing. Where in hell are you going to?" The mate replied "Genoa" and then said, "Tom, you only want a few good shots of whiskey," and Patterson asked if he had any on board. The mate replied he had plenty, and Patterson then said, "I'll chase you to hell for a drink of whiskey."[15]

*Maiden
Voyage*

All of these affidavits were transmitted by the American consul general at Genoa to the secretary of state, Washington, D.C. The consul general's letter was rather benign, except that he pointed out that Mate Lamb endeavored to justify the incident. The consul also noted that Captain Wry did not report the matter to the consul office upon his arrival and that Patterson only made his complaint on August 1 when a new master was about to take charge. The letter made no suggestions other than to say it was for the information of the Department of Commerce. All of these documents were transmitted by the Department of State, letter dated September 4, 1917, to the secretary of commerce.[16]

That was as far as the official record files went. One would expect that when a citizen's freedom is taken away from him against his will, somebody would be called to task. But the *City of Orange* existed in a different time, when human rights were not looked upon as they are in contemporary society. Besides, the United States was in one of its popular wars; a national draft had been started that would eventually result in casualties, and shirkers were not popular. Personal rights were not paramount in this era and became even less so after America entered the war.

Sometime not long after the alleged shanghaiing, the *City of Orange* left for the next stop, the Port of Gibraltar. Whether this was a scheduled stop is unknown; however, it is probable that all ships going into the Mediterranean Sea had to stop at Gibraltar, as the British had a blockade there.

The City of Orange *at Gibraltar and Other Places*

On July 25, 1917, William A. White, a black cook and steward on the *City of Orange*, made two sworn statements to the American Consul General at Genoa, Italy. White was British and from Bridgetown, British West Indies. His first statement alleged that on June 21, 1917, while in the Port of Gibraltar, Captain Wry beat him up quite severely. The affidavit began with the statement that the captain had given White orders on June 21, 1917, to prepare supper for a party of four that might or might not come, and they were to dine before the officers. They came—seventeen strong. In spite of the fact that the galley was forward and the officers' dining room was aft, the captain became quite upset over what he perceived as unusual delay on the part of the cook and went forward to remedy the situation.

When the captain came into the galley, White was coming out with a plate of bread but stopped long enough to tell the kitchen man to straighten everything up for the evening. The captain verbally attacked him as they walked aft, and White spoke up for the first and only time saying, "You treat me as if I was a slave." According to White,

> We were then abreast of the two engines. He promptly slew around and struck me under the jaw and one on the left temple which floored me and while down kicking me about the body when I got up and try to collect the bread and plate he landed on me again and after being down he kicked me all over the body. When I got up he said if I am going to be in trouble I am going to give it to you good and don't give a dam if they string me here—he came at me again and down I went, getting kicked until the Mate (1st) pull him away with the admonition that he was getting himself in

trouble. The result of the beat me I have a lump over the back of the right ear my left ear was cut and it is now black and blue—my body is sore my kidney now is so, that when I stand up any length of time—I have to urinate about ten minutes or so. I also have some minor scratches about the face the marks of his ring where he struck me.[1]

This alleged incident occurred in the Port of Gibraltar, on June 21, 1917, and while at sea from Gibraltar to Genoa, another incident took place, according to White. The captain came to the galley and ordered White to clean the floor and varnish it. White demurred, telling the captain he had forbidden the boys (the waiters and galley boy) to go for stores aft, as he had plenty of time for that. Then White indicated he was refusing to clean the floor as long as there was a boy occupying the room with him. He said, "I had already clean the paint work and that was enough."

He then caught me hold by the throat and called me a God damned son of a bitch you will do as I order you—I told him with two helpers I'll not scrub the floor He then began jabbing me on the nose with his finger meanwhile calling me a c—s—. and this was done after promising the Consul at Gibraltar that he would not molest me in the future—I have the Consul written words to that effect. Now, Mr. Consul—my plea is that you will summon the following witnesses, who will testify to the brutal treatment I received at the time. Should it be in your opinion that my case can best be settled in the States you will please have me sent back or put my case so that it will not be in jepirdy for future use.[2]

White then asked the consul to call several witnesses. Seven witnesses provided affidavits in this case, and their personal data is presented in the table 7. The first mate and the next two affiants stated that the first assault took place on June 21, 1917.[3] The statement of First Mate Lamb on July 23 corroborated White's affidavit on the first assault and added a couple of enlightening statements: "The Captain then went down below to rejoin his guests who were seated at the table in the dining room. The Captain appeared pleased that I had intervened in the matter. The cook also went below to his room. The Captain was under the influence of drink at the time."

The next two men, F. C. Pjerrou and E. C. Garrett, former engineers on the *City of Orange*, gave a joint statement that both signed. This again substantiated the previous affidavits. Garrett was from Merkle, Texas,

TABLE 7. CREWMEN MAKING AFFIDAVITS
CONCERNING ALLEGED ASSAULTS

Name	Job	Age	Nationality	Address
W. W. Lamb	first mate	39	American	Mobile, Ala.
F. C. Pjerrou	former engineer	—	American	Omaha, Nebr.
E. C. Garrett	former engineer	—	American	Merkel, Tex.
T. A. Jackson	donkeyman	—	British	Grand Cayman, B.W.I.
W. P. Hurlston	sailor	21	British	Grand Cayman, B.W.I.
D. W. Patterson	sailor	33	American	Atlanta, Ga.
L. O. Goodwin	3rd engineer	32	American	Kansas City, Mo.

and the only Texan found in crew identifications. The crews were a broad cross section of American and foreign seamen.[4]

One might also wonder why these two men were former members of the crew. Did they decide to leave the ship before or after Captain Wry left? Since the *City of Orange* was making a trip to Genoa and back, it is very likely that all hands signing on at Orange and Key West had to sign on for the round-trip. Until 1915, American seamen jumping ship in foreign ports were subject to arrest and imprisonment, another function of our foreign consuls. The LaFollette Act, commonly known as the Seamen's act, passed March 4, 1915, was legislation that abolished imprisonment as a penalty for desertion of American seamen in all ports.

The act also called for the payment of half of all earnings when demanded at any port of lading or discharge.[5] Since the two engineers apparently quit in the port of discharge, they would not be considered deserters but would have to forfeit half of their pay. This probably was not a big consideration, as it would usually all be gone for liquor and female entertainment in a short time anyway. Aside from the bullying captain, they may have decided that a steamship, with its government-supplied armed guard, would be safer from German submarines.

The next affidavit, by T. A. Jackson on July 24, matches the others. He said that the captain and White came up on deck on the deck load, indicating that no passageways were left on deck, which was normal for deck-loaded schooners. He also mentioned that the captain went down aft to join the party of four ladies and a few gentlemen.

W. P. Hurlston made his statement July 24, and indicated he witnessed both alleged assaults. He was also a witness for both previous incidents. D. W. Patterson, the alleged shanghaiing victim, also made a sworn statement on July 27, reiterating previous statements concerning both alleged assaults. He stated that White was complaining because the captain told him there would be four people, and instead there were eight. Patterson observed that the captain appeared to be under the influence of alcohol.

This is the second statement in which a reference is made to the captain being under the influence of alcohol. Patterson also wanted to call the harbor police but was prevented from doing so by one of the mates. His knowledge of seaman-to-captain protocol was rather limited despite his long cruise from Key West. It appears that Patterson was completely detoxified and in good health. Since the ship had been in port for more than twenty days, why had not Patterson left the ship with his half pay and returned to the States? He had not even been to the American Consulate to make his complaint about being shanghaied, as evidenced by the absence of his affidavit on that matter, which was not made until August 1, 1917. Perhaps Patterson has grown fond of the sea, bearing out the stories that many an alcoholic ended up in the forecastle as a way to survive.

The last statement, dated July 27, was made by L. O. Goodwin, who had also made statements on both previous incidents. He made several allegations not made by the other affiants. He quoted the captain as telling the cook, "No, I'll not make a slave out of you, I'll do worse than that. I'll kill you." He indicated that a Captain Roberts of another American schooner in port, helped the mate stop the assault, the only reference to such an occurrence.

Goodwin also indicated that about the third morning after the assault, the cook told the captain that he had written a letter to the consul, to which the captain replied, "It won't do you any good here. I've got you here. You may get me in Genoa, but it won't do you any good." The cook told the captain that he had a letter from the consul, to which the captain replied, "I told the Consul that I would not hit you anymore but that I would kill you."

Goodwin put in a good word for the captain by saying, "The captain was not known to mistreat or brutally assault any other member of the crew, but he did on diverse occasions curse various members of the crew and threaten to shoot them if his orders were not carried out to the letter." He went on to observe that the captain consumed enormous quantities of whiskey and was drunk two-thirds of the time while en route from Orange to Genoa.

Goodwin would have done well to stop there or even a little sooner, but he went on to accuse the captain of stealing a solid silver percolator given to the ship by the Board of Commerce for Orange. The captain was also accused of selling ship's provisions, including rope, paint, gasoline, and several barrels, and of buying 6,000 gallons of saltwater out of 14,000 gallons of fresh water. The last accusation was that the captain bought a hundred-pound sack of flour at Gibraltar and told the cook to count it as a barrel.[6] Unfortunately, these latter accusations, whether founded or not, had nothing to do with the assault and served to confuse the issue later on.

The affidavits of the eight crew members were transmitted by the Consul General at Genoa to the secretary of state with a letter dated July 28, 1917. Consul General Wilber summarized the affidavits and indicated he felt they were well founded. According to Wilber, Captain Wry only appeared at the consulate on Saturday, July 5 (the day after arriving), and left on the following Wednesday for the United States on the American SS *Pisa*. As a result, there was no time to obtain a statement from him, and he volunteered no explanation.

Captain Wry rather unceremoniously left his ship in the hands of the mate, on July 9, and returned to the United States, stating that he had orders to bring other schooners to Genoa for his owners. The secretary of state again transmitted the documents to the secretary of commerce with the same short letter as before, dated September 10, 1917, and it arrived at the Bureau of Navigation the next day.[7]

Some background on cruelty to seaman, including its possible origins and slow decline, is in order. Early seamen were slaves, and the dreadfulness of their existence can only be imagined. They were followed by the medieval seamen who were subject to laws that were brutally severe in punishing sins of omission and of commission but that showed little if any interest in the individual's welfare or human decency.

Two things became paramount: cargo space and saving money. These were important if midcentury American sailing ships were to compete with steamships. As a result, sailing crews came to be made up more and more of misfits, ne'er-do-wells, and unprincipled adventurers who were driven under brutal discipline by "bucko mates" at sea and victimized by a vicious system of commercialized exploitation ashore.

Hours of work, on a normal watch-and-watch (four or six hours on and four or six hours off) basis, were long, broken, and entirely at the disposition of the master; food and bunk space were execrable; and pay was very low.[8] A commission working under the direction of the U.S. Treasury Department reported urgent need of some legislation to prevent brutality on shipboard, and one member stated that it was only too true that American seamen were "underpaid, underfed, overworked, and generally driven about like slaves."[9] Although conditions had improved by 1917, some of the traditional early behavior continued for years, as evidenced on the *City of Orange*.

Some sailors and officers were reluctant to sign on slow-moving, unarmed merchant vessels, especially sailing ships going into submarine-infested waters during World War I. The German U-boat was very well developed by the latter part of the war, and many ships were sunk, especially in the Mediterranean. So felicitous was the basic design of the U-boats that years later, when Germany again went to war, the U-boats it turned loose on Britain were not substantially different from the U-35 used in World War I.[10]

Did this consideration cause the *City of Orange* to have officers and crew who couldn't find less hazardous jobs because of limited experience and talent, or were they just more patriotic and adventuresome? What was the status of seamen in this somewhat belated era of sail and wooden ships?

The merchant seaman is a civilian, but in many respects his life resembles that of a soldier. His signature of the shipping articles places him in a position that is strikingly similar to a short term of enlistment. He has narrowly prescribed duties, obligations, and responsibilities, as well as rights and privileges; and he must formally sign away his freedom of action for a given period of time. He lives in close quarters that are essentially floating barracks, with a negligible amount of privacy; he is removed for long periods from the influence of home life and from association with women; he takes part in drills and many forms of disciplined group activity; he is tied to his ship as the soldier is to his camp, and if he leaves it without permission he is termed a deserter; he must obey the orders of his officers without question, and if discipline is less strict than in the army it is also more uneven, less impersonal, and more likely to be influenced by subjective factors such as prejudices, idiosyncrasies, and antipathies.[11]

Some of these factors occurred on the maiden voyage of the *City of Orange*.

AVERAGE SPEEDS OF THE *CITY OF ORANGE*

A look at the time at sea for the three legs of the trip provides average speeds of the *City of Orange*. Table 8 summarizes the trip based on dates from the various affidavits. There was no indication of the departure

TABLE 8. TIMES AND AVERAGE SPEEDS
FOR THE *CITY OF ORANGE*

Port of departure	Date	Port of arrival	Date	Days	Miles statute	Average speed*
Orange	Apr. 24	Key West	May 4	10	891	89.1, 3.7
Key West	May 21	Gibraltar	June 20	30	4669	155.6, 6.5
Gibraltar	June 23	Genoa	July 4	11	974	88.5, 3.7

*Miles per day, miles per hour

date from Gibraltar. Was the captain's party, when the alleged assault of White took place, a final fling before sailing? In lieu of any better indications, the day after the party was selected as the departure date, since that would be the earliest time of departure.

The first leg, from Orange to Key West, was rather slow, perhaps owing to the learning process always necessary with a new ship. Another more likely factor that slowed the ship down is that in the spring the prevailing winds in the eastern Gulf of Mexico are strong and out of the southeast, right on the nose of the ship. That means the engines alone would not have pushed the vessel through the seas upwind with the massive wind resistance inherent in a five-masted schooner, so the ship would have had to take long tacks upwind. The distance traveled was much farther than the straight-line distance, so there is no way of determining the ship's true average speed. Of course, the important thing is the port-to-port time; nobody paid by the day but rather for cargo delivered.

The next leg, from Key West to Gibraltar, was a good average for that trip. In the ocean, the winds are usually stronger and more consistent than on land, and a sailing vessel could pick the latitude, depending on the time of year that provided favorable winds. Obviously, the winds were more favorable across the Atlantic than in the Gulf, averaging 6.5 mph for thirty days. The stays at Key West and Gibraltar were not revealed and may have been longer than the estimates; if so, that would have improved the time for those two legs also. The total time for the trip from Orange to Genoa was approximately seventy days, partially extended by the lengthy stay at Key West and Gibraltar.

THE PAPER CHASE OF CAPTAIN WRY

The Department of Commerce sent the assault report from the Consul General at Genoa, Italy, to the acting secretary of the Bureau of Navigation. This was E. F. Sweet, who was active in the ISC problem concerning the lack of qualified officers when the *City of Orange* was ready to sail. On September 13, 1917, Sweet sent three letters concerning the incident.[12] The first was to the secretary of state, acknowledging the report and indicating that, according to the facts presented, Captain Wry was subject to criminal prosecution.

Sweet went on to say that his department would endeavor to secure the prosecution but that Captain Wry had left the vessel, rendering the matter difficult, as the witnesses were scattered and Captain Wry's whereabouts were unknown.

The second letter was to the collector of customs, Galveston, Texas, with copies of related documents. Sweet stated that if the facts were proven, Captain Wry would be subject to imprisonment. He wanted the collector to endeavor to locate Captain Wry, and, if successful, confer at once with the U.S. attorney looking to his prosecution. It is not clear why Sweet sent this letter to the customs collector at Galveston instead of at Port Arthur. The third letter was to the Ship Ownery Company (ISC) at Orange and included copies of the report. Sweet suggested that the addressee would agree that the action of Captain Wry, if the facts were substantiated, was inexcusable and that he should be prosecuted. Sweet also asked for any information the company might have on the whereabouts of Captain Wry.

Perhaps Sweet sent this information to several Gulf Coast custom collectors, as the next communication was a telegram dated September 21, 1917, from the collector at New Orleans, Louisiana.[13] It informed Sweet that the collector at New Orleans had forwarded the letter and enclosures to Mobile, since Captain Wry was due in that port that day or the next on the *City of Pensacola*. He asked that necessary instructions be given to the collector and U.S. attorney. A confirming letter followed.

The next letter was from an official of ISC at Orange to Sweet, dated September 20, 1917. This letter disputed the shotgun approach taken by Goodwin in his affidavit. The main paragraph of the letter reads:

I know nothing of the charges made against Captain Wry, but the affidavit of L. O. Goodwin where he stated that Captain Wry stole a "solid silver percolator," which was given to the Ship by the Board of Trade of the City of Orange, Texas, is not correct, inasmuch as this percolator was not the property of the vessel, but was presented to Captain Wry, personally, by a few of his friends here on which occasion the writer happened to be present. I also seriously doubt that part of Goodwin's affidavit wherein he claimed Captain Wry sold certain equipment from the vessel, as Captain

Wry's accounts were checked up in a satisfactory manner to the Owners.[14]

Goodwin gave the owners a nice smoke screen to hide behind, and none of the other affidavits was mentioned. Why should they have been? The owners were apparently sure they were all in the same category.

The last sentence of the letter indicated that Captain Wry sailed from Orange on September 18, on the schooner *City of Pensacola* for Mobile, Alabama, and should arrive at that point on September 21 or 22.

The next letter, dated October 18, 1917, was from the special deputy collector at Mobile, Alabama, to the commissioner of navigation, Washington, D.C.[15] He acknowledged a letter concerning the case of Captain Wry and stated that it had been referred to the U.S. attorney for further consideration. He said also that as soon as he heard anything the bureau would be notified immediately.

The next letter, dated October 19, 1917, was from an assistant U.S. attorney to the special deputy collector mentioned in the preceding paragraph. He informed the collector:

> The case is in this condition. Captain Wry as you remember, gave bond to answer any indictments that may be found against him when our Grand Jury meets. Our Grand Jury convenes the Fourth Monday in November. It will be absolutely necessary for one or more of the witnesses whose affidavits are on file with the Bureau to be present before the Grand Jury, in order to get an indictment, and also to be present when our Court meets and the case is set for trial.
>
> I would suggest that you keep a watch for this vessel, should it come to some Gulf port and find out whether any of the witnesses are still on board her. Also you had best write to them at the addresses given in the letter of the Commissioner, to see if any of them can be reached that way.[16]

Captain Wry had to post some sort of bond, according to the letter.

That official wrote a letter, dated October 27, 1917, to the commissioner of navigation bringing him up to date. He informed the commissioner that he had addressed communications to Lamb, Jackson, Pjerrou, Garrett, and Patterson to secure them as witnesses in the case. He omitted Hurlston, Goodwin, and the alleged victim, White.[17]

The commissioner of navigation wrote a subsequent letter to the collector of customs at Mobile (date covered up by file binding), acknowledging the two previous letters. He also mentioned that in another case against Captain Wry, the department had evidence that Hurlston and Goodwin were still on the vessel (the *City of Orange*). He went on to request that the collector communicate with these men (including the other five) to secure at least one of them as a witness in the case. He further stated: "The treatment of the cook, Mr. White, in this case was of such a nature that, in the opinion of the Bureau, there should be a prosecution of Captain Wry, and any assistance you can render to secure these witnesses will be appreciated."[18]

The last letter, at least in these files, was to the U.S. district attorney, Eastern District of Texas, Beaumont, from the special deputy collector at Galveston, dated December 26, 1917. The letter transmitted the set of documents received from the secretary of commerce concerning the alleged assaults, and the last paragraph explained the reason for the transfer:

> The papers referred to were transmitted to this office with a communication from the Secretary of Commerce, copy of which is hereto attached, requesting that the facts be reported to the U.S. District Attorney as soon as the whereabouts of Captain Wry became known. Information has been received recently that the party involved is now living at Orange, Texas, and in the employ of Piaggio's ship yard at that place, and as Orange is within the jurisdiction of your district, the matter is respectfully referred to you for such action as you may deem necessary in the premises.[19]

That was the end of the paper trail, at least as far as the official files went, and apparently Captain Wry escaped prosecution on all three incidents. The primary reason for this was the nomadic nature of the seamen at that time. Without at least one witness, the courts could not do anything.

NO NEWS IS GOOD NEWS

When ships went missing, burned, collided with another vessel, or ran aground, their misfortune was widely publicized. Other ships sailed the high seas for years without mishap, and so nothing was heard about them. So it was with the *City of Orange*. With the new Captain Imke, nothing more happened for some time that was sufficient to gain the government's attention.

The next two letters regarding the ship pertained to the deaths of two seamen. The first letter was from the acting commissioner to the United States Shipping Commissioner, Barge Office, New York, dated

December 5, 1918: "I enclose a dispatch from our Consul at Cette, France dated the 4th instant and its enclosures in regard to the wages and effects of Bengt Hagdahl, a deceased seaman of the schooner CITY OF ORANGE."[20] Cette (Sète) is located on the southern coast of France on the Mediterranean (see figure 8.2 in chapter 8).

Another letter was sent the same day with contents exactly the same, except it pertained to another seaman named Peter Nestaby.[21] Information and the circumstances of these two deaths that appear to have happened on the same day were not in the file. It is a mystery as to whether their deaths were owing to an accident on shipboard or something that happened ashore. By this time, Captain Imke was gone, and F. N. J. Nordberg of San Francisco was the master of the *City of Orange*.

The next letter, from what appeared to be a law firm in New York City was to the commissioner of navigation, dated February 1, 1919. The first paragraph stated that all of the stock of the *City of Orange*, except directors' qualifying shares, stood in the name of Herbert W. Mills. Mills, a British subject, was acting solely as agent and trustee of the Italian beneficial owners of this stock. The actual owner was one Alfonso Clerici, who died in November, 1917.

The Italian interest was acquired in July, 1917, which was only three months after the ship was documented and had started on her maiden voyage. The letter pointed out that it was, of course, impossible at that time to secure Shipping Board approval of change of flag. Mills was going to Italy, and the Italian interests wanted to have the ship transferred to the Italian flag. Mills was described as being exceedingly glad to be relieved of all responsibility connected to the matter. The *City of Orange* was in a United States port. The writer of the letter understood it was going to proceed to an Italian port, and he wanted to determine if the ship could be transferred to the Italians after arrival.[22]

This letter was answered by the commissioner, presumably soon after receiving it (date illegible), as he referred to "your letter of the first instant."[23] He told the Italian owners that, as they stated, it would be necessary for them to first secure the approval of the Shipping Board for the transfer. Then the vessel could proceed to Italy under the American flag, provided that the transfer was not made before the ship arrived in Italy. Once there, the transfer could be completed, and the papers, as required by law, would be delivered to the consul, who would subsequently forward them to the United States.

It is interesting to note that the Italians acquired this ship shortly after she was completed, a practice apparently repeated for many of the ships. That answers the question of where at least part of the money came from for what was a very large project for private enterprise at that time. This was a project fraught with high risk, especially considering the near obsolescence of sail and wooden ships.

THE FINAL REPORT

Although it may have been fortunate for some and unfortunate for others, the transfer to the Italian flag was never completed. On May 26, 1919, the consulate general at Marseilles, France, sent the following telegram to the secretary of state, Washington, D.C.: "Twenty-sixth. Schooner CITY OF ORANGE totally destroyed by fire. Origin unknown. No casualties. DAVIS."[24]

On August 7, 1919, the consulate general at Marseilles sent the ship's papers and a description of the circumstances of the burning of the vessel taken from the Marine Extended Protest. The Protest was signed by Frederic Nils J. Nordberg, master; George T. Foley, first mate; John Duncan, third mate; Thomas C. Ward, first assistant engineer; Akel Ericson, seaman; and Olaf Westgard, seaman.[25]

According to the statement, the vessel arrived at Marseilles on April 5, 1919, and completed discharge of its cargo on April 27, 1919, then took in 200 tons of earth ballast. When ready to sail April 30, its rudderstock was discovered to be twisted. Measures to have the rudderstock replaced were taken immediately, and the ship's papers were redeposited at the consulate on May 5. The rudder was to be reshipped on May 25, as the decision was made to put in a new rudderstock instead of strapping the old one.

About nine o'clock in the evening of May 24, smoke was noticed coming from between the mast wedges of the spankermast (fifth mast aft on a five-masted schooner).[26] On board at the time were Frederick Nils J. Nordberg, master; John Duncan, third mate; Thomas Ward, first assistant engineer; and Captain Erik P. S. Erikson and two seamen from the American schooner, *Percy R. Pine II*. The smoke was first seen by Duncan, the only one on deck, and this was followed almost immediately by an explosion. The others were in the master's cabin and, when they came on deck, flames were issuing from the after hatch.

Immediately after the explosion, the cabin filled with heavy black smoke, and it was impossible to enter the cabin again except on one occasion. Duncan went at once to the donkey room to get steam up on the boiler, as the fires had been banked. Considerable water was thrown from buckets into the after hold and was also used to extinguish the burning mizzen gaff sail and boom that had been set ablaze by flames coming from the hatch.

A hose from the Brazilian steamer *Itu* was brought over and its pumps started. A French torpedo boat and later a fire tug and the fire department arrived on the scene. The fire department took charge of operations. The vessel was abandoned at about eleven o'clock on May 24, with the personnel reeling in their hoses and drawing off. At the request of the consul, a vessel that appeared to be a patrol or guard-boat fired about twenty shots into the ship to try to sink her, but without success. An attempt was also made to open the seacocks, but the fire and smoke made it impossible to get to them.

No further effort was made to extinguish the fire, and the ship burned fiercely all night. The main fuel tanks exploded at about 3 A.M. on May 25. The rigging with jibboom went overboard at about 5 A.M., and the vessel sank at about 9 A.M. on May 25, having then burned to the water's edge. The master declared that the cause of the fire was entirely unknown to him, but it appeared to have started between the jibber and the spankermasts in either the lower hold or the tween-decks.

Though there was no cargo on the ship, it was carrying 200 tons of earth ballast and about 60 tons (approximately 20,000 gallons) of fuel in tanks in the engine room, the poop, and on the main deck. The ship was moored to a buoy astern and had two anchors out forward. It sank in about forty feet of water.

At the request of the owners, the French Police made a full investigation of the matter without coming to any final conclusions as to the cause of the fire. The consul stated: "It appears probable that gasoline vapor from the fuel tanks was ignited by accident, and that the resulting explosion scattered the fire so widely and thoroughly that it could not be extinguished. It is my opinion that most, if not all, the men on board had been drinking rather freely at the time."[27]

The question here is whether the consul is referring to the fuel tanks for the propulsion engines, which was fuel oil, or gasoline for some other use. Indications are that some or all of the ships carried approximately 1,300 gallons of gasoline, and at least one of the lifeboats on each ship had a gasoline engine. The ships may have also have had some motor generator sets for electricity. Fuel oil has low volatility and a relatively high ignition point, but gasoline is opposite in both characteristics and is very much a fire hazard in poorly ventilated areas, especially if a leak occurs.

As for the consul's reference to drinking, that is a factor in many fires, but whether it contributed in this case is not known.

The hulk of the vessel was raised at the direction of the port authorities, as it was an encumbrance in the basin where it sank. Everything on board was ruined by the intense heat, and the owners abandoned the hulk to the underwriters on July 14, 1919.

The Italian underwriter was Assiouazions Generale di Venezia, represented by Messrs. R. de Campou and Fils, Marseilles, agents. The underwriters insisted on one month's notice of abandonment and thus were not going to take over the hulk until August 14, 1919. It was thought they would hardly get enough for the hulk to pay the cost of salvage.

The fourteen-man crew of the vessel were taken on official relief by the consulate general on May 26, 1919. Their wages were paid up to and including May 25, 1919, and they were discharged from the ship as of May 26, 1919, and repatriated according to law. The crew had to be sent to Havre, for transportation, as none was expected at Marseilles.

This report, with enclosures, was sent by the secretary of state to the secretary of commerce with a letter dated September 5, 1919. That would be the last known correspondence concerning the *City of Orange*.[28]

The *City of Orange* was in active service from April 24, 1917, until arriving at Marseilles, France, on April 5, 1919, or approximately twenty-three and a half months. A conservative estimate of round-trip times for this ship was six months, even though the vessel only took two and a half months for the first trip to Genoa, Italy. The voyage time may have improved, but time was needed for loading and unloading and unexpected delays such as the holdup at Marseilles for the rudder reshipping that extended to more than three weeks time.

The ship might have made four round-trips, possibly more; but even with only four trips, the cargo delivered would have been the equivalent of 6 million board feet of lumber. It is probable that Italy's need for lumber declined before the end of World War I on November 11, 1918. If not lumber, the cargo discharged at Marseilles could have been grain, coal, packaged petroleum products, or some other bulk cargo. The ship did well to have survived her trips, especially into the Mediterranean, for German U-boats sank a large number of ships in this area.

Apparently the ship also did some work on the East Coast, as it obtained Temporary Consolidated Enrollment and License No. 19, limiting it to the coasting trade, November 6, 1917, at the Port of Norfolk and Newport News, Virginia, which was retained for nine months, or until August 6, 1918.[29] It may have carried coal along the eastern seaboard, but this was not confirmed.

The *City of Orange* appears to have accomplished her primary function, to deliver Gulf Coast pine lumber to Italy in support of their war effort. ISC probably made some money on both the lumber and the transportation, and since the Italians apparently paid for the construction and the ship was insured, it is doubtful that Piaggio lost anything. The subtleties of the financial arrangements, however, are essentially a mystery.

This ship was well designed and well built by Texans in Texas, as proved by the successful completion of several transatlantic voyages without serious mishap at sea. Its problems appear, as was almost always the case, to have been man-made and not the result of a flaw in its design, construction, or materials.

The *City of Orange* Certificate of Registry No. 17 was surrendered August 7, 1919 at Marseilles, France. Reason: "Vessel burned May 24, 1919."[30]

The Next Two Ships

We must go back to 1917 and Orange, Texas, for the story of the next two ships, the *City of Houston* and the *City of Pensacola*.

THE *CITY OF HOUSTON*

The *City of Houston* was a four-masted barkentine, close in length and cargo capacity to the *City of Orange*. She was being loaded with lumber by the time her Certificate of Registry was issued at Port Arthur on July 28, 1917.[1] Her career was exceedingly short, for only nine days later, on August 6, 1917, disaster struck in the form of fire. Her Certificate of Registry was surrendered August 9, 1917 at Port Arthur, Texas. Reason surrendered: "Vessel Lost, Burned Aug. 6, 1917; shipyard Orange, Texas; total number persons on board 17; number of lives lost, none." (See figure 6.1.)

The owners must have been very disappointed to lose this elegant ship before its first voyage. Since the surrender document stated, "Vessel Lost," a reincarnation might not be expected, but some time later the ship was rebuilt.

A Temporary Certificate of Registry was issued at Port Arthur, on July 2, 1919, almost two years later, and significant changes had been made. The new Certificate of Registry indicated that the vessel had been rebuilt at Moss Point in 1919, and remeasured at Pascagoula the same year. Moss Point is very close to Pascagoula, and both are on the Mississippi Gulf Coast not far from Gulfport. The Certificate of Registry was temporary because the ship's Port of Registry was no longer Port Arthur.

The ship was renamed the *Jessie Bounds*. The new owners were Jesse Bounds, owning 99/100 and being managing owner; and his partner, Leslie L. Rogers, owning 1/100. Both resided at Moss Point, Mississippi. With the proper application and approval, vessels can be re-

fig. 6.1. The City
of Houston
burning.
Courtesy
Dr. Howard
C. Williams
Collection

named. The official number, however, is never changed, even if the vessel is rebuilt and modified substantially. This is the one constant that allows tracking of the vessel, regardless of changes of owners, rig, name, locality, or service.

The ship was registered for ocean freight with a crew of ten, down from sixteen; other changes made this a rational number.[2] Modifications included converting the ship to a schooner, removing the engines, and installing water tanks in part of that space. This eliminated requirements for steam-qualified mates and engineers and square-rig sailors, reducing crew number and skill requirements.

The owners sent the ship on her maiden voyage, reportedly to England.[3] On the way over, the *Jessie Bounds* ran into trouble. The Temporary Certificate of Registry was surrendered at Gibraltar, Spain, on November 3, 1919. Reason surrendered: "Vessel abandoned at sea 37° 30'N, 42° 25'W Oct. 10, 1919."[4] No details were given as to whether any of the crew was lost. One can only imagine the disappointment of the owner Bounds to lose his namesake on the first voyage.

THE *CITY OF PENSACOLA*

The *City of Pensacola* was a four-masted schooner and the smallest of the fourteen ships built by ISC. Her Certificate of Registry was issued

September 6, 1917 at Port Arthur, Texas, with D. R. Christopher the first master.[5]

The same problems occurred in obtaining officers with steam licenses as the time came for the ship to sail. On September 7, 1917, a telegram bearing Piaggio's name was sent to E. T. Chamberlain, Commissioner of Navigation, Department of Commerce, Washington, D.C. This indicated that the vessel would be ready to sail in a day or two in ballast for Mobile but they could not find licensed officers and certified seaman. They could procure experienced officers and seamen, but without steam license and authorization to sail under these conditions was being requested.[6]

The files did not contain any response to this communication. A likely reason for sailing in ballast to Mobile was to pick up a cargo of lumber in that area rather than at Orange; that was closer to Piaggio's lumber operations. We also know from the owner's letter in chapter 5 that Captain Wry was along on the voyage of the *City of Pensacola* from Orange to Mobile. The reason for Captain Wry's trip was not stated; however, this appears to be when the assistant U.S. attorney served Captain Wry with papers and obtained a bond from him to answer any indictments when the grand jury met in November, 1917.

ONE OR TWO TRIPS

Like the previous two ships, the *City of Pensacola* did not last long. The Certificate of Registry No. 10 was surrendered May 5, 1918, at Port Arthur, Texas. Reason surrendered: "Vessel lost. Sunk near Garrucha, Spain, April 29, 1918; no lives were lost. (As per B/N letter No. 93521-N of May 1, 1918.)"[7] All documents related to this loss described the seas as calm and the wind at one knot. The ship did not run aground, nor was she sabotaged. The surrender document did not tell the full story, omitting one important fact: the ship was sunk by a German U-boat.

The master had changed from D. R. Christopher to Robert A. Sanderson, who was born on Prince Edward Island and had become a naturalized citizen of the United States. His home was Mobile, Alabama. On May 1, 1918, two days after the sinking, Captain Sanderson appeared before the Consulate of the United States of America at the Port of Almeria, Spain, and rendered a Marine Note of Protest.[8] In actuality, he underwent a rather formal interrogation, having to answer a document with 131 standard questions. The answers indicated that the ship had departed Genoa, Italy, on April 22, 1918, and had stopped at Marseilles, France, on April 24. Almeria, Spain is shown on the map of the Mediterranean in chapter 8 (figure 8.2).

The attack occurred at 2:30 A.M. The submarine fired its deck gun at the schooner, expending some twenty-five rounds, hitting the ship approximately five times; no torpedoes were used. The engine room was hit, stopping the engines and initiating a fire. Not long after the attack started, the crew took to two boats. No rounds were fired after the ship was abandoned.

To the question of how the watches were taken, the captain answered six hours on and six off, five men to a watch. The captain was on watch at the time of the attack and had just taken a sighting so was quite sure of the vessel's position. The position was: "Approximately, in Latitude 36' 58" [36° 58'] north, Long. 4° 20' 40" East. San Fernando, Cadiz. April 29, 1918 at 2:30 A.M."

No guns or radio apparatus were on board; smoke was not used; and the ship did not zigzag as an evasive measure. The wind was very low, the seas calm, and the ship was headed west at 5 knots, the speed the engines could achieve in calm conditions. The sky was clear, with the moon near the last quarter. In answering how the ship was maneuvered after the attack, the captain stated that he headed for land, but the second shot that hit the vessel stopped the engines. A Spanish schooner was about a mile and a quarter east northeast.

The ship was pillaged by the enemy after the submarine captain made the occupants of the lifeboats board the U-boat. Equipped with gas masks, five or six of the U-boat crew rowed one of the lifeboats, accompanied by their own boat, to the *City of Pensacola*, which was then burning. They remained on the burning ship for about half an hour. While aboard, they took the chronometer, sextants, and other instruments, some provisions and clothes, then put two bombs aboard and rowed back to the submarine. The two bombs exploded within ten to fifteen minutes. A while later, the vessel settled level with the water and rolled over on its side.

Asked if there were any confidential documents on board, the captain answered, "None except the sailing instructions from the Italian dispatch officer in Genoa and the French dispatch officer in Marseille. These went down with the boat."

The number of the submarine looked like U-34 or U-37, and the sub was about 125 feet long. The conning tower and bridge looked to the captain like a diagram of Model U.C.1–15, and it had one deck gun forward of the conni+ng tower that looked to be about four inches. One collapsible canvas boat was on deck.

The captain, when asked to describe the officers and crew of the submarine, responded, "Captain of the submarine wore a leather coat-dark, a yachting cap of dark blue with an insignia, the sailors wore dark jerseys and trousers. Names not known. Captain appeared to be about 35 years old, tall, blonde, about 180 pounds in weight, spoke fairly good English with a German accent. Number of the crew seen: About 12 or 14. One who seemed to be a gunner's mate on board of submarine, spoke very good English and said he had lived in New York and would return there after the war. He said he left New York about a year ago on a Scandinavian liner."

In answer to what questions the captain of the schooner was asked, he stated the following: "Captain of submarine seemed well informed with reference to the CITY OF PENSACOLA. The first thing he said was, 'Captain, I am sorry I had to sink your ship, but war is war.' He added 'She is only seven months old.' [The ship received her papers in September 1917.] The Captain also asked if there were any chronometers aboard."

Captain Sanderson, in answer to questions, also indicated that he had carried out the war and local instructions, that he did all in his power to prevent capture, and that naval instructions were followed. In answer to a casualty question, the captain indicated that both mates hurt their hands getting into lifeboats.

When queried what became of passengers (none were onboard) and crew after abandoning the ship, the captain answered: "Crew rowed ashore to Carboneras where the authorities sent them on muleback to Garrucha. At Garrucha they were interrogated by the Spanish Naval authorities and a statement written obtained from all the crew. As this statement was obtained through an interpreter and only the first mate who is an Austrian speaks Spanish, it was signed on the assurance of this man that the testimony was properly translated."

In the questionnaire, the names and addresses of the crew were requested—first the Americans and then the foreigners. The data are consolidated in tables 9 and 10. The captain also stated in the questionnaire, "The officers and crew of the CITY OF PENSACOLA consider that the submarine officers showed consideration for them. The captain of the submarine said this was the first American boat he had attacked."9

A listing of items saved included 2 lifeboats, 16 life belts, 50 gallons of gasoline, 1 keg of sea oil, 2 masts, 2 sails, and various tools. The two boats saved were described as a horsepower gasoline lifeboat 33 feet long and a metallic lifeboat 20 feet long. The estimated value of both was $500.

The captain earlier stated that after the submarine left them, the crew rowed off, and they were sent by the authorities on muleback to Garrucha. Captain Sanderson's statement was also read and sworn to by the officers of the *City of Pensacola*, Hayley A. Wilson, Paguzzino

TABLE 9. DATA ON AMERICAN CREW MEMBERS

Name	Age	Job	Married	Address
Hayley A. Wilson	39	chief engineer	yes	128 Dresden St., Brooklyn, N.Y.
George Gart	20	2nd asst. engineer	no	644 East 170 St., New York, N.Y.
James Scanlon	37	unknown	no	808 Cader St., Sault Ste. Marie, Minn.
Robert A. Sanderson	67	master	widower	253 Church St., Mobile, Ala.
Peter Brandt	33	1st asst. engineer	no answer	255 22nd St., New York, N.Y.
Gustave A. Carlson	27	second mate	no	2 Linden St., North Easton, Mass.

Giovanni, Peter Brandt, Gustave A. Carlson, and George Gart. Their titles are indicated in tables 9 and 10.

Peter Brandt the first assistant engineer stated:

> At the time of occurrence I was on watch, watch commencing at 12,m.night. About 2.45 A.M. my attention was called by a noise sounding like someone striking the funnel with a heavy board, me being used to that paid no attention to same but when a second sound came within 15 seconds of the first one I knew we was being shelled. I then waited for instructions to stop the engines but as I received none, I after waiting 15 minutes for signals and receiving none went up the emergency entrance to see what was going on. I met Chief Engineer Mr. Wilson and upon his instruction I went and got my life belt and got ready with him to get to our position in the motor boat being boarded at the stern of the vessel.
>
> When getting clear of vessel to a distance of about 200 yards we noticed the crew of our other life boat being picked up by the submarine. In the meantime a two masted schooner painted white which was very close by was passed by on its port side by the submarine and as this occurred I heard voices and rather greetings exchanged between the crews of the two vessels. Directly after passing this schooner the submarine came alongside our boat and asked for the captain and upon acknowledgment that he was in our boat asked him to pull alongsid [sic] the submarine. We pulled

TABLE 10. DATA ON FOREIGN CREW MEMBERS

Name	Age	Job	Married	Address
Nicolai Roos	18	mess boy	no answer	Arendal, Norway
Alexander Olson	30	seaman	no	3 State St., Brooklyn, N.Y.
Karl Persson	24	seaman	no	25 South St., New York, N.Y., Petrograde, Russia
Paguzzino Giovanni	64	1st mate	no answer	Via Antochia 3, Geneva
Arnold Centil	22	no answer	no	Auckland, New Zealand

alongside and was asked to step on board the submarine. While I was on board said submarine my attention was immediately called to the effect that there were several of the crew of the submarine who had been in the States and spoke quite good English and one of the first questions I was asked by one of these was to the effect "WHAT DOES THE UNITED STATES THINK OF THE WAR NOW." I did not give him any direct answer as I thought better not under my present circumstances. I was asked by one of the German sailors to go to 328 Hudson Street, Hoboken, New Jersey, and give his best regards to a German woman living there. Said sailor told me that he left America in 1915 on the Scadinavian [sic] American Line for Copenhagen, Denmark, and got back to Germany in that way. One of the officers in the submarine asked our crew if any of us understood German and as I had learned German for six years in college I answered, yes. Said officer thereupon engaged me in conversation in German telling me that they had a 10 1/2 inch gun in the submarine, which I knew was an infernal lie as the gun was only 4,5 inches at the very most. He also told me that they were going ashore regularly in the Spanish coast and that we only had 4 1/2 miles to the nearest town in the coast of Spain and gave me a lot of stories about girls and good times they used to have in those places.

While I was on board the submarine I heard a remark passed between the crew that the Spanish 2 masted schooner I gave the description of previously, in German DAS IST UNSERER MUTTER SCHIFF WISSEN SIE. The submarine Commander asked his sailors to go on board of our Schooner to get whatever food and things they could gather and they went in our lifeboat and brought back a lot of stores from the Galley and a lot of other articles from the cabin including the signal flags and the old glory of our Vessel. They planted two bombs in the schooner and coming back to the submarine with our boat ordered all of us in our boat and start for the Spanish coast which we did and the submarine went to sea but on the surface. I am not able to give our position or distance from shore at the time of being shelled but I know we were pulling oars for 2 hours before we landed on the beach of a small village on the Spanish coast. Trusting you are accepting this statement subject to oath and totthe [*sic*] best of my ability, I beg to remain Yours most respectfully, BRANDS (SIGNED) 1st Asst. Engineer.

This statement was subscribed and sworn to before me this second day of May, 1918. Signed Gaston Smith, Consul of the United States of America.[10]

The Spanish were supposed to be neutral at this time, so this testimony elicited the United States Navy's interest. This was indicated in a communication from "U.S. Navy, C.O. U.S. Naval Forces operating in European Waters" on the subject of sailing vessel *Paco Bonmati*, with the date and addressee missing. The writer quoted Brandt and went on to say: "The PACO BONMATI arrived at Almeria on May 1st, 1918 and the Captain JOSE MORENO, told me that he came from Barcelona. The schooner is painted white, and is about 180 tons. Her register is from the port of Santa Pola and the Captain JOSE MORENO is from Torrevieja, these ports near Alicante. The owner of the PACO BONMATI is Paco Bonmati. He is considered a wealthy man. He owns salt pans (salinas) and other property in Santa Pola."[11]

A similar letter dated June 3, 1918, was sent to a Lieutenant Commander Gilpin (Operations), State Department, and to the British and French Naval attachés. The subject: "Spanish vessel assists submarine." It again quoted Peter Brandt's information and was similar to the first letter. The only addition, apparently, was a photograph of the *Paco Bonmati* attached to the letter (which was not in the file).

On June 11, 1918, Giovanni Ragusin, first mate on the *City of Pensacola*, was interrogated on board the American SS *Orion* in New York Harbor by C. B. M. Demuth. Presumably, Demuth was a U.S. Navy official, and possibly the first "C" is for Commander; the documents did not provide that information. Captain Sanderson also made a statement on that ship on the same date, which was very much a repeat of his first statement. The first mate substantiated the other statements with a few additions and his personal history.

Ragusin stated he was of Italian nationality and an Austrian subject. He indicated he was always at sea on Austrian boats but Italian was the only language spoken. Just before Italy went into the war, he took all of his family back to Italy and put himself at the disposal of the Italian government. While waiting, he was employed as chief officer on various steamers run by the Italian States Railway Company. Ragusin had just signed on the ship on April 11, 1918, at Genoa. He was asked to tell, in his own words, what happened. His answer throws more light on the lifeboat situation and why they had to row ashore:

I was asleep, just coming off watch. The Captain was on watch and of course when I heard the first shot I arose and took my coat and went out. Just as I came out I heard the second shot. Then I saw the Captain and I went to my place and took the davit fall to lower the boat, because the ship got sunk at the third shot, and very heavy smoke came from the ship. We lowered the boat and we left the ship. It was impossible to free the motor boat.

The submarine ordered the two boats containing our entire crew to come alongside, and they took the Captain on board the submarine. The German officer said in English to our Captain, "I am very sorry, but war is war." He also said, "You are too far off shore, you are about 4 1/2 miles," But from my experience of 36 years at sea, I am sure that we were about 2 1/2 or 3 miles from the shore, and then the Captain of the submarine said to his crew in German, "You go aboard the steamer and you take every thing you can find, we have plenty of time." Then they went on board with masks because because [*sic*] the ship was burning. They took the sextant, chronometers and various ship's papers and books and all the shoes and blankets they could find.

When the submarine captain heard that the schooner was in ballast, he exclaimed in German "What a pity." When asked if anything else was said, Ragusin stated, "The Germans were very kind to the American ships, in that they treated us with the utmost courtesy, and very, very nice in every respect. They even gave cigarettes to the members of our crew." He also stated that the submarine had one deck gun about 75 or 76 centimeters (this should be millimeters).

The last Ragusin heard of the submarine was four shots about twenty minutes later. His description of their location at the time of the attack was about 2 3/4 miles from Torre de le Messa di Roldan. He made a sketch of the U-boat. When asked how he could make a sketch of the boat at night, Ragusin indicated that the close proximity allowed some vision.

The concern with the distance of the *City of Pensacola* from the coast of Spain and the interplay between the Spanish schooner and the German submarine are relevant because Spain remained neutral throughout World War I. Supposedly the ship was in neutral waters as long as it stayed within three miles of shore. Furthermore, a neutral country is not supposed to aid either side.

In Spain at that time, "the working classes, most of the intellectuals, and the trading communities—the Liberal left—were pro-Allies. The clergy, most of the army and the bureaucracy, and the 'idle rich'—the Conservative right—were pro-German." All agreed on the one essential, and that was avoiding the war. Germany was not kind to Spain in this war: by September of 1916, Spain had lost more than 80,000 tons of shipping, 30,000 tons of which were by torpedo attack. When on January 31, 1917, Germany intimated an "absolute blockade" of the Allied coasts, Premier Alvaro de Figueroa y Torres, conde de Romanones delivered a spirited answer partly to test public opinion. He resigned the following April. In the end the submarine war cost Spain 65 vessels, or a total of 140,000 tons.[12]

Based on this information, it is difficult to understand why the Spanish schooner was helping the German submarine, unless it was for money. It also would not appear that hugging the Spanish coast was a very effective strategy for avoiding U-boats.

The Germans seemed quite proud of this victory at sea, as a report in the enemy's camp on May 17, 1918, indicated:

Berlin, May 17. Our submarines sank in the Mediterranean 25,000 gross tons of ships space. A main part in these successes is due to the submarine boat under the command of Lieutenant Marschall. The English armed steamers "KUT SANG" (4896 tons) and "CONWAY" (4003 tons) were shot out from strong convoys. The entirely new four masted schooner "CITY OF PENSACOLA," which was equipped with two auxiliary motors (706 tons) was sunk by means of explosive cartridges. The Chief of the Admiralty Staff of the Navy.[13]

Captain Sanderson came to the attention of the U.S. Navy for what they considered a major indiscretion. On June 1, 1918, the director of naval intelligence, Roger Willis, Captain U.S.N., wrote the commissioner of navigation with a serious complaint about Captain Sanderson: "It is reported by the Italian Admiralty that secret instructions were allowed to fall into the hands of the enemy by the Captain of the CITY OF PENSACOLA."

He went on to summarize the information obtained from the affidavits, which in no way added anything incriminating except to say that all documents were lost. His last sentence was "In view of the fact that the Captain allowed secret orders to fall into the hands of the enemy kindly advise us what steps are taken in this case."[14]

The commissioner replied promptly with a letter dated June 5, 1918, to the Navy. The commissioner merely looked at the available evidence to provide answers to questions. Question number 64 of the captain's interrogation was: "Were there any other confidential documents on board? If so, state what disposition was made of them": "None except the sailing instructions from the Italian dispatch officer in Genoa, and the French dispatch officer in Marseilles. These went down with the boat." While it is possible that the submarine crew picked up such documents, if they only pertained to the *City of Pensacola*, this would not appear to be a major security breach, especially since no radio codes should have been involved. The commissioner put things in place with his final paragraph: "Before proceeding further in the matter I will be pleased to be informed if the Italian Admiralty has information that the sailing directions actually fell into the hands of the enemy instead of going down with the ship as claimed by the master, or if the charge is against the master for failing to throw overboard or otherwise destroy these sailing directions as instructed therein."[15]

The *City of Pensacola* deserves one last look to see what she may have accomplished in her short lifetime. First, her net tonnage was 602 tons, and calculations indicate that she could carry approximately 600,000 board feet of lumber in the holds and on deck. This load also would not exceed her deadweight tonnage capacity of about 1,000 tons. The question was, was she sunk on the first trip or a later trip? The ship sailed on her maiden voyage, leaving Orange on September 18, 1917, according to the owner's letter, quoted in chapter 5. Using the *City of Orange*'s best time, which was 6.5 mph, and applying it to the total distance of 6,500 miles, the travel time would have been forty-two days. To have delivered two loads of lumber to Italy, the ship would have made one round-trip plus a one-way trip. The travel time would then have been at least 126 days, or 4 months and 6 days. The total time available was about seven months, so two deliveries were possible. But, with all of the stops they seemed to have made and the unforeseen delays, it does not appear likely. It is also very improbable that the ship would average 6.5 mph for the total trip. One other possibility is that she made a round-trip to the East Coast with packaged petroleum products or other bulk cargo; however, if this occurred, there should have been a document change.

Many sailing vessels were sunk in World War I because of greedy owners eager to make money during this period of extreme demand for anything that would float. The crews obviously knew of the risks, so perhaps some of their motivation was the extra pay for the additional hazards.

Two Barkentines Go South

The next eleven ships built for ISC were five-masted barkentines. The first was the *City of Gulfport*, probably named in honor of Piaggio's adopted home in America. She and the *City of Mobile* avoided the perils of the German U-boats by going to South American ports. This probably was not a consideration of the owners but, rather, a choice of destinations based on the cargo consignments.

THE STRAW THAT BROKE CAPTAIN WRY'S BACK

The *City of Gulfport* received her Certificate of Registry at Port Arthur on March 12, 1918.[1] A picture of the finished ship is shown in figure 7.1. All of the sails are bent on and furled, including the topsails. Sailcovers are on the gaffsails, and the ship appears ready to sail except for loading. A man in a boatswain's chair is working at bulwarks level forward.

The ship has twelve shrouds and stays on the foremast going to chainplates on each side of the hull, and eight on each side of the remaining masts. Foremasts on schooners will have one or two more shrouds than the following masts, because more loads are transmitted to the foremast from the after masts. In the case of the barkentines additional shrouds are required because the foremast being square-rigged is made up of three masts instead of two and so requires even more shrouds and stays. The ship has four headsails going to a spike bowsprit, without a jibboom or martingale.

Her master for the maiden voyage was Captain Wry, and the first destination was New Orleans, Louisiana, in ballast. The departure took place on March 28, 1918, and subsequent plans for cargo and destination were not stated. On March 9, 1918, ISC sent the following letter to Captain Wry: "Please be advised that we have a clause in our Insurance Policies requiring a continuous running of your Motor Engines from the time you leave Port until you arrive at your destination. Also please be advised that under no circumstances are you to permit any visitors, regardless of who they may be, aboard the 'CITY OF GULFPORT'; in other words no one is allowed on the vessel, except your crew and the pilot, when this vessel leaves this Port. Please acknowledge receipt in writing with your full understanding."[2]

Apparently ISC was not pleased with Captain Wry's practice, in Gibraltar or other ports, of entertaining on board the ship. This letter was very clear, but Captain Wry was undaunted by its contents, as indicated in the next letter from the collector of customs at Port Arthur to his counterpart at New Orleans, dated March 29, 1918.[3] The primary message was that when the ship left Orange, it had on board Judge J. B. Bisland, a lawyer of Orange, as a passenger on the vessel. The master tried to get the collector to sign the judge on as a member of the crew, but, as it appeared to be an evasion, he refused. The certificate of inspection for the *City of Gulfport* did not permit the carriage of passengers. This was the final straw for the owners, and on April 4, 1918, at New Orleans, an Indorsements of Change of Master

fig. 7.1. The City
of Gulfport.
Courtesy Blud-
worth Collection

form indicated that Captain Rupert Wry was replaced by Captain M. W. Geldert.[4]

Captain Wry was not going to give up without being heard from, and on April 8, 1918, he appeared before a notary and made a sworn statement.[5] Captain Wry's concern was that his infraction had an automatic penalty of $500. He knew ISC was not going to take him back, and he was probably not one to get overly worried about his reputation. He stated that up until April 4, 1918, he was master of the *City of Gulfport* when she left Orange on March 28, 1918, on her maiden voyage bound for New Orleans. On that voyage, the ship was in ballast and carried no passengers whatsoever, every person on board having been properly signed on and received wages in accordance with the positions held by them. He submitted this statement to the customs collector at New Orleans, who forwarded it with a two-page letter of his own dated April 9, 1918, to the secretary of commerce, Washington, D.C. Everyone concerned gave this matter prompt attention.

The customs collector discussed the background and the fact that Captain Wry told him verbally that Judge Bisland actually waited on the table during the voyage. According to the records of the U.S. shipping commissioner at the port, it appeared that the judge was paid off per Mutual Release as "Asst. Cabin Boy," at the rate of $25 per month. This did not fool the collector, and he went on to say that, in the master's sworn statement, it did not appear that the judge rendered any service whatsoever. The collector then stated that the judge was not a professional seaman but an attorney-at-law who made no statement in the matter. The master offered no evidence that the judge's services, if any were rendered, were absolutely required for the safe navigation of the vessel. Based on this, the presumption is that he was really carried as a passenger, and his signing was a mere evasion of the law, particularly so since the deputy collector at Orange refused to ship him as a member of the crew. Enclosures were Captain Wry's statement and the letter from the collector at Orange.

The acting secretary replied to the collector at New Orleans in a letter dated April 19, 1918.[6] The first paragraph of this letter revealed that this was really about Captain Wry's trying to avoid paying the fine of $500. The secretary agreed with the two collectors and further mentioned: "It might also be stated that Captain Rupert Wry has been before the Department on a number of occasions for violations of law." He added: "In view of the circumstances the Department declines to intervene in this case." The acting supervising inspector general had also reviewed this action on April 18 (the day before) and recommended that the full penalty be imposed.

On April 25, 1918, a letter was written, on Piaggio's Gulfport Pitch Pine and Timber Export business stationery, over the stamp of HENRY PIAGGIO and signed by a person named Dickman to the Honorable Calhoun Fluker, special deputy collector, New Orleans.[7] This letter made a case that Captain Wry acted entirely without the writer's knowledge, and enclosed was a copy of the letter to Captain Wry stating that no passengers or visitors were to be allowed on board their boats. He further stated that the captain was dismissed for this action and that a master would not be tolerated who would act contrary to the instructions of a collector in any port. Dickman asked that in view of his innocence in the matter a mitigation of the fine be allowed.

The writer was pleading not for Captain Wry but rather for the company that would be responsible for the fine when, inevitably and probably soon, the captain would go to sea on another ship. The anonymity of the life of a seaman had a high appeal, especially to less conforming individuals, and Captain Wry appeared to fit that description.

The next day, the vice president and general manager of the South Atlantic Steamship Line wrote a letter of appeal again to Fluker in an attempt to help Piaggio. The writer stated that the ship came into New Orleans consigned to the steamship company. The writer restated the case, adding that the fine would fall on Piaggio after he discharged Captain Wry. He felt that Piaggio would far rather pay a larger fine than retain in his employment any master who would act as Captain Wry did. His closing paragraph is of interest: "Mr. Piaggio is a well known citizen of Gulfport and the public prints speak almost daily of Mr. Piaggio's large part in building vessels and in bringing his every talent and effort towards re-establishing the American merchant marine. It seems to me that your department might well show some leniency to such a citizen when the record will clearly disclose that he was entirely innocent of any wrong doing and was simply the victim of Capt. Wry's violation of orders."[8]

Fluker, the collector at New Orleans, then wrote a favorable letter to the secretary of commerce, dated April 29, 1918, with the two previous letters as enclosures.[9] Since the department declined earlier to intervene in the case, the agents for the vessel had to put up the full penalty, which was held in a special deposit. He reviewed the two letters, emphasizing the positive aspects, and closed by making a recommendation for favorable consideration. The climate changed when the officials found out that Captain Wry was not going to suffer the penalty, and the recommendation for favorable consideration would seem the just answer.

The supervising inspector general reviewed the letters and submitted his recommendation to the commissioner in a letter dated May 4,

1918.[10] He was not in favor of any leniency, stating that the principal was responsible for the acts of his agent and brought up the earlier statement about Captain Wry's previous violations. He felt that this should have alerted the owner as to what might happen on a vessel owned by him when he employed Captain Wry. In the end, the commissioner gave everyone a concession, as the last paragraph in his letter to the collector at New Orleans dated May 10, 1918, showed: "The Department cannot entirely excuse this violation as the owner of a vessel must be held responsible for the actions his masters take. In view of the circumstances, however, the penalty incurred is hereby mitigated to $50."[11]

That brought this episode to a close, and reluctantly we bid Captain Wry farewell, for, if nothing else, he livened up this bit of history and again proved that truth is stranger than fiction. He was the only captain I have ever run across in truth or fiction who jettisoned cargo without a good cause and who further proved that shanghaiing was still in vogue as late as World War I. Cruelty to a seaman, possibly based on racial prejudice, was not, however, a rarity during this time, on land or sea. Sadly it persisted for many years.

Neither the cargo carried by the *City of Gulfport* nor the ship's destination after the trip in ballast to New Orleans was known, but in mid-August, the vessel was back in the Port Arthur area. Because the previous incident revealed she arrived in New Orleans on April 4, 1918, there is a four-month unaccounted for gap. That amount of time would have permitted a round-trip to the East Coast but not to Europe. Such a trip would not have been unusual at that time, with some product of the South such as cotton, lumber, or packaged petroleum products, although the latter would be more likely to come out of Port Arthur. A change in documentation from Certificate of Registry to a Consolidated Certificate of Enrollment and License should have been made for such a coastal trip, but none was found. Many such things, however, became lost or were overlooked.

THE *CITY OF GULFPORT* GOES SOUTH

The next communication was a letter from the American Consulate at Montevideo, Uruguay, concerning the death at sea of Charles S. Lee, seaman of American auxiliary barkentine *City of Gulfport*.[12] The master was still M. W. Geldert, who took over from Captain Wry, and the letter states that he had made oath to the death at sea of Charles S. Lee, steward and a Japanese subject. Lee shipped at Port Arthur on August 19, 1918, and died November 21, 1918, on the voyage from Port Arthur to Montevideo. The distance, at 7,150 miles, is greater than the distance to

Genoa.[13] The master stated the cause of death to have been dropsy, and the body was buried at sea.

The consulate goes on to say that the vessel would proceed from Montevideo to La Plata, Argentina, and from there to the United States, probably by way of Cette, France. The Consul also included a statement of the seaman's account, certified by the master.

Of interest is the pay of the steward, which was $150 per month plus 25 percent bonus, making the accrued pay $581.25. Lee had some debt, as he received a ten-dollar advance at Port Arthur, and he owed Antonio Gonzalez nine dollars.

In addition, Lee owed the slop chest twelve dollars for two pounds of tobacco, one suit of underwear, and five pairs of bath towels. His total effects in the hands of the master were three suits of underwear, one pair shoes, four dress shirts, one straw hat, seven ties, one pair of trousers, one belt, one pair of suspenders, three pairs of socks, one safety razor, one drinking cup, and one comb—but no towels.

One further letter followed, dated April 19, 1919, from R. E. Latimer, collector at Port Arthur, to the commissioner of navigation and in effect said that they had been unable to communicate with the next of kin.[14]

The *City of Gulfport* arrived at La Plata, Argentina, on December 26, 1918, with a part cargo of case oil (kerosene in tinned containers).[15] After her previous stop at Montevideo and after apparently unloading the remaining cargo, she was waiting to load a cargo of cereals for Cette, France, consigned to the Swiss government. This information came from the consul general at Buenos Aires in a letter to the assistant secretary for navigation, E. F. Sweet dated May 2, 1919.[16] The main thrust of the letter, however, was that some members of the crew wanted to be discharged on the grounds that they had only signed up to go to South America and back and to go by way of France would be in direct conflict with the ship's articles.

The consul did not feel their case was justified because the war was over but made a compromise settlement, withholding the authorized transportation costs back to the United States that the crew would be due if they were in the right. The list of job titles requesting release (names were not legible) included third mate, chief engineer, first assistant engineer, carpenter, and five seamen. Of those, three were American, two Norwegian, two Spanish, and the nationalities of two were illegible. Captain Geldert asked the consul to add that his former chief engineer on the list, David Walsh, was the cause of considerable trouble and annoyance to himself and the vessel. The captain also had reliable information that this man allowed some 1,800 gallons of fuel oil to run into the bilges and later to be pumped into the open sea.

Sweet did not agree with the consul at all and stated that the terms of the employment were specific, and any variation from the terms entitled the seamen to discharge, on the grounds that the voyage was continued contrary to that upon which they had agreed. His word in this case was law, and the letter was mailed May 12, 1919.

DISASTER STRIKES

The *City of Gulfport* did not get to sail for France. The Certificate of Registry No. 43 was surrendered at Buenos Aires, Argentina, on May 17, 1919. Reason surrendered: "Vessel burned, March 13, 1919, at La Plata, Argentina."[17]

The *City of Gulfport* arrived December 26, 1918, and was still there March 13 when she burned. This was two and a half months. The reason for such a long delay was not revealed. Did the fuel oil dumped into the bilge cause the fire? Probably not, as the master's statement to the consulate indicated that the fire was caused by the ignition of waste in the engine room while testing the engines preparatory to sailing. The fire reached the bunker fuel oil, causing two explosions. Thereafter the fire spread rapidly until the vessel burned to the water's edge. According to the captain's statement they were preparing to sail, so the full cargo had been delivered before the fire.

The American consul general at Buenos Aires, Argentina, in a telegram dated March 15, 1919, indicated that the consulate's surveyors had condemned the vessel, and he was discharging and relieving the crew, with the exception of the foreigners, who were shipped abroad. Apparently, the crew was held by the port authorities pending an investigation of the fire. Nothing of a suspicious nature, however, was found by the Brazilian authorities or the American consul.[18]

Perhaps it was some legal or administrative formality, but a confusing factor was the burning date (verified), which was almost two months before the consul's letter pertaining to the crew's complaint about going to France.

THE *CITY OF MOBILE*

The *City of Mobile* received her Certificate of Registration at Port Arthur on July 17, 1918.[19]

The master for the maiden voyage of the *City of Mobile* was Captain R. A. Sanderson, a native of Prince Edward Island, who became a naturalized American in Boston about 1880. He was in command of the *City of Pensacola* when it had the U-boat encounter. He lived at

253 Church Street, Mobile, Alabama, and had an excellent reputation in that city.[20]

The *City of Mobile* loaded packaged petroleum products at Port Arthur, Texas, and sailed from there sometime in August of 1918. The ship had been freighted by the Texas Oil Company (Texaco) and the cargo of kerosene and gasoline in cases was consigned to the company's agents at Montevideo and Buenos Aires. On the way, the ship struck bottom on the Bahama Banks, and the vessel had to put into Jacksonville, Florida, for repairs. She did not again start on her voyage to the River Plate until January 21, 1919. During the stay at Jacksonville, about half the cargo had to be discharged and reloaded, resulting in a badly mixed cargo that slowed down the discharge.[21]

The next communication was interesting:

> The Acting Secretary of State presents his compliments to the Honorable the Secretary of Commerce, and has the honor to state that an undated telegram has been received from the American Consul at Montevideo, Uruguay, stating that the master of the American vessel, CITY OF MOBILE, and Mr. Smith, the representative of the owners, have been arrested in Montevideo, accused by the third mate of having caused the loss of the vessel. The Consul requests official advice as to whether the vessel was insured and the amount of the policy, and also requests information regarding the antecedents of the owners, the master of the vessel and Mr. Smith, the representative. He requests that notification be sent to Alvi [*sic*] Bragadin, 71 Broadway, New York. However, inasmuch as Alvi [*sic*] Bragadin is unknown to the Department of State, the information has not been forwarded to him, and it is respectfully requested that the information be forwarded through the Shipping Commissioner for the Port of New York in order that, if the party addressed is unreliable, the information may not be given to him.
>
> It is also respectfully requested that an investigation of the antecedents of the owners, the master and Mr. Smith be made through the appropriate representative of the Department of Commerce in order that appropriate information may be sent to the Consul at Montevideo for use in connection with the trial of the master and Mr. Smith.[22]

The writer was asking for a check on the antecedents of the parties concerned—perhaps what today would be called a background check.

What really happened? Was the captain another villain? The next three letters, dated May 26, 1919, are from Sweet, the acting secretary, and are addressed to the collector of customs, New York City; the U.S. shipping commissioner, New York City; and the secretary of state, Washington, D.C.[23] The first two letters had the letter from the secretary of state as an enclosure and Sweet asking the recipients to respond. He asked the collector to notify Bragadin of the conditions without any admonitions concerning Bragadin's reliability. In the first two paragraphs, to the shipping commissioner, he said:

> I enclose copy of a letter dated 22nd instant from the Secretary of State in regard to a charge against the master of the steamer CITY OF MOBILE that he assisted in the loss of the vessel at Montevideo Uruguay.
>
> I wish you would furnish the Department with any information you may have in regard to the loss of this boat, his antecedents, etc.[24]

The correspondence still contained no mention of the master's name. The ship was erroneously referred to as both a steamer and a boat in the letter.

The third letter was a response to the secretary of state, informing him of the action taken. What happened to the *City of Mobile* was a mystery, but, in looking at the surrender statement on the Certificate of Registry, the puzzle appeared to be at least partially answered. The Certificate of Registry was surrendered at Montevideo, Uruguay, on June 11, 1919, and it is the same story told again. Reason surrendered: "Vessel burned, May 14, 1919, in Montevideo Roads."[25]

One has to wonder how this could happen again after all of the previous losses by fire. (Actually the *City of Orange* did not burn until shortly after the *City of Mobile*, as the latter's end did not come until May 24, 1919. For reasons of completing her career, however, her demise was presented in an earlier chapter.)

The consul paraphrased the telegram that he sent May 14, 1919, in a letter to the secretary of state, dated May 21, 1919:

> On the morning of May 14th the American auxiliary barkentine CITY OF MOBILE became probably a total loss from fire which followed the explosion of the gasoline cargo, occurring at Montevideo Roads. The Marine Superintendent of the owners is here and will probably take charge. The following members of the crew shipped at Jacksonville, Florida, and are missing and are supposed to be dead: De Witt Harp and R. Howard Thomson, American citizens, and Carl Peterson, a subject of Denmark. All the others

of the crew are safe. The home port of the vessel was Port Arthur.[26]

The ISC record was not good to this point. Of the first five ships, four burned and one was sunk by a German submarine. Suspicions were being aroused, especially after the loss of the *City of Orange* only ten days later. A letter from the acting secretary of state to the secretary of commerce, dated May 31, 1919, that transmitted news of the burning of the *City of Orange* alluded to those suspicions in the second paragraph: "Attention is respectfully directed to the fact that three American schooners apparently owned and operated by the same company have been destroyed by fire within the past few months. The last vessel to be destroyed by fire was the CITY OF MOBILE in the port of Montevideo, Uruguay, the master and owners representative having been arrested, charged by the third mate of the vessel of having set fire to the vessel purposely."[27]

This event was much more of a tragedy than the other vessel losses, in that three crew members were lost.

On June 4, 1919, the acting commissioner of navigation, A. J. Tyrer, wrote to the collector of customs at Port Arthur:

> The Department of State calls attention to what it thinks may be suspicious circumstances in connection with the loss by fire within a few months of the gas screws CITY OF GULFPORT, CITY OF MOBILE and CITY OF ORANGE, all belonging at Orange, Texas and possibly to the same persons. The master and owners' representatives in the case of the CITY OF MOBILE have been arrested at Montevideo, Uruguay charged by the third mate with having set fire to the vessel.
>
> The above statement is submitted to you in order that you may call the matter to the attention of the Marine Underwriters if you think the circumstances warrant such action. It seems unnecessary to tell you that whatever action is taken should be with great caution.[28]

Not mentioned was the burning of the *City of Houston* that occurred August 6, 1917.

The American consulate at Montevideo had a more complete report on the loss in a letter to the secretary of state dated May 28, 1919. The consul reported that the ship was lost as a result of an explosion and fire on the morning of May 14, 1919, and that the ship continued to burn for the better part of two days and was virtually a total wreck. Most of the kerosene had been unloaded, and only a few hundred cases were left on board at the time of the explosion. The rest of the cargo was consigned to La Plata, Argentina, and consisted of 33,000 cases of gasoline (330,000 gallons), which were lost.[29] A few thousand cases of oil were picked up in the water or from the beach and were sold at auction by Lloyd's Agent.

The consul went on to say that the cause had not been established, but there seemed no doubt to him that the fire was accidental. He thought it was probably caused by the ignition of gases escaping from the cargo and accumulating in the hold, the ignition being the result of a spark from an engine, a cigarette, or some other agent. With the unloading and reloading that had taken place at Jacksonville and the apparent lack of fire-prevention discipline on the ship, the explosion, though probably not intentional, was likely to happen. The explosion occurred around 7 A.M. on May 14.

The incarceration of Captain Sanderson and Smith was brought about by charges preferred by third mate, Karl Henrickson. First, Smith represented Alvise Bragadin of New York. Bragadin was the person the secretary of state asked the Department of Commerce to inform concerning the explosion of the *City of Mobile*, at the request of Smith. The writer went on to suggest that if the party addressed was determined to be unreliable, the information should not be given to him. Bragadin wore several hats, according to his New York office letterhead on a letter dated July 22, 1919. First he was listed as a director for four companies including a Piave mill company and was a vice president for three of the companies. He was also general agent for several of the wooden sailing ships, starting with the *City of Beaumont* but not including the *Macerata* or *Monfalcone*. Two barkentines built at Pascagoula, Mississippi; the *City of Biloxi* and the *City of Pascagoula* are included for a total of nine. The letterhead also indicated that he represented seven Italian companies including the Societa Annonima Riccardo Gualino. His office address was 71 Broadway. Riccardo Gualino was chairman of ISC, indicating a strong financial tie with Italian interests.

On the ISC letterhead, Bragadin was listed right under Henry Piaggio as a vice president, and, although the main address for the company was Gulfport, Mississippi, just below that was listed the New York address of Bragadin. The location on Broadway was near Wall Street. His signature might have appeared on any of the various letterheads, depending on the subject and recipient.

Henrickson claimed to have overheard a conversation between Captain Sanderson and Smith on the morning of May 4, 1919, when Smith visited the master on board the ship. Smith was alleged to have said, "Well, I guess we will let her burn," or words to that effect. The consul also indicated that both men had been released on bail: "I believe that

TABLE 11. CREW MEMBERS OF
THE *CITY OF MOBILE* DESERTED OR
PAID OFF BEFORE EXPLOSION

Name	Job	Nationality
Daniel O'Brien	sailor	British
John Serback	sailor	American
Karl Henrickson	third mate	Finn
E. L. Bailey	cook and steward	American
Mary E. Bailey	stewardess	American

there can be no doubt but that both men are innocent and that the accusation of the third mate is to be attributed either to ignorance or willful calumny. He had deserted the vessel on or about May 6, 1919, but was still at Montevideo and endeavoring to obtain money from the master. The case of the master and Smith is still pending and I shall report more fully in the matter at as early a date as practicable. From the first the Consulate has cooperated in every way practicable with the accused, their attorney, agents and friends."[30]

Tables 11 and 12 provide data on the crew taken from the consul's letter. Table 11 lists the crew members who had deserted or had been paid by the time of the explosion and contains a rather surprising crew member, namely Mary E. Bailey. Not many women went to sea in this period. Since the cook and steward's last name was also Bailey, it is probable that the two were a husband-and-wife team. Table 12 lists the surviving crew members.

The total number of crew from both tables is twenty, and twelve were officers and idlers, leaving eight sailors to sail the ship. The vessel had a large number of foreign crewmen, typical of the time. Another letter from the consulate to the secretary of state, dated July 18, 1919, throws more light on the accusation.[31] The consul wrote that Henrickson, after allegedly hearing the incriminating conversation, also warned several members of the crew in the forecastle that the ship would burn and that he was going to leave. Four members of the crew confirmed this. Henrickson left the ship around May 6 and went to a sailors' lodging house, where he told the same story to the proprietor, who later confirmed this. Henrickson apparently did not make any effort to warn the local authorities or the consulate, and it was only after trying repeatedly to secure a regular discharge after the ship loss that he denounced the master.

On May 15, Henrickson came to the consulate to find out whether the master could be compelled to pay him off despite his desertion. He

TABLE 12. SURVIVING CREW MEMBERS

Name	Job	Nationality
R. A. Sanderson	master	American
J. L. Warren	first mate	American
J. D. Halliday	second mate	British
L. T. Forlaw	chief engineer	American
Roger Ware	first assistant engineer	American
Claud Wolvin	donkeyman	American
John Ernstein	boatswain	Russian
L. Sveinsson*	carpenter	Dane
Jerre T. Wills	second cook	American
Torstein Kristiansen	sailor	Norwegian
Knut Wallin	sailor	Swede
D. O. Flannigan	sailor	American
Axel H. Larson	sailor	Swede
Lauritz Peterson	sailor	Norwegian
A. Anderson	sailor	Norwegian

* Sorrenson on crew list

was informed that, as a deserter, he was not entitled to wages (for some reason, the half-pay rule did not appear to apply). To this, Henrickson replied that he knew the master would do nothing for him, so he was going to show the master up. Shortly after this conversation with Vice Consul Fonda, Henrickson denounced the master and Smith to the local authorities.

Had it not been for these verified warnings, Henrickson's accusations probably would not have received much attention, but in this case, the police turned the matter over to a court of investigation, which ordered the detention of the master and Smith on the evening of May 16. They were deprived of all communication, as was customary pending certain legal formalities. The consul decided, after consultation with the ship's agents on May 17, to request that Dr. Daniel Garcia Avevedo, a well-known local attorney, undertake the defense. The consul carefully explained that he could assume no responsibility whatsoever for the payment of fees.

The consul went on to state that Karl Henrickson appeared to be a man of low type, as shown by the fact that, as he himself admitted, he would never have brought the matter up to the authorities had he gotten the money from the master. As for the statements he claims to have overheard, his own statement showed him to be so far from the master's cabin that it would have been very easy for a foreigner to misconstrue phrases. The only circumstances giving weight to his denunciation were his warnings to his shipmates and a boarding master, given well in advance of the loss of the ship and subsequently confirmed by his interlocutors. The man may have honestly believed that he had overheard some phrases such as that reported, or the whole story may have been invented.

The consul thought it significant that none of the crew given the warning left the ship. It also appeared that Henrickson had told various shipmates that he would leave the vessel at Montevideo, where he could make more money. He was also reported to have obtained considerable sums from the crews of Norwegian whalers. By this latter date, July 18, 1919, no specific cause for the explosion had been found, and it was still thought to be accidental ignition of accumulated gases from the cargo. De Witt Harp, the second assistant engineer, was in the engine room when the explosion occurred and was one of the three dead seamen.

The consul also went on to say that there were no circumstances of any sort connected with the explosion itself that could cast suspicion on the master or Smith. Some time delay in communications accounts for the fact that the master and Smith had been released in Montevideo but were thought still to be in jail by the Bureau of Navigation in Washington.

The question concerning the antecedents was answered on July 22, 1919, by the New York collector of customs, who, because the ship had not been to New York, had requested information from Jacksonville and Port Arthur. His answer indicated that the principal owner was said to be Henry Piaggio, son of the Italian consul at Gulfport (a check with the Department of State would have shown there was no Italian consul at Gulfport). The reputation of the company and of the officers of the company was good, although they had other vessels that had been destroyed by fire. Smith was a young man sent from the office of Alvise Bragadin in New York. Nothing critical concerning the company or its officials was found.[32]

In the case of the death of an American in a foreign country, consular form 192, Report of the Death of an American Citizen, was required. The form for De Witt Harp, age thirty-five, gave some brief details of the circumstances surrounding his death and indicated that he was interred in grave number 960 at the Cementerio del Buceo, Montevideo, Uruguay. It further indicated that his body could be removed at the expiration of five years and that he had a wife, Nellie Harp, living at 27 Hubbard Lane, Jacksonville, Florida. In a separate letter from the consulate to the secretary of state, his account, according to the master's statement and based on wages of $162.50 per month for the period from January 18 to May 14, was $639.17. From this was subtracted $200 cash advance and an allotment of $62.50 per month for three months, leaving a balance due the seaman of $251.67.

Since the master expected to return to the United States, the consul stated he deemed it advisable not to require him to hand over the monies due the deceased. If, however, his return were greatly delayed, the consul would require the master to hand over the money in compliance with consular regulations. The consul stated that the very slow mail service between the United States and Uruguay made it impossible to settle estates of this kind expeditiously. He wrote to the widow of the deceased informing her of the status of Harp's account with the vessel, as stated by the master.[33]

The other American killed was R. Howard Thompson, age twenty, whose body was not recovered and presumably burned with the vessel. He had a survivor, his father, Dr. R. W. Thompson of Gainesville, Florida. Seamen on the ship at the time of the explosion made sworn statements verifying the fact that the deceased sailors were on board at the time of the explosion, and, in the case of Thompson, that they did not again see him. Thompson's pay was $75 per month, and he got an advance of $115, leaving a balance due of $172.50. The consul again wrote the survivor with this information.[34]

In another letter to the secretary of state, the consul indicated that the master informed him that he did not desire to retain half of the register. The ship's copy of the Certificate of Registry would be cut in half diagonally and half given the captain if he desired.

The last accounting was that of Carl L. Peterson, with wages of $75 per month, for a total of $297.50. Unlike the Americans, he was charged an 8 percent tax, or $23.80, and he owed $144 for cash and slops, leaving a balance due of $129.70. According to the articles and crew list, he was twenty-eight years old and a Danish subject. A shipmate stated that he hailed from Aarhus, Denmark, but no other information that might assist in locating his relatives was available. The cemetery certificate spelled his first name Karl, which was probably correct.

In a letter to the commissioner of navigation, dated June 2, 1919, the deputy collector at Jacksonville, Florida, explained why they had been unable to ascertain the address of the next of kin of Peterson. In answer, the commissioner of navigation wrote: "Referring to the Bureau's request as to what effort is made at this port to obtain addresses on shipping a crew for a foreign voyage, each member of the crew always has an opportunity to have the name and address of his next of kin inserted in the shipping articles; but it is sometimes the case that, through indifference or for other reasons, seamen refuse to give such information. Usually, however, the addresses of the next of kin are inserted."[35]

On March 13, 1920, the secretary of state wrote to the secretary of commerce, indicating that the Danish Legation had inquired as to whether the available records of the *City of Mobile* disclosed any information that might lead to the deceased sailor's kin. In a previous communication, they thought some information might be obtained from papers or other available personal effects. Advertisements in newspapers at Aarhus, Denmark, did not produce any information about Peterson. The assistant secretary of commerce, Sweet, answered March 19, 1920, indicating that nothing new had been found concerning Peterson.[36]

That was the last communication concerning the *City of Mobile*, and it marked the end of the first two barkentines. The *City of Gulfport* survived from March 12, 1918, until March 13, 1919, one year and one day. The *City of Mobile* survived from July 17, 1918, until June 11, 1919, slightly less than eleven months. Hauling packaged petroleum products in lieu of going to the war zone still resulted in lost vessels. Nevertheless, many ships hauled case oil and gasoline all over the world, so the cargo was not the real problem.

Neither the *City of Houston* nor the *City of Orange* had petroleum products as a cargo when they burned, and, in fact, the latter ship was in ballast. Indications are the first five ships carried a thousand or more gallons of gasoline onboard for a gasoline-powered lifeboat that was also used as needed when the ship was anchored off shore. Some of the ships may have used gasoline for other purposes, such as for a donkey engine. Gasoline was also a favorite solvent for cleaning parts, tools, and hands. The engine maintenance manuals called for the use of gasoline to clean various screen filters followed by drying with compressed air. This was a dangerous combination especially in an enclosed engine room and there were no safety cautions offered as one finds today with almost everything we do. Indications were that, while the drinking of alcoholic beverages while in port was at least tolerated, it may have been a contributing factor as well. It would appear that some major lack in fire prevention and discipline contributed to at least some of the ship losses.

The City of Beaumont

The next two ships completed were the *City of Beaumont* and the *City of Dallas*. The hulls were built at a yard in Beaumont. Both were about 255 feet long and had two 100 horsepower Fairbanks-Morse marine oil engines and could carry 26,000 gallons of fuel oil. In addition, they had tankage for approximately 1,300 gallons of gasoline, probably for a gasoline-powered lifeboat, although the specific usage was not given. This is a large quantity of fuel if it were for emergency use only; however, the motorized lifeboat was also a taxi for the ship. At ports other than the loading and unloading port, the ships usually anchored offshore, so ship-to-shore transportation was mandatory.

It was mentioned that the *City of Pensacola* had a gasoline-powered lifeboat, and the *City of Beaumont* had a motorboat (fuel not mentioned), so one would expect that all of the ships had something similar. Papers for the *City of Dallas* listed twenty tons of coal, and the presumed use would be for the donkey boiler and possibly heating and cooking. All of the ships had donkey engines, but the coal supply was not usually given. The form giving this information was often only partially filled out and sometimes not at all, suggesting this information was not considered important. Donkey engines for hoisting and pumping were available and were powered by steam from a coal-fired boiler or were internal combustion with gasoline or oil as the fuel.

Both ships are mentioned here because they were built at a Beaumont yard and were the last two of the slightly smaller length barkentines that also had the two smaller 100 horsepower engines. The remainder of this chapter is devoted to the *City of Beaumont*.

THE *CITY OF BEAUMONT*

The *City of Beaumont* was launched March 28, 1918, and received her Certificate of Registry No. 8 at Port Arthur, Texas, July 22, 1918, some three months and three weeks before the end of World War I.[1] She was owned by the City of Beaumont Ship Company of Gulfport, Mississippi, maintaining an office at Orange, Texas. The master listed on the registry was S. A. Simmons, although he did not take her on the maiden voyage, and the vessel was described as a gas screw (auxiliary barkentine).

Figure 8.1 shows a head-on view of the *City of Beaumont*. Here one can see the fineness of the hull; these ships were not sailing barges, and with a length-to-breadth ratio of 5.6:1, were typical for the size. The clipper ship *Flying Cloud*, discussed earlier, had a fineness ratio of 5.5:1. A pair of struts with tailshaft bearing is in the foreground and may have been intended for installation in one of the ships.

These ships were described in a variety of ways, such as oil screw, gas screw, and auxiliary barkentine, the latter being the correct terminology. Erroneous were "steamer" or "steamship," terms used by the Bureau of Navigation's acting inspector general. To a true sailor, calling these ships anything but auxiliary followed by their correct rig descrip-

fig. 8.1. The City
of Beaumont
head on.
Courtesy
Bludworth
Collection

tion was unjustified. Further it was an insult to the men who sailed them, for sailing required many skills and a higher level of intestinal fortitude not learned or required on steamships.

Several naval powers required training in sail before receiving commissions in their navy because of the extra physical and psychological demands of sail. Such training was instrumental in weeding out the less dedicated and valiant individuals. Many governments subsidized commercial sail to support apprentice programs, which in turn provided officers for their merchant ships.

THE MAIDEN VOYAGE OF THE *CITY OF BEAUMONT*

We are fortunate in that the first captain of the *City of Beaumont* wrote a very descriptive letter to the ship's launch sponsor, Mary Anna Crary of Beaumont, describing what started out to be the maiden voyage and ended up in divorce. The master who took the ship to sea on her first trip was W. B. Butler, and the trip started September 14, 1918, a little less than two months after its documentation. The letter, which was typed in purple, according to the recipient, reads:

AT SEA.

The "CITY OF BEAUMONT"; Sunday, November 23rd; 1919.

On passage From SPEZIA, in ITALY, to HAMPTON ROADS. U.S.A.

Latitude 26.28 North.

Longitude 31.35 West.

In the saloon of this good vessel there hangs a framed photograph of a young lady, to which the Master has attached a note which informs the curious people who repeatedly inquire "is that your daughter"? that it is a Miss Creary? who christened the vessel at time of launching; whose father is a friend of Mr. Piaggio, and who lives in Beaumont, Texas.

The said master, approaching as he is, the sere and yellow leaf period of life, does not consider it either wise or prudent to repeat anything which might induce pride or vanity in the heart of that young lady; but he does not mind admitting that he would be a proud man if he had a daughter resembling your fathers daughter.

It has occurred to him to day that you, the young lady in question might be interested in a brief outline of the history of the *City of Beaumont* since she started out on her career of adventure on the 14th day of September, 1918. That was the day she sailed from Ship Island, bound for South Norwalk, Conn.

This was before the Armistice was signed, and while the public mind was concerned about the action of German submarines on the American Coast.

I do not recall that the crew expressed, or manifested any concern regarding any possible danger from that source. We however were made conscious of the concern of Uncle Sam for the welfare of his proteges, by the appearance of aeroplanes every day in our vicinity.

With light and variable winds we were 17 days reaching New York. From there we proceeded to South Norwalk, through Hell Gate, into Long Island Sound, thence to our destination, which we reached on October 3rd.

Having discharged the cargo there, we left for New York on the 26th day of October, arriving the same day. On this trip thru the Sound, and the East River, we had as passengers the respective wives of the Master and Chief Engineer. It was an ideal day, and they keenly enjoyed the experience. When approaching the first Bridge—Queensboro—they became so afraid that the vessels masts would strike it that they fled into the saloon. Going clear, they remained on deck while passing beneath the other Bridges.

After considerable delay in New York, we at last got loaded with a valuable general cargo ostensibly destined for Switzerland, but actually for Germany. If I were required to prove that this was the truth, I am afraid I could not do so, any more than I could prove that this old earth of ours is a fragment thrown off from the sun, many many years ago. I am only morally certain of it.

On the 18th day of December we went to anchor in New York harbour, pending certain official formalities to be complied with before sailing. On the 19th of December while lying peaceably at anchor, the steamer "Westland" deliberately ran into the "Beaumont", doing her considerable damage. Our departure was delayed by that incident until the 25th of January, 1919. All repairs being completed, we sailed on that day for Cette, a small seaport on the Mediterranean coast of France.

All went well until the night of February 1st, when during a heavy gale, with rain, thunder and lightening, a fire broke out in the Engine room. Of all the perils of the sea, fire is probably the most dreaded. When it was first discovered by myself, and located near the gasoline tank, I had to decide quickly what had to be done. Taking weather conditions into consideration I concluded that we could not get clear of the vessel in our boats. There was but one alternative therefore, which was to fight fire for dear life.

Fortunately we had fire extinguishers; water alone would never have put the fire out. Carbonic acid gas did the trick. Everybody worked like Trojans; worked for their lives. The Chief Officer especially deserves great praise. After more than an hour of strenuous struggle we believed we had overcome the fire, and were standing around congratulating ourselves, when one of the Engineers making an effort to enter the engine room, came running back to say that he heard wood burning, that is he heard it crackling.

A call was made for someone to go below and direct the hose immediately on the fire. Without hesitation the Chief Officer responded, and after some hesitation he was followed by the Third Officer. With water soaked coats over their heads, and with ropes around their waists, they went into that Inferno of heat, gas, and smoke; groped their way to the Ventilator, down which the hose was thrust, and played a stream of water on the wood sheathing inclosing the gasoline tank. We hauled Mr. Peterson on deck more dead than alive; but the fire was extinguished.

Later on we kept the vessel away on her course again, and after the gas had been blown out of the engine room I went below, and viewing the charred wood work around the gasoline tank concluded that something very much resembling a miracle had taken place in that engine room. As I am not a believer in miracles however, I am forced to admit the human factor, and good luck. That suggests Mascots, but before I treat of that subject, I will mention a bit of bad luck which happened at the same time.

My Second Officer seemed to be in the way during our fight, so I sent him to help the Steward put some Extra Provisions in the motor boat. It was a formality. We could not have lowered the boat successfully. He exceeded his instructions, cast the lashings off the boat, it broke adrift from the davitts—due to the heavy rolling of the vessel—and fell into the raging sea. For one minute I forgot about our seeming greater misfortune. That boat was worth 1500 dollars. Absolute Ignorance is at a premium in the U.S. merchant service today. To answer YAH for YES, and to be able to write ones name intelligibly, are all the qualifications necessary for the obtaining a license, and a big salary, that effectively drives all recollections of codfishing in the Baltic out of ones memory.

Now I come to the subject of mascots. On the day after the fire our Japanese Steward was wiping the soot off the furniture in the saloon. He was a little chap, while I am a descendent of Anak. He had some difficulty in reaching up to the Photo before referred to. I therefore took the cloth from him and cleaned it myself.

While doing so it was revealed to me why we were saved from destruction the night before. We had a mascot; a guardian spirit on board, of whose existence we had been unconscious. I did not hesitate to declare the fact, or to attribute our escape to its presence. My statement was accepted, and now whenever any of them have occasion to enter my quarters, they turn to look at our Mascot, with undoubtedly as great reverence as does a devoted Christian view a Cross, a Mohomedan a Crescent, or a Parsee the rising Sun.

I believe that very few people understand the origin of Mascots. Our men in the Navy have them on shipboard; our soldiers carry them with them on their marches, and into foreign lands, and I am convinced that many men in civil life find it easy of belief that some object which they habitually carry on their persons, or keep in their office, has the merit of bringing them good luck.

Such beliefs may be traced back to a remote and barbarous age, when household gods occupied every home, and were considered necessary as preserving the home from misfortune, as well as the occupants thereof.

A Jewish tradition recounts that Terah, the father of Abram, was a manufacturer of idols, or wooden images, which he sold to the public, and which were purchased because the people believed that they would keep danger and misfortune from them and their homes.

It goes on to relate that Abram was left in charge of his fathers shop one day; and while viewing the stock in trade was seized with such a frenzy of rightous indignition, and such contempt for his fathers hypocrytical Profession, that he took a large mallet and smashed all the little gods in the shop; all but one big one standing in a corner: this he pried out near the centre of the shop, piled all the mutilated little ones around it, put the mallet in its hand, went out and shut the door.

Of course when his father opened up for business on the following morning, and discovered the wreckage; there was the old Harry to pay. IT was no use for Abram to tell him that the big image had destroyed all the little ones; Terah knew better than that; the object lesson Abram hoped to bring home to his father was entirely lost on the old man; all he could realize was that 500 dollars worth of gods had been maliciously smashed up, and his 40 year old kid had done it. He therefore haled him off to the Great Temple, and inquired of the priests what should be done to that irreverant boy. When Abram declared that he believed in only one God, and that both his father and the priests themselves were rank imposters, they became furious, and threw him into a fiery furnace kept especially for heretics. But as like Daniel many years later, he did not burn, they let him go.

As it was impossible for him to live in that community any longer, the upshot of the matter was that Abram went West, where he succeeded so well that Horace Greeley more than 4000 years afterward got the notion in his head that any young man who went West was bound to get rich. Mr. Greeley evidently overlooked the fact that one swallow does not make a summer.

We reached Cette in 24 days. It is a dirty little town in the south of France, which had been allotted to Switzerland for the importation of goods from America and elsewhere. That most of these goods were destined for Germany was an open secret, which was apparently confirmed by the fact that after the armistice was signed the docks and warehouses became so congested that later imports were stacked up anywhere in the open. Germany had no longer any use for the goods.

Sailed from there on the on the 29th of March, and arrived in Genoa on the 31st. This is one of the interesting cities in that land of romance and thrilling history. It is the most cosmopolitan city in Italy, and the least conservative. One of the interesting objects to be seen there is the house where it is alleged Columbus was born. It is in a very dilapidated condition, the bricks of which it was built are crumbling to dust. Another object of interest is the Cementry, where lie the remains of many of Genoa's illustrious dead. I noticed the name "Piaggio" on several of the exquisite marble monuments.

We took in some cargo at Genoa, and sailed for Licata, in Sicily. That is a very old town, dating probably from Phoenician days. It is a dirty ramshackle place, its only industry is the shipping of Sulphur. We took one thousand tons on board for a paper manufacturing company in Bucharest, and then sailed for Naples, where we completed our cargo for the Balkans.

Sailed from Naples on the 4th of June, bound for Constantinople. If you have an Encyclopaedia in your home, you might look up and read the historical account of these two cities, which you will find there. The Encyclopaedia Britannica gives very interesting matter concerning them; and as they both have figured largely in history, I think you will be interested.

After a few days delay at Constantinople we were ordered on to Constanza, in Roumania. Stayed there five days, and again was ordered to proceed to Galatz, which is the commercial capitol of Roumania.

It is on the Danube, some 82 miles from the sea. During the late war it was in possession of the Germans for some time, and shows the marks of the Vandals. There we discharged our cargo, composed mostly of cloths, wearing apparel, and footwear.

The sale of the goods was controlled by two of the employees of the Gualino firm, Messrs. Guglielmi and Perrara. They had an interesting and a strenuous time, dealing as they did with Roumanians, Armenians, Russian Jews, Turks, Greeks, Gypsies, and some others, all of whom are born thieves and liars. Perhaps I should Qualify that by stating that the only possible exception to that sweeping statement are the Turks, who I am satisfied are the only gentlemen in the Balkans.

We left that malodorous region on the 3rd of August, with some cargo for Varna, in Bulgaria; having as passengers Messrs. Guglielmi and Perrara, and an American soldier named Arthur Meyer; who had more recently been engaged in Red Cross work in Roumania.

An interesting experience was the smuggling of the freight money out of Roumania. Mr. Guglielmi, who received the money for the goods sold, conveyed the impression that he was banking it from time to time, in Bucharest; whereas he was bringing it on board and entrusting it to me. I had a supple and slender Canadian boy on board in whom I had confidence, and we hid that money where only a ferret could have found it.

As a law existed which made it a felony to carry more than 2500 Lei out of the country, Mr. Guglielmi was naturally considerably concerned over the matter; and when the total amount of money hidden was 7,800,000 Lei, he got on tenter hooks, fearing most of all that the vessel would be searched by the authorities on the eve of sailing. However no search was made, but he hardly drew a peaceful breath until Roumania faded away on the horizon.

Seven million eight hundred thousand Lei sounds like a tremendous sum of money; but if it was converted into American money at the current rate of exchange, it would amount to something more than 500 to 1000 dollars.

Sailed from Varna on the 7th of August, arriving at Constantanople on the 9th. Coming thru the Bosporus, while trying to round to, in response to orders from a Naval vessel, we went ashore; but were hauled off almost immediately by a Naval tug without having received any damage. A very strong current sets thru those

Straits from the Black Sea. Going into the Black Sea we were obliged to be towed, as our engines were not strong enough to enable us to stem the current. At Constantinople Messrs. Guglielmi and Perrara purchased 44 Bales of Turkish Rugs which were put on board the *Beaumont* to bring to Genoa. Mr. Meyer continued with us; the other two gentlemen took steam for Genoa, after first depositing in the Bank the money with which they were burdened.

Sailed for Genoa on the 20th of August, and arrived at Genoa on the 6th of September, via the Straits of Messina.

On the 9th of September we left Genoa for Spezia, Italy's principal Naval Station. There we went into Dry-dock.

When we arrived there, it was estimated that all work would be completed in 15 days. We were there one month and 20 days!!!

It was outrageous; but it was a mistake to get into the clutches of Government workmen, where malingering and red tape was rampant, and from which there was no escape.

We thankfully left Spezia on the 31st of October, homeward bound. When we left New York it was supposed that we would return directly from Cette. The Black Sea is a region which I never expected to visit, but having done so, I am not desirous of repeating the experience.

It is intended to send this vessel back to Italy with a cargo of coal. It is my intention to leave her as soon as I can be relieved.

The *City of Beaumont* has many good qualities, but to me she seems like an extravagant woman, who insists on having a new hat every month, and who willfully does things which vexes her best friends.

Because of this weakness in her character I am divorcing her. I trust she will get a more complacent guardian than I find it possible to be.

I trust, moreover, that this letter from the sea will give you some pleasure. If it does, than am I repaid.

Gradite i nostri distinti saluti
W. B. Butler[2]

A map showing the Mediterranean and Black Sea ports of call, based on the letter, is shown in figure 8.2. The total trip covered some 15,000 miles and involved at least fifteen ports of call. This is quite different from the earlier voyages of the ISC ships that hauled a single cargo to Genoa, Italy, or other ports and then returned in ballast to the Gulf Coast. This would seem to indicate that the market for lumber products in Italy had disappeared.

A fire in the engine room occurred early in the voyage and was successfully extinguished, initially with carbon dioxide and then water. This makes sense, in that the initial displacement of oxygen extinguished the fuel fire but was useless against the fire embedded in the wood. This was put out with water by quenching the coals and getting all of the materials below their ignition point.

It is very likely that the fuel was not gasoline as stated but rather the fuel oil used by the propulsion engines. There would be no point in storing the gasoline in an area so remote from its use. Moreover, the absence of an explosion after what was described as a fairly lengthy and severe exposure to a significant ignition source suggests a fuel less volatile than gasoline.

Where did the voyage start, and what was the initial cargo to South Norwalk, Connecticut? Ships Island, mentioned by the captain as the starting point, is approximately ten miles south of Gulfport, Mississippi, in the Gulf of Mexico. Since Piaggio's exporting business was headquartered in Gulfport and his primary interest was selling lumber, it is likely that the cargo was lumber, possibly railroad ties or pilings. Nothing else would seem to be a logical cargo from that region except possibly cotton; however, the cargo was not revealed.

With this in mind, I painted the ship loaded with lumber, as seen in

fig. 8.2. The route
of the City of
Beaumont.

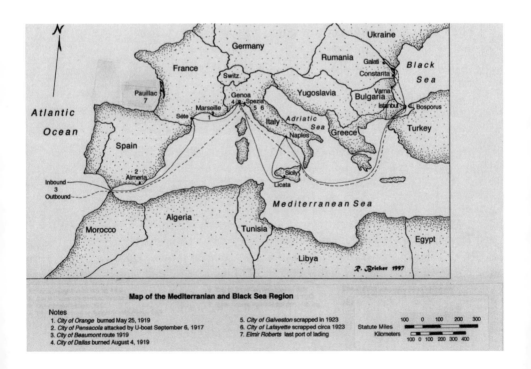

the insert of color plates in this book. The objective of the painting was to depict a five-masted barkentine sailing, since no photographs of the ships under sail were found. Fortunately, pictures of two of the ships with sails up were available, showing the sail plan. This was one of the early barkentines with the drop-down poop at the stern. In the painting, the square sails are set at a different angle aloft compared to the lower sails. This is seen in most photographs of square-rigged ships under sail and is caused by a significant wind speed gradient from the water surface to higher levels because of the wind energy lost to wave making. This is called wind shear and results in the apparent wind coming from more aft aloft than at deck level, requiring the range of sail settings seen, to obtain maximum efficiency.

The trip to New York took seventeen days, and the sea distance was approximately 1,800 miles, for an average speed of 4.4 miles per hour. The next leg, from New York to Cette, France, was approximately 4,300 miles and was reached in twenty-four days. This resulted in an average speed of almost 7.5 miles per hour, the best for trips that had enough data for the calculations. The *City of Orange* also had her highest average speed on the transatlantic leg, and a look at Atlantic Ocean wind charts shows that very favorable winds could be found by choosing the right latitude. Again, one must remember that the actual distance sailed was greater even with engines, for, in brisk headwinds, the ship could not go straight upwind because of insufficient power, even with the square sails furled.

The engines were of considerable use on this trip because of the many narrow channels the vessel traversed. The East River through Hell's Gate and back, the Dardanalles, Bosporus Strait (towed one way), eighty-two miles up the Danube River and return, and perhaps other channels and confined areas not mentioned. The Dardenanelles and Bosporus straits, especially, were rather long and narrow and had strong surface currents.

Finally, the Gualino name mentioned in the letter seemed to be the instigator of many of the cargo transactions and is the same name seen in other companies involved in the ISC ship business. Riccardo Gualino was the chairman of ISC and, as such, was one step above Piaggio as president.[3] He was also listed as president of the Marine and Commerce Corporation of America, with offices at 71 Broadway New York, New York, so perhaps he was the primary connection with Italy.[4] One of the companies that Alvise Bragadin, also at 71 Broadway, listed on his letterhead as representing was the Societa Anonima Riccardo Gualina. This was also the letterhead used on the captain's letter to Mary Anna Crary. The captain's typing concerning the freight money collected was rather confusing but my guess would be that he meant $500 to $1000.

Based on the coordinates in the captain's letter, the ship was approximately 3,300 statute miles directly east of West Palm Beach, Florida. The date was November 23, 1919, so the arrival time at Hampton Roads (Norfolk, Virginia, area) would be near Christmas at best.

Shortly after the ship returned, she was sold to another American company, indicated by Certificate of Registry No. 8, being surrendered February 27, 1920, at Wilmington, Delaware. Reason surrendered: "Ownership, District, & Hail Changed PE No. 10 issued."[5] Certificate of Registry No. 10 listed the new owner as Sanford D. Stockton, Jr., president of the City of Beaumont Ship Corporation of Wilmington, Delaware, incorporated under the laws of the state of Delaware. The rig was unchanged, the service stayed as ocean freight, and the number of crew was retained at twenty-three.

On May 19, 1922, a little more than twenty-six months later, the ship was sold to William F. Probst of Staten Island, New York.[6] This resulted in a change of district, rig, tonnage, ownership, and issuance of Consolidated Enrollment and License No. 121. The rig was changed from a gas screw (auxiliary barkentine) to a barkentine, which meant the engines were removed. The change from Certificate of Registry documentation to Consolidated Enrollment and License meant the ship was authorized to engage in the coastal trade only, and all subsequent Permanent Enrollment (PE) changes were in this category.

The changes resulted in an increase in net tonnage for the engine room and fuel tankage space recovered when the engines were removed. The ship was remeasured at Newport News, Virginia, in 1922, reflecting the net tonnage increase and change in rig. This meant the owner did not have to have any steam-qualified captain, mates, or engineers in the crew. The service, ocean freight, was retained, as was the crew level of twenty-three. The ship probably sailed with a lesser number, owing to the reduced crew needs.

This owner kept the ship for three years and four months. It is probable that the ship was hauling cargo during most of the time with these various tenures, as an inactive ship quickly deteriorates—much like an unoccupied house. Owners were not likely to maintain unused ships, and wise owners could still make a profit with a miserly approach that did not include frills such as stewards or more than one or two mates at most.

A postwar building boom in south Florida had many vessels, including sail, hauling lumber there during the twenties. Again, ships that stay out of trouble did not get in the news. Safe voyages went unnoticed by the media and the government.

The next change in ownership came September 21, 1925, when the ship was sold to Frances J. Ruth of 241 North Lakewood Avenue, Baltimore, Maryland, and Herman Block also of Baltimore. Each owned one-half.[7] Reason surrendered: "Property and hail changed, Consolidated Enrollment and License No. 34 issued." The ship remained a five-masted barkentine, and no other significant changes were made.

This PE was surrendered January 10, 1927, a little less than sixteen months later. Reason surrendered: "Ownership and District Changed, PE 41 issued."[8] The *City of Beaumont* appears to have been a useful citizen in the community of ships for nine and a half years until this transaction.

The new owner was Ferriss P. Merritt, of 25 West 43rd Street, New York, New York, and he transferred ownership of the vessel a little more than two months later to James V. Reddy, of New York, New York, secretary of the Buccaneers Club, Incorporated, at 25 West 43rd Street, New York, New York.[9] A new PE No. 57 was issued because of this ownership change. This document indicated the service as passenger, with a crew of twenty-three.[10]

A new PE No. 5 was issued four months later on August 2, 1927. Reason surrendered: "Name changed to Buccaneer by authority of C/N letter 158866-N dated July 16, 1927." Wallace F. Goodnow, of New York, New York, is listed as vice president of the Buccaneers Club, Incorporated, the sole owner of the vessel called the *Buccaneer*, with the same address as above and incorporated under the laws of the state of New York.[11]

Now the *City of Beaumont* had lost her original identity, but she was still built by Texans of Texas materials. When enough care was taken to avoid loss by fire, the mortal enemy of wooden ships, she showed her built-in durability and toughness. The Texas ship became a New York nightclub and possibly was a gambling ship, as she apparently did not stay docked all the time, based on the following addition.

PE No. 9, issued less than a year later on August 2, 1928, indicated that a 450 BHP Winton diesel engine had been installed. Surrender reason on PE No. 5 was: "Copy supplied, Original lost and corporate officer changed."[12] Pictures of the ship as the *Buccaneer* show her painted black with simulated gun ports down the sides of the hull.

On September 6, 1931, the *Buccaneer*, ex *City of Beaumont*, was in good company. The USS *Constitution*, after an extensive rebuild, was on tour of the East Coast and docked at the West 79th Street Pier in a slip right next to the *Buccaneer*.[13] The *Constitution* called on Beaumont and several other Texas coastal cities later on during this same tour. Although capable of doing so, she did not sail, so as to adhere to a tight schedule and, instead, was pulled by a navy minesweeper, the *Grebe*, that also provided power in port.[14]

The next change might have been worse than being a floating speakeasy and gambling ship in New York City (though many people may have been attracted to such). The PE No. 9 was surrendered at Los Angeles, California, on June 24, 1932, so it would appear that *Buccaneer* lasted approximately five years as a nightclub, or whatever it was, in New York. Reason surrendered: "Property, district, service and rig changed, document lost." PE No. 226 was issued, in which the ship was described as an oil screw, although it still had five masts.

The new owner was J. B. Philbin of Hollywood, California, 8435 Sunset Boulevard. He was president of the Famous Story Pictures, incorporated under the laws of the state of Delaware and having its principal place of business at 1040 Las Palmas Street, Hollywood, California. The service listed was "Moving Pictures," and the number of crew excluding master was eighteen.[15] So now, our Texas ship is in the movies—at least it would appear. The *Buccaneer* was still five-masted and how the rig was changed was not specified; however, there was no reference to barkentine or schooner—simply oil screw.

This romance with Hollywood was short-lived, as PE No. 226 was surrendered at New York, New York, on May 20, 1933, approximately eleven months later.[16] Reason surrendered: "Property and District Changed." PE No. 474 was issued, and the new owner was James A. Kenyon, of 1012 Grace Terrace, Teaneck, New Jersey. The service was listed as stake boat, with a crew of two, excluding master. It would seem that the career status of the ship was declining with age. But, she was not finished yet, as less than two months later, on July 11, 1933, she was sold back to the Showboat Buccaneer, Incorporated.

The PE No. 15 issued for this transaction was surrendered just six weeks later on August 31, 1933, in New York, New York, and the reason was: "Original lost, tonnage changed, Bureau of Navigation letter 128206N, August 11, 1933 & rig changed to schooner barge, engines and three masts removed."[17] PE No. 2 was issued to document these changes.[18] These were rather drastic changes, leaving the vessel with only two masts and no engine, and its designation stayed schooner barge with a crew of two, excluding master. Its gross tonnage and net tonnage were the same at 2,053 tons, indicating that there were no living facilities left onboard.

Apparently these changes were made to convert the vessel to a showboat, with the three middle masts removed to provide room for an enclosed theater and stage with seating for an audience of 1,000. It was anchored on the Hudson River close to Piermont, New York, and its showboat status lasted three years. An advertisement ballyhooed the nightly presentation of Bobby Sanford's dynamic revue, with glorious girls and glittering stars.[19]

Sometime in 1936 or 1937, the ship was sold and towed over to the Robinson Oil Corporation dock to protect the company structure from waves and ice in winter.[20] This was at nearby Hastings on Hudson, New York, a couple of miles south of Irvington, New York, the ship's listed graveyard. A noteworthy fact is that although the *City of Beaumont* was the longest lasting ISC ship (twenty years), she did not have one piece of correspondence in the Bureau of Marine Inspection and Navigation General Correspondence files. This resulted from having reliable and skilled masters like Captain Butler with some minor element of luck thrown in.

Figure 8.3 shows an aerial view of the ship at Hastings on Hudson. The center three masts have, of course, been removed; however, the picture shows the drop down poop very well. Supports for the two forward lifeboats can also be seen in the region just forward of the foremast

City
of Beaumont

fig. 8.3. The
Buccaneer *ex*
City of Beaumont
at Hastings-
on-Hudson.
Courtesy Texas
Seaport Museum

on each side of the forecastle. At the time the photograph was taken (1940s) the ship also protected the Tower Ridge Yacht Club.[21]

Her end did not officially take place until January 17, 1939, with the final surrender of PE No. 2 at New York, New York. Reason surrendered: "ABANDONED, Used as breakwater at IRVINGTON-ON-HUDSON, NY."[22] This location is approximately ten miles north of the Bronx on the Hudson River. Although this was the ship's official end, it drew the considerable interest of numerous marine historians and citizens of the region. It was the last of the fourteen ships built in Texas by ISC to go out of registration.

Eight More Barkentines

The known careers of the last eight ships built by ISC in Texas will be discussed in this chapter. The last two ships did not have any propulsion engines, and the documents that provide this information, the back of the Application of Owner or Master for Official Number, did not show any fuels, either solid or liquid. Such an absence was very unlikely and merely showed the lack of attention this part of the form received, for these ships had some sort of donkey engine with fuel requirements, and fuel for cooking and heating was needed.

THE *CITY OF DALLAS*

The *City of Dallas* received her Certificate of Registry No. 18, at Port Arthur, Texas, on September 25, 1918.[1] This was the ship against which the champagne bottle failed to break at the christening, portending bad luck, according to superstition. The *City of Dallas* made at least one trip with cargo to Genoa, Italy, for ISC. This was verified in a letter to the U.S. Shipping Board dated June 14, 1919, from the Marine and Commerce Corporation of America, 71 Broadway, New York, signed by Alvise Bragadin.[2] The letter stated: "The 'CITY OF DALLAS' is now in Genoa on her first trip, and is the only one at sea."

The situation was becoming very complex about this time, as ISC was trying to transfer the remaining ships, including some not down the ways yet, to the Italian flag. The U.S. Shipping Board had to give approval for any flag transfer, and they appeared to have a modicum of bureaucracy and were not lacking in inertia. The letter, written by Alvise Bragadin, went on to state that the *City of Dallas* was unloaded, awaiting the Shipping Board's cable to the American consul in Genoa to transfer the flag.

The approval was fairly prompt, for the Certificate of Registry No. 18 was surrendered at Genoa, Italy, on July 24, 1919. Reason surrendered:

"Sold to alien, Italian flag." That was the end of the *City of Dallas*, so far as her American flag career went. The ship was renamed *SNIA Dallas* (SNIA being the abbreviation for the company Societa Di Navigazione Industria E Commercio) and on August 4, 1919, just eleven days after the transfer, she burned at Genoa, Italy.[3]

THE *CITY OF AUSTIN*

A temporary Certificate of Registry No. 19 was issued for the *City of Austin* at New Orleans, Louisiana, on February 12, 1919.[4] The Request for Official Number did not list any gasoline tankage onboard, unlike the preceding ships, but did list twenty-three tons of coal.[5] The ship is shown in figure 9.1 as she was being fitted out. The yards had not been installed on the foremast yet. The vessel had a white or light gray paint job and looked very good.

Starting with this ship, the length was increased to 282 feet and the total horsepower to 400. The master was S. A. Simmons, who apparently took her on the maiden voyage to Genoa, Italy. This was her first and last voyage for ISC, according to a letter from the special deputy collector at New Orleans, to the commissioner of navigation, dated July 11, 1919:

fig. 9.1. The City
of Austin.
Courtesy
Texas Maritime
Museum

This office transmits herewith one-half of T.R. No. 19, issued at New Orleans, on Feb. 12th 1919 to the gas screw "CITY OF AUSTIN".

This vessel was sold to aliens at Genoa, Italy, in the early part of June. This portion of the Register was delivered up by Capt. S. A. Simmons, who arrived in New York on the 9th instant.[6]

The Temporary Certificate of Registry No. 19 had been surrendered at Genoa, Italy, on June 30, 1920. She apparently was renamed *Mortara* while in Italy.[7] Mortara is a small town approximately fifty miles north of Genoa.

In 1922, the Italians sold the vessel to William F. Probst of New York, New York, who was also a onetime owner of the *City of Beaumont*. Provisional Register No. 1, issued at Genoa, Italy, on August 8, 1922, was surrendered and vessel home, ownership, rig, dimensions, and tonnage changed. The ship was altered from an auxiliary barkentine to a barkentine (engines removed). These changes were documented on Consolidated Certificate of Enrollment and License No. 97, indicating, among other things, that the vessel was going to engage in the coastal trade.[8] All subsequent PEs were in this category.

The ship was remeasured at New York in 1923, as removing the engines and fuel tanks increased the net tonnage, and PE No. 97 reflected these changes. PE No. 97 was surrendered April 6, 1923, for ownership change, and PE No. 99 was issued.[9] That PE was surrendered a short time later on May 25, 1923, at Norfolk, Virginia, as the rig was changed, and PE No. 74 was issued.[10] The rig was changed from barkentine to a schooner barge, and this appears to have been the reason for the trip to Norfolk, for it was not there very long.

A schooner barge, as the name suggests, is a schooner rig that can sail or be towed with the topmasts usually removed. Another administrative change resulted in PE No. 74 being surrendered July 25, 1923. Reason surrendered: "Name changed to Smith and Terry No. 4 by authority letter 134995-n (7/2/23) (3850/1124)." PE No. 8 was issued.[11] This lasted less than a year, as the vessel was sold, and PE No. 84 was issued April 8, 1924. The vessel was then moved to the Port of New York, until it was sold on March 18, 1928.[12] The last document, PE 59, was surrendered August 15, 1935, at New York. Reason surrendered: "Dismantled and abandoned."[13] Here was another one of the ISC ships that had a long and useful life, without burning. The hulk ended up at Port Johnson, Bayonne, New, Jersey, formerly one of the largest wooden ship graveyards in the world.[14]

The Certificate of Registry No. 28 for the *City of Galveston* was issued February 27, 1919, at Port Arthur, Texas.[15] The owner was the City of Galveston Ship Company, incorporated in the State of Mississippi, and maintaining an office at Orange, Texas.

A voyage was made to Funchal, Madeira, about 475 miles west of Casablanca, Morocco, in the Atlantic Ocean. The master had an exciting time with the ship after arriving, as the next several communications indicate. The first is a letter from the American consul in Funchal, Madeira, dated March 9, 1920.[16] The subject of the letter is "Ship's Papers of the 'City of Galveston,'" which the consul was transmitting to the secretary of state because the ship had left that port on March 2, 1920.

When a ship reaches a foreign port, the Crew List, Shipping Articles, Certificate of Registry, and other ship's papers must be deposited with the American consul, who retains them until the ship is cleared to leave. Normally, the consul would not be transmitting them to Washington unless the ship were destroyed in port. It is, of course, a serious violation for a vessel to leave port without getting clearance and picking up the ship's papers from the consul.

The consul went on to state that for several days a violent gale had been blowing and the ship was in considerable danger. Captain E. M. Richard informed him on the morning of March 2, 1920, that the ship was dragging her anchor, and the windlass was broken, so he could not drop the other anchor. If he went adrift, it would be difficult to return, but he would try his best to do so.

He did go adrift soon after and was blown out to sea. No mention was made of the auxiliary engines, and this ship had a total of 400 horsepower. Even so, that would have been inadequate to hold the vessel in high winds. The gale continued all of that day and the next. As a result, the consul presumed the ship had blown so far out that the master had decided to proceed to Mobile, Alabama, since he had received sailing orders for that port, 4,600 miles away.[17]

The ship had been in port for fifty-eight days, having been arrested on the alleged charge of a shortage of cargo. The ship's owners were the Marine and Commerce Corporation, 71 Broadway, New York (telegraphic address was Gualino—New York), and they had apparently failed to inform the captain that the deposit had been sent that would allow the ship to sail before the case came up for trial.

This was the address of Alvise Bragadin, and the company was one of those for which he was a director and vice president. Gualino was the chairman of ISC, although nothing was heard about him directly. Based on frequent conversations with the master, the consul was convinced that Captain Richard intended to stay until all matters had been taken care of and only left for the safety of the vessel.

Along with the ship's papers, the consul sent a supplemental bill of health and a copy of two entries in the Ship's Daily Journal regarding certain disputes on the vessel, requesting that all be sent to Mobile. A manifest of aliens in the crew had not been presented to the consul for visas, but he did not see any objection to letting them land, with the exception of three Chinese, unless the required bonds were furnished.

The secretary of state sent the papers to the secretary of commerce, mentioning that the *City of Galveston* was blown to sea by a violent gale. He requested that the recipient make appropriate disposition of the enclosed papers, which included a copy of the consul's letter.[18] The acting commissioner for navigation, with the knowledge of the assistant secretary of commerce, mistakenly sent the papers to Galveston, Texas, instead of to Mobile, although the consul's letter had stated that the vessel would go to Mobile.

On April 15, 1920, the master, E. M. Richard, made an affidavit on the matter before J. S. Callahan, the special deputy collector at Mobile:

Your letter regarding the Bktn; City of Galveston received and contents noted. In reply I beg to say the above named Vessel was blown away from her anchorage at Funchal Madeira in a Hurricane on the 2nd day of March, in which we lost our anchor and chain. The gale continued six days and when it was over we were over a Thousand miles from there and the Ship being very foul and without ballast we found it impossible to beat back against the prevailing North East winds. So was forced to proceed to Mobile where we could haul out and dock the Ship. I was aware at the time we were liable to fine as you have enumerated them, but under the circumstances I think no fines should be assessed as I was in no way to blame as it was an act of God. I am informed that all my papers have been forwarded to the Department of State at Washington with a full report of the circumstances by the U.S. Consul which will substantiate all I claim when you receive them.[19]

The affidavit was forwarded to the secretary of commerce on April 16, 1920, stating that the special deputy collector had not imposed a fine and requesting that such action meet the approval of the department. This was the final resolution, but it took six more communications, including a request by the Department of Labor to finally get the ship's papers to Mobile after being sent to Galveston.

What does a captain do with his ship when it is blown offshore as the *City of Galveston* was? He might put out a sea anchor to hold the ship's bow into the wind and waves until the wind subsides. The anchor itself, with several fathoms of chain and cable out, would be a fairly effective sea anchor. In this case, however, the captain indicated he had lost his anchor and chain at some point.

The ship could turn and run downwind under bare poles. The ship would move pretty fast under these conditions because of all the windage area of the masts and rigging. This entails certain hazards because of the enormous following seas, which may poop the ship (an overtaking wave that goes faster than the ship and swamps the poop deck). The high poop deck design and enclosed wheelhouse of the ship were certainly advantages in these conditions.

The master of the *City of Galveston* had many sail options, as he had some twenty sails to work with, several of which had at least two reef bands. With the lack of ballast, the captain would probably not want a strong side force on the ship that would result from beating or reaching. If the engines were working, the ship could be held with the bow pointing toward the most advantageous direction upwind, or to control the speed downwind to prevent getting pooped.

Last, the ship could heave-to by setting just enough sails and the right sails to keep the ship stable. The ship had the disadvantage of not having any ballast, so she would be cranky or very tender, wanting to heel with any side component of wind. The foul bottom was a disadvantage for the ship trying to go upwind. These are the times when the captain's experience and leadership in a crisis are important, and ships are saved when the right decisions are made when needed.

The ship arrived at Mobile, Alabama, on April 13, 1920, according to the special deputy collector there, forty-two days after being blown out to sea, according to the captain's affidavit. The distance, as previously stated, was 4,600 miles, with an average speed of 4.6 miles per hour.

A frontal quarter view of the ship at sea is shown in the insert of color plates in this book. This is perhaps the best view for seeing all of the unique features of a barkentine. The raised poop area and enclosed wheelhouse are visible in this view. The spike bowsprit without jibboom or martingale was the system used on all of the barkentines built by ISC. This view shows the five square sails to advantage and also the many chainplates.

Temporary Certificate of Registry No. 2 was issued July 7, 1920, at Port Arthur, indicating the ship had been sold to a company in Wilmington, Delaware.[20] The owner was again listed as the City of Galveston Ship Company, incorporated under the laws of the State of Delaware and maintaining an office at Wilmington, Delaware. The agent for the ship was Paul Boulo of Mobile, Alabama, and the master was A. E. Crowell.

The new owners removed the engines, and the ship was remeasured at Beaumont, Texas, in 1920, showing an increase in net tonnage from 2,060 to 2,148 tons. Again, one can see how unpopular auxiliary engines in these vessels were with experienced ship owners. The new register still showed a crew number of twenty-five, although a reduction would be expected.

The master foresaw a problem with the authorities and made an affidavit July 30, 1920, at Gulfport, Mississippi: "I, M. E. Crowell, Master of the American Barkentine 'City of Galveston' have tried to secure the required number of licensed A.B. Seamen in Gulfport, Miss. New Orleans, La. and Mobile, Ala and have been unable to obtain them."[21] This was signed by the master and sworn to by a notary public. The problem was not with finding steam-qualified personnel but with finding able-bodied seamen. The Seamen's Act of 1915 specified that 65 percent of the deck crew be able seamen, exclusive of officers and apprentices. Qualifications for an able-bodied seaman were that he be at least nineteen years old and have three years on deck.[22]

The captain appealed to the secretary of commerce by telegram on July 31, 1920, requesting permission to proceed to England with uncertified seamen. The commissioner for navigation telegrammed to customs office at Gulfport the same date: "If you permit barkentine CITY OF GALVESTON clear without required able seamen report case navigation fine usual manner Collect."

This appeared to have bounced around between the Bureau of Navigation and the deputy supervising inspector general, again, both of them referring to the barkentine as a steamer. Of course, the IG, as always, recommended that the full penalty be imposed—after all, that was his job. The assistant secretary of commerce, E. F. Sweet, reviewed the case, and on September 11, 1920, mitigated the $500 fine to $50.[23]

What happened next is not clear, as not all of the story is in the files. Another letter from the secretary of state to the secretary of commerce dated January 25, 1921, stated that a report relative to a marine casualty to the "schooner" *City of Galveston* received from the British Embassy was enclosed.[24] The second paragraph stated that the enclosed copy (not found) was the only one available in the files of the Department of State, so the Department of Commerce was respectfully requested to make appropriate disposition of it. The document was delivered to the deputy collector of customs at Wilmington, Delaware, to pass on to the owners.

Apparently, whatever happened to the *City of Galveston* was serious enough that she never went to sea again. The next letter was an enclosure of the letter from the American consul at Genoa, Italy, to the secretary of state, arriving at the Department of Commerce in November, 1922. SNIA emphatically informed the consulate that the sailing vessel, *City of Galveston*, under the American flag, was absolutely and exclusively owned by their company, contrary to what appeared in the Certificate of Registry.[25] The letter went on to beg for authorization for the demolition of the vessel, which was in Spezia, Italy, in a condition of absolute unseaworthiness.

The ship was still under the American flag; otherwise, the consulate would not have entered the picture. The connection between the Wilmington, Delaware, company and SNIA is not clear, but the Italian company seemed to have been the driving force in trying to dispose of the ship. The American consulate general's letter indicated the ship had entered the Port of Genoa on February 16, 1921, and the crew was paid off on February 21 and 25, 1921, so the vessel was active for almost two years. The ship was moved to the Port of Spezia on September 23, 1921, because of congestion in the Port of Genoa.

The last sentence of that letter is of interest, since mention was made several times (about half the register) when some of the previous ships burned: "Since the barkentine has been dismantled and the former Master is no longer present the entire Certificate of Registry is sent, herewith, instead of being cut into two portions."[26] This letter was dated October 13, 1922, and this was also the date the Certificate of Registry No. 2 was surrendered at Genoa, Italy. Reason surrendered: "Vessel Dismantled."[27]

THE *CITY OF ORLEANS*

This ship was finished May 6, 1919, and was issued Consolidated Enrollment and License No. 49 (indicating coastal trade) at Port Arthur, Texas. A picture of the finished *City of Orleans* at the ISC yard in Orange is shown in figure 9.2. The gaff sails are on with covers, and the stay sails and square sails are up, showing that much of the sail plan.

PE No. 49 was surrendered June 17, 1919, at Gulfport, Mississippi, and the ship was transferred to the Italian flag on June 17, 1919.

The engines may have been removed in Italy, as Probst of New York purchased her shown by PE No. 129, on June 12, 1922, and the vessel was listed as a barkentine. She was remeasured at Newport News, Virginia, in 1922, indicating a change in measurements, and the new documentation showed no deduction for propelling power. The PE No. 129 was surrendered November 2, 1923, as the rig was altered to a schooner barge with one mast removed, and PE No. 43 was issued. As can be seen, the Italians, like ISC, were divesting themselves of the ships fairly promptly after their transfer to the Italian flag.

PE No. 43 was surrendered at New York, New York, on November 28, 1923. Reason surrendered: "Vessel foundered 5 miles South West of Fenwick Island Lightship on November 13, 1923, Total loss (vessel). 5 persons on board, no life lost. Casualty report filed."[28]

This happened only eleven days after the new documentation had been issued. The crew number had dropped from more than twenty to five, the only way these vessels could compete with steam. This also might have contributed to the sinking; however, many schooners sailed the eastern seaboard with similar size crews for years without mishap. (Fenwick Island is on the Atlantic Coast where the southern border of Delaware meets Maryland's border.)

THE *CITY OF LAFAYETTE*

On June 5, 1919, the following unsigned note was sent to Monty, an official of the U.S. Shipping Board in Washington, D.C.

Referring to previous correspondence, we now beg to make formal application for permission to transfer registry of the following

fig. 9.2. The City of Orleans. Courtesy Dr. Howard C. Williams Collection

four auxiliary barkentine to Italian flag, all to be in the name of the S. N. I. A. Co., (Societa Navigazione Italie-Americana Turin). The vessels are:

CITY OF DALLAS, already running under American flag and now at or due Genoa.

CITY OF ORLEANS, now loading at Gulfport, but not fully documented.

CITY OF BILOXI, now under construction and undocumented.

CITY OF LAFAYETTE, now under construction and undocumented.

The writer is senidng [*sic*] this note to you by hand while in Washington, and will have pleasure in calling on you sometime suring [*sic*] the day.

Yours very truly,[29]

As we already know, the *City of Dallas* was transferred to the Italian flag in Genoa, on July 17, 1919; the *City of Austin* in early June, 1919; and the *City of Orleans* on June 17, 1919, but apparently not without a lot of frustration on the part of ISC. Before delving into that matter, however, some background on the *City of Biloxi* is needed.

ISC was building ships at Pascagoula, Mississippi, as well as at Orange, and the two built there were the *City of Biloxi* and the *City of Pascagoula*, both five-masted barkentines. These were probably the only two built in Mississippi; they were not finished until sometime in 1919, and no earlier vessels were documented by ISC in that area.

ISC was also building wooden steamships at Pascagoula, Mississippi, for the Italian government. Between June 12, 1919, and July 25, 1919, at least thirty-eight communications transpired in the form of letters, telegrams, and interdepartmental memorandums concerning the transfer of the sailing ships to the Italian flag. The stated reason for the requested transfers was "economy of operation."

The main players in this bureaucratic drama were, on the U.S. Shipping Board side, W. E. Monty of the law department and J. H. Rosseter, director of operations. Trying to get the ships transferred were the Robert J. Tod Company, Ship and Steamship brokers of New York, representing SNIA, and submitters of the application for transfer; and ISC, represented by Bragadin. The Marine and Commerce Corporation of America had Riccardo Gualino as president, with Bragadin as vice president, and they wrote letters to the shipping board also.

Two standard forms of the shipping board were filled out pertaining to the *City of Lafayette*, one by pen and one typed, but with differing answers. One question asked for terms of the contract. The answer, in ink, was "built at cost plus 10 percent profit." The typed answer was: "NO SALE INTENDED, NO CHANGE OF OWNERSHIP, SIMPLY CHANGE OF TITLE."

To the question of total price and price per deadweight-ton the answer on this penned form was "$450,000, near $120 per deadweight-ton." The typed form answer was "NO PRICE INVOLVED." It is not clear what the significance of this was, except earlier indications were that the Italians paid for the ships as they were being built. But no flag changes could be made during the war. This seemed to be a no-lose setup for ISC, except for the fact that ISC was also intertwined with other Italian companies.

The transfer process was slowed, at least in part, because several government entities had to concur in the transfer. The law division sent requests for approval to Military Intelligence of the War Department, Naval Intelligence of the Navy Department, and the Department of Justice of the Bureau of Investigation. Of course, their responses were needed before anything could be done.

Another stumbling block was J. H. Rosseter, director of operations for the shipping board, who objected to the transfer of motor auxiliary schooners of more than 2,500 deadweight tons to foreign registry. He wrote a memorandum June 18, 1919, to the legal division, to the attention of Monty, concerning the four auxiliary barkentines, *City of Biloxi*, *City of Dallas*, *City of Orleans*, and *City of Lafayette*: "In line with previous memorandum of date, recommending the reopening of cases in which we have previously requested that action be deferred or denied. I would suggest that the question of change to Italian registry of the above vessels be docketed for consideration at time of reopening of the other applications."[30]

Despite this objection, Monty recommended approval for transferring the four ships in a memorandum to the shipping board, dated June 19, 1919, and all were approved for transfer by the end of July, 1919.[31] Monty's memorandum had several gross errors in it, worth mentioning to avoid the confusion that might occur in future research based on these records alone.

The *City of Dallas* was called a wooden auxiliary schooner instead of the correct auxiliary barkentine. In addition, it was stated that she was built at Pascagoula, Mississippi, when, in fact, the hull was built at Beaumont and fitted out at Orange, Texas. The *City of Orleans* had the same incorrect rig designation, and it was stated she was built at Gulfport, Mississippi, instead of the correct Orange.

A letter from ISC, dated June 28, 1919, over Bragadin's signature, to the U.S. Shipping Board advised them that two ships were finished. These two were the *City of Lafayette* and the *City of Biloxi*, both finished and begun loading. This indicated that the *City of Lafayette* carried cargo to Italy on her maiden voyage.

The transfer to Italian registry was approved by U.S. Shipping Board Order No. 627, dated July 18, 1919, so no American Certificate of Registry was issued for the *City of Lafayette*. The ship was renamed *Miramare* in 1921 while laid up at Genoa, Italy, and was broken up at Spezia, Italy, in 1923.[32]

THE *CITY OF WACO*

*fig. 9.3. Launching
of the* City
of Waco.
Courtesy
Bludworth
Collection

No papers were found for the *City of Waco* after two searches at the National Archives. Another source indicated that the *City of Waco* was moved from Orange to Gulfport on her carpenter's certificate, and at Gulfport, she was registered as the *Modena* (the name of a town close to Bologna, Italy). In 1921, the ship was sold at Buenos Aires by court order and renamed *Columbia*.[33]

Figure 9.3 shows the ship being launched. It is almost clear, but the forward cradle is still on the ways with smoke from the frictional heat-

ing rising. A tent was installed on the poop deck in the wheelhouse region.

THE *MACERATA*

The last two ships were named for small Italian towns on the Adriatic Sea. These two barkentines did not have engines installed, and because they were of the same dimensions as the previous five ships the net tonnage was increased. Why ISC waited to leave out engines until the last two ships was not revealed. Perhaps they were tired of the steam requirements hassle, or it may have been a measure to cut crew costs, or both. The last two ships may have been built on speculation by ISC and they were sold to American companies with no apparent Italian connections. The Application of Owner or Master for Official Number was submitted on November 18, 1919, at Port Arthur, Texas.[34]

The *Macerata* received its Certificate of Registry No. 31, on December 29, 1919, which was surrendered the same day, as the ship was moved to New Orleans, Louisiana. No change in ownership was involved.[35] According to Karppi's paper, the ship was not active while at New Orleans and may have been waiting for a buyer.

Temporary Registry No. 32 was surrendered May 22, 1922 at New York, New York, when the ship was sold to William F. Probst, purchaser of several of the previous ISC ships.[36] The ship remained a barkentine, although the Consolidated Enrollment and License No. 122 issued indicated the vessel would be utilized in the coastal trade, with the crew reduced to twelve, more typical of East Coast sailing ships.[37] This was a no-frills system, and there were no stewards or mess attendants, no engineers, and probably only one mate who alternated watches with the captain. This was the only way sail could compete with steam before World War I and after the war was over. The ships were called workhouses—and worse by the crews.

The PE No. 122 issued to Probst was surrendered a little less than two years later when the ship was sold to the Fair Oaks Steamship Corporation, 11 Broadway, New York, New York, represented by Joseph Morecraft. The ship remained a five-masted barkentine, and PE No. 83 was issued on the effective date of April 8, 1924.[38] The next change came a little more than two months later on June 25, 1924, when PE No. 83 was surrendered at Boston, Massachusetts, and PE No. 165 was issued.[39]

The ship's name was changed August 29, 1924, resulting in a new PE No. 19, issued on that date.[40] The new name was the *H. W. Brown*. This ownership and location remained unchanged until March 5, 1929, when the ship was sold to the Durham Navigation Corporation of 17 Battery

Place, New York, New York, incorporated under the laws of the state of Delaware, and PE No. 43 was issued.[41] The ship was still a barkentine and retained this rig to the end, which came February 13, 1936. Her papers were surrendered at New York, and the reason surrendered was that the ship was abandoned. The vessel had a long and apparently useful career, and she remained a barkentine without engines for the full time.

This is one of the ships that became a part of the large wooden-ship graveyard at the abandoned coal-loading docks at Port Johnson, Bayonne, New Jersey.[42] This area is not far from the Statue of Liberty and faces Staten Island.

fig. 94.
Monfalcone *at
launching.*
Courtesy
Bludworth
Collection

THE *MONFALCONE*

The application for Official Number designated the rig for the *Monfalcone* as "Sailer Barkentine" ("sailer," not "sailor"), meaning this was a ship that sailed and was square-rigged on the foremast, with no engines involved. The application was submitted at Port Arthur, Texas, on

December 29, 1919.[43] The owner was listed as the City of Houston Ship Company of Gulfport, Mississippi.

Figure 9.4 shows the ship being launched. This was the only picture that showed an ISC ship being launched with the bowsprit on. This may have been a result of being the last ship built. Another difference on this ship not seen on any other is the recessed section in the hull from the hawse holes downward several feet. Other pictures showed this to run the full length of the hull. In the background to the right can be seen some wooden steamship construction at the Southern Dry-dock and Shipbuilding Company of Orange.

The Certificate of Registry No. 3 was issued at Gulfport, Mississippi, September 8, 1920. Why eight months elapsed after the Application for Official Number is not known.[44] The City of Houston Ship Company owed $25,000 to the Interstate Trust and Banking Company, due October 20, 1920. The ship was sold to the A. J. Higgins Lumber and Export Company, Incorporated, of New Orleans, Louisiana, and PE No. 39 was issued November 29, 1921.[45] The mortgage was transferred to the new owner; however, it had increased to $28,161.70.

According to one report, the ship sailed for Los Angeles sometime in 1923 and was partially dismasted en route to Panama. She was later towed from Balboa, Panama, to San Pedro, California.[46]

On November 9, 1923, the vessel was sold by a U.S. marshal at Los Angeles, California, free of all encumbrances. The ship was registered at the Port of Los Angeles, December 3, 1923, for the coasting trade, with Consolidated Enrollment and License No. 73 issued.[47] That was a very temporary move, for a little over a month later, on January 25, 1924, the enrollment was surrendered. The new owner was the Curtis Corporation, organized and existing under the laws of the State of Delaware and having its principal place of business at Long Beach, California.

This company kept the ship more than three years, until April 30, 1928, but in what trade is unknown. She remained a barkentine, and the Certificate of Registry No. 102 was for foreign trade.[48] The new owners were of Newport Beach, California, and each owned a third share (PE No. 270).[49] The ship was derigged, converted to a fishing barge, and PE No. 84 was issued.[50] Sixty shares were split among five owners. The ship retained one mast and a crew of one, excluding the master.

It is not known when the *Monfalcone*'s end came, for PE No. 84 was surrendered a month later on November 17, 1928, as she was exempt— not in trade and her sailing days were over.

The *Monfalcone* was the fourteenth and the last of the ISC ships built at Orange and Beaumont. Each of these ships ended its career far away from its birthplace.

More of the Story

All of the ships examined thus far, with the exception of the two hulls built at Beaumont, Texas, in 1918 (*City of Beaumont* and *City of Dallas*), were built at the ISC yard in Orange, Texas. Taking into account the size of these ships, this was a phenomenal construction feat that no other sailing shipyard in the country, or the world for that matter, had ever, in the long history of sailing shipbuilding, come close to accomplishing.

The careers of the fourteen ships are summarized in table 13. The official beginning and ending dates for each ship are also included. A recap of this major sailing ship construction project is in order, based on the documentation dates provided in this table. Three ships were completed in 1917; four, all five-masted barkentines, were completed in 1918; and seven, again, all five-masted barkentines, were completed in 1919.

As seen in numerous construction views, the ISC yard was set up with several gantry cranes, rail and monorail systems, and shops with electrically operated woodworking equipment and dust collection systems. Most yards at this time were not as well equipped.

The skills and potential for facilities to perform such a task were probably available in New England yards, but two very important things were missing in the north. They were the 15 to 20 million board feet of lumber required for the construction of fourteen ships and a climate that only infrequently interfered with construction. The cost and time consumed by transporting the required lumber from the south by ship or rail in an era when shipping was in very short supply would have been prohibitive. No, this task could only have been performed by the people who had the lumber in hand and near the construction site.

The logistics and climate were absolutely right for building these ships on the Gulf Coast, and Orange, Texas, which, in its well-protected location, was the prime choice of the region. The fact that the United States government was also having large numbers of wooden steamships built in Orange and Beaumont, Texas, during the years that the barken-

TABLE 13. SHIP CAREERS

Ship/number*	Completion date	Date lost or surrendered	How and where lost
Orange/214819	Apr. 23, 1917	May 24, 1919	Burned, Marseilles, France
Houston/215246	July 28, 1917	Aug. 6, 1917	Burned while loading at Orange
Jessie Bounds ex *Houston*/ 215246	July 2, 1919	Oct. 10, 1919	Abandoned at sea, 37° 30'N, 42° 25'W (Spanish coast)
Pensacola/215584	Sept. 6, 1917	Apr. 29, 1918	Sank by U-boat near Garrucha, Spain
Gulfport/215942	Mar. 12, 1918	Mar. 13, 1919	Burned, La Plata, Argentina
Mobile/216350	July 17, 1918	May 14, 1919	Exploded and burned at Montevideo Roads, Uruguay
Beaumont/216473	July 22, 1918	Jan. 17, 1939	Abandoned, Irvington-On-Huds on, New York
Dallas/216909	Sept. 25, 1918	July 24, 1919	Sold to alien, Italian flag, burned August 4, 1919
Austin/217160	Feb. 12, 1919	June 30, 1919 Aug. 15, 1935	Vessel sold alien, Italian flag, came back 1923, became schooner barge, hulk at Port Johnson, Bayonne, N.J.
Galveston/217482	Feb. 27, 1919	Oct. 13, 1922	Vessel dismantled, Genoa, Italy
Orleans/217696	May 6, 1919	Nov. 13, 1923	Vessel foundered 5 miles SW Fenwick Island Lightship
Lafayette/No number issued	June 7, 1919	July 18, 1919	Transferred to Italian flag, S.N.I.A.
Waco/No number issued	Nov. 21, 1919	None, sold 1922	Sold at Buenos Aires by court order.

Ship/number	Completion date	Date lost or surrendered	How and where lost
Macerata/192862	Dec. 29, 1919	Feb. 13, 1936	Abandoned, Port Johnson, Bayonne, N.J.
Monfalcone/ 219468	Dec. 29, 1919	Nov. 17, 1928	Exempted, not in trade (had become fishing barge)

* Names preceded by *City of* except the *Jesse Bounds* and last two ships.

tines were built indicates there was an almost unlimited supply of Texas pine timber available, not only for all kinds of domestic construction but also for export to Europe. In fact, Texas still has a large lumber and pulpwood industry.

The late Frank Karppi, formerly a naval architect at Levingston Shipbuilding Company at Orange, Texas, did some research on these ships in the 1970s. In his paper titled "Shipbuilding on Harbor Island," he wrote:

> These vessels built [by] the International Shipbuilding Company and its predecessor firm, F. H. Swails, were very well constructed, and had it not been for the severe postwar slump in shipping, they might have continued in service for the ten or fifteen years which was the expected life span for large wooden hulls. . . .
>
> It may be interesting to note that these barkentines, along with some similar ones on the west coast, were among the last cargo carriers ever to [be] built with square sails, thus ending over six thousand years of history.[1]

Some, in fact, did survive for several years in one form or another, as seen in the ships' careers detailed earlier.

Port Arthur did have another large sailing ship active while the ISC ships were making their mark. Because of the wartime shortage of shipping, in 1916, Texaco at Port Arthur bought the 332-foot-long *Edward Sewall*. This ship was an all-steel, four-masted, square-rigged ship launched in 1899 at Bath, Maine, and she still had an AI rating. She had no mechanical propulsion and routinely carried 5,000 tons of packaged petroleum products for Texaco to Buenos Aires or the East Coast of the United States. Captain Richard Quick prided himself in bringing his "fine white yacht" into port looking better than when she left. He once put seven sailors in irons when they refused to go over the side to paint

plate 1. Juanita *Homeward Bound*

plate 2. Bonita *in Campeche Bay*

plate 3. The Dawning of Houston

plate 4. The City of Orange

plate 5. The City of Beaumont

plate 6. The City of Galveston

plate 7. *The* Edward Sewall *and a Barkentine*

at sea in a calm. The ship may have been painted a dark color at some time after becoming a Texaco ship, though not by Captain Quick's choice. She is shown in the insert of color plates in this book, crossing tacks with one of the barkentines at Sabine Banks light. With all of the barkentines at Orange, surely one of them and the *Edward Sewall* crossed paths, although several barkentines sailed out that never sailed back.

As the end of World War I approached, it appeared that neither ISC nor Piaggio had any desire to stay in the shipping business. Piaggio's real business was lumber, not shipping. Shipbuilding was a means of selling more lumber, both for the ship construction and for export to Italy. ISC was very good at disposing of the ships and put a lot of pressure on the U.S. Shipping Board to expedite transfer of the vessels to the Italian flag. The last two ships apparently belonged to ISC and were inactive until they could be sold. Several of the ships went to the East Coast, even after transferring to the Italian flag.

WHO WAS HENRY PIAGGIO?

Letters from Piaggio were usually on his Gulfport, Mississippi, lumber company letterhead. His letters were stamped Henry Piaggio in large letters and signed by Dickman. Some of his early letterheads also indicated a branch office in Pensacola, Florida. The letterhead, describing him as an exporter, leaves a question as to whether Piaggio was just a timber broker or had timber holdings of his own. In three land purchases in 1917 and three in 1919, Piaggio spent $38,250, which probably resulted in the acquisition of several acres, but there was no indication that this was timberland. He may have owned land under the name Nino Enrico Piaggio and in other counties. Neither this nor ownership of the timberland to support the Piave mill, which is discussed later, was investigated.

In 1916, Margaret Piaggio, his wife, made land purchases for $100 and $700 and, in 1917, made a purchase for $600. The deed for the $700 purchase described the property as a 102-foot-wide lot and depth from a described point inland to the Gulf of Mexico.[2] Based on the legal description and another reference, this lot was a part of the property on which the Piaggio mansion was built.[3]

Additional information concerning lumber supplies for ISC is contained in the following documents. In an oral history source, a native Mississippian, Ben Earles, made the following statements:

> Now there was one fellow—I think this has been pretty well authenticated so I guess it's safe to tell it. A fellow from Italy, an Ital-

ian, had come over to this country and seen the opportunities here. And he was a pretty big man in his own right. But he had gone back to Italy and interested some money people there in supplying money and he accumulated a fleet of ships of his own. He had put up a sawmill out here at—what's the name of the town out here that's got an Italian name? I'll think of it in a minute.

His name was Piaggio, Mr. Piaggio. In coming back from Italy with his empty ships, he put Italian marble on there as ballast, and he built a marble mansion there on the beach at Gulfport, between Gulfport and Biloxi, a very elaborate marble mansion built with the marble he brought back as ballast.

Piave is the name of the town I'm talking about.

In response to the interviewer's comment, "Yes, I bet that was quite a house down there," Earles replied:

It was. It has been torn down in the last twenty years. It was almost destroyed in the hurricane of 1947. They never did live in it, never did get it built during his lifetime. They caught up with him on his embezzlement, or whatever you want to call it, and he died a broke man. His widow lived in a wooden house, more or less a cottage, behind the mansion, and during World War Two, that was a night club place and was called the "Merry Mansion."

I remember Mr. Piaggio very well. He liked to scare me to death when I was a kid. He had two automobiles, one of them was an Atheston Jack Rabbit and the other one was a Stanley Steamer. The Stanley Steamer was supposed to do one hundred and twenty-five miles an hour although nobody had ever done that in one.

He took me riding in it one time, when I was about nine years old, and we got to going so fast I took off my cap and put it over the speedometer so I couldn't tell how fast we were going.[4]

Piaggio's car evolved from a fast breed. In 1906, one of the Stanley Brothers' steam cars set a world's speed record of 127.66 mph that held for many years.[5] Earles also indicated that there were several hundred thousand railroad ties on an island off the coast of Mobile, Alabama, as his father had been hired by the British Army to pick out the good ones.

In his typewritten document "Hometown Mississippi," James F. Brieger provides a description of Piave: "Located six miles north of Bothwell, Piave is the remains of a lumber town which was established during the boom of the early 1900's. One of the largest mills in the South was built here, bringing to the backwoods a prosperity never known before. Aside from the neat rows of Mill-houses, a great many larger homes, several stores, and a movie house were built. The prosperity was short-lived; the mill closed, the houses were deserted, and the remains of a once large forest stretched out for miles in all directions."[6]

Piave was approximately fifty miles north of Gulfport, Mississippi, and lumber could be sent there, to Moss Point, Mississippi, or to Mobile, Alabama. Piave is also the name of a river on the northeast coast of Italy.

A documented connection of Piave to ISC was found on Alvise Bragadin's letterhead. Bragadin was one of the directors of the Piave mill, and it appears this was the source of some of the lumber going to Italy and possibly for ship construction. Some or all of the ties may have come from Piave.

A Marine Iron Works company was also listed on the ISC letterhead with the address in Houston, Texas. Whether it supplied any of the large quantities of iron fittings and castings required for the many ships is an interesting, but unanswered, question.

An enlightening letter to the British Embassy in Washington, D.C., on March 8, 1922, after Piaggio's death, throws a little more light on his operations: "There is pending in the United States District Court for this district a libel and cross-libel growing out of the failure of the Schooner 'Elizabeth T. Doyle' in the Spring of 1917 to transport a cargo of lumber from Moss Point to Genoa, Italy, under a charter party with one Henry Piaggio, the cross-libelants being Fratelli Feltrinelli of Milan, Italy, claiming as assignees of said charterer."[7] The writer of the letter, the proctor for the owners of the schooner, is, in essence, trying to find out if the British will provide some information that will support his case.

The schooner loaded with lumber at Moss Point (possibly from the Piave mill) the latter part of February 1917, but Genoa had ceased to be a safe port, and the "Doyle" was unable to secure a crew at any of the Gulf ports. On April 3, she proceeded to Norfolk, Virginia, and got a crew there but was refused clearance because of the submarine threat in the Mediterranean.

The writer went on to state that it was by then impossible to deliver cargo to Genoa because of the existing blockade by the British Fleet that he understood was detaining all sailing vessels bound for Mediterranean ports. Captain Wry, with the *City of Orange*, and Captain Sanderson, with the *City of Pensacola*, did not seem to have any great problem with this—at least on the way over.

The proctor had discussed this defense with the proctor for the cross-libelants, who claimed such defense was untenable because two other schooners chartered by Henry Piaggio had secured crews and delivered

their cargoes safely to Genoa at about the same time the *Doyle* should
have sailed.

Piaggio leased the *Frank Huckins* (three-masted, 153 feet long, 545
tons) and the *Samuel P. Bowers* (four-masted, 174 feet long, 623 tons)
from the Hirsch Lumber Company of New York the latter part of
May, 1917.[8] These Bath-built schooners were detained by the British
fleet at Gibraltar, and they tried, through the State Department, to per-
suade the Italian government to get permission for them to pass through
the Straits and proceed by convoy.

Almost two months later, they were informed through the State Department that the Italians had declined to act on the matter. The reason given was that the consignees, who were Feltrinelli (previously
mentioned) and (no first name given) Piaggio, brother of the charterer,
refused to sell the lumber to the Department of Railways for the Italian
government. In the latter part of August, after the Italian government
understood they had made arrangements for the purchase of the cargoes, the two schooners were allowed by the British to pass through the
Straits. They were met by an Italian destroyer and convoyed to Genoa,
arriving in late August.

The interesting information here was the fact that Piaggio's brother
was acting for him in Italy, and only after the lumber was committed to
the Italian government was the impasse resolved. Another fact was, in
addition to ISC ships, Piaggio was leasing other vessels to haul lumber to
Italy, an indication of the massive amounts of lumber he had available,
probably in large part from the Piave mill.[9] Resolution of the Doyle case
was not revealed in the records and is only cited because it indicated the
extensive operations of Piaggio. Other aspects of Piaggio's career follow.

Based on documentation obtained I would like to clarify some of the
previous information concerning Piaggio that is in error or misleading.
A direct quote from the *Orange Leader Sunday Magazine Section (Spice)*
is first.

> International Shipbuilding Co. by the close of the war was to run
> into problems with government laws and regulations. Eventually
> the owners were told to complete the series of vessels that had been
> contacted [contracted probably], but no new vessels could be built.
>
> After the war, the company was liquidated at a heavy loss to
> creditors and stockholders.[10]

The writer appears to be mixing oranges and apples here, because the
sailing ships were neither contracted to nor funded by the U.S. government. Some of the other companies in Orange and Beaumont that built

wooden steamships for the government may have had problems with canceled contracts and unfinished ships, but ISC was not building ships for anyone except themselves and the Italians.

A letter from ISC to the U.S. Shipping Board, dated July 25, 1919, with Bragadin's signature, mentions wooden steamships, but even these were built for the Italians.[11] The letter concerns ISC's request to transfer eight steamers, then under construction at their Pascagoula yard, to the Italian Registry immediately after their completion. The date of the letter is more than eight months after the end of the war, and the ships were still under construction. The National Archives documents listing shipyards that were building ships for the U.S. Shipping Board did not list ISC as a builder of wooden steamships for the Emergency Fleet Corporation.

Outstanding mortgages are normally indicated on ship documentation. Only one of the documents pertaining to the fourteen ships had a mortgage indicated (the *Monfalcone*), and it was taken over by the buyer. At a later time the buyer appeared to have defaulted on the mortgage, which was recovered by an auction, but this was not against ISC.

The newspaper article also mentioned that Piaggio was an exporter and Italian vice-consul at Gulfport, Mississippi. Other sources reported that Piaggio was the son of the vice-consul. Only one document with the name Piaggio was found among the records of the Department of State. On August 18, 1915, a Nino Enrico Piaggio was appointed consular agent at Gulfport, Mississippi.[12] Some may have thought this was Henry Piaggio's father because of the name. Piaggio's father's name, however, was listed as Daria Piaggio on Henry Piaggio's Record of Funeral.[13] Piaggio's middle name shown on the Record of Funeral, and the only record that showed it, was Nino.

Circumstantially, it appears that Piaggio's Italian name was Nino Enrico Piaggio, and at some time, he had it officially changed (or just changed it) to Henry Nino Piaggio, Henry being the English form of the Italian Enrico. Unless a name change record were found, however, the assumption that this answers the consular status of Piaggio is still just an assumption, although a rather strong one. A consular agent is defined as a consular officer of the lowest rank, often a designated foreign national stationed at a place where no full consular office is established. To represent the Italian government, Piaggio would have probably needed to use his Italian name. In the Department of State records, one only finds vice consuls in major cities having consuls, and there are many more consular agents than other consular officers. Gulfport, Mississippi, did not have an Italian consul, the nearest being at New Orleans, Louisiana.

According to one source, the International Shipbuilding Company's yard closed late in 1920, and a year later, Henry Piaggio died. Sometime in the 1920s, the buildings, ways, and piers were destroyed by fire.[14]

The Gulfport-Harrison County Library has a Diamond Jubilee Photo Album covering Gulfport from 1898 to 1973, which contains the following statements concerning Piaggio: "AN ITALIAN DIPLOMAT named Piagio [*sic*] came to the Mississippi Gulf Coast to build ships for the Italian Government at the National Shipyard in Pascagoula and another shipyard in Texas. He imported the materials and statuary to construct and landscape his palace on the beach in Mississippi City. Unfortunately he died before the palace was completed. Mr. Salvadore Bertucci purchased the property during World War II and opened a club known as 'The Merry Mansion'. Mrs. Piagio [*sic*] lived in a cottage on the grounds until her death."[15]

The Biloxi Public Library, an entity of the Harrison County Library System, was most helpful and supplied Piaggio's obituary and funeral notice from the *Biloxi Daily Herald.* The obituary is provided verbatim, except for the lengthy listing of pallbearers, as it summarizes the life and career of Piaggio as well as newspapers can. Additionally, it provides answers to age and the early life of Piaggio:

HENRY PIAGGIO
ANSWERS SUMMONS
Prominent Business Man Died
Last Night after an Illness of
About Three Months.

Henry Piaggio, one of the prominent business men of the Coast, died at his home in Mississippi City last night at 10 o'clock after a lingering illness of about three months. G. O. Carlovitz of Gulfport, a life-long friend, was at his bedside when the end came. Mr. Piaggio had been ailing since last April and had been taking treatments both from specialists and from local physicians. Mr. Piaggio was born in Genoa, Italy, March 17, 1874, and came to the United States when a boy. His father engaged in the saw mill business and later in the lumber exporting business in Pensacola, Fla., and the son was trained in this work which he followed afterward.

He was a Spanish War veteran, having gone into the service from Pensacola, Fla. Later he came to Gulfport and opened a lumber exporting office under the name of Henry Piaggio and Company. Visiting Italy about this time he became interested in building ships for the Italian Government and finally organized the International Shipbuilding Company which was located at

Pascagoula. He was also president of another company known as the Marine Commerce Corporation. Previous to his illness he was engaged in exporting lumber under the name of the Henry Piaggio Exporting Company, with offices at Gulfport.

During all this time he maintained offices in Gulfport. He loved the coast and built a magnificent home on the beach in Mississippi City making it a veritable Italian Villa.

The wife, two sisters and a mother remain to mourn his loss. The mother and one sister live in Genoa, Italy and the other sister, Mrs. John Ryan lives in Mobile, Ala. The funeral services will be held at the family residence on the beach in Mississippi City tomorrow morning at 10 o'clock. Burial will be made at Evergreen Cemetery, it being his desire to be laid to rest on the coast that he loved so well.

Mr. Piaggio was a generous hearted man and gave to every charitable movement. He had an engaging personality and made friends readily. His passing will be regretted by the entire Coast.[16]

The active pallbearers, numbered seven, including three colonels and a judge. Among the twenty-eight honorary pallbearers were four doctors, an admiral, and a judge. The floral display was extolled as extensive and elaborate, and the funeral procession was estimated at over a half mile long, at a time when only the well-to-do had cars. Although this does not sound like the funeral of a destitute man, indications are that his estate was not substantial enough to allow his wife to live in the mansion.

Murella Hebert Powell, local history librarian at Biloxi Library, had some telephone conversations with Savadore Bertucci's daughter in the summer of 1997. She learned from these conversations that Mrs. Piaggio was left penniless upon her husband's death and could neither complete the mansion nor afford to live in it. Consequently, she lived, as mentioned earlier, in the small cottage on the grounds, which had been meant for a caretaker.[17] According to another reference, the cottage was referred to as a spacious bungalow, and it is quite possible that Mrs. Piaggio chose to live in it instead of the mansion.[18]

The Record of Funeral listed Piaggio's occupation as lumber exporter and indicated that his mother, Angelina Bozinna (her maiden name is not clear), was born in New Orleans.[19]

The Archives I Record Branch at the National Archives made an extensive search of all the pertinent Records Groups and Indexes for each service to determine what Piaggio's participation in the Spanish American War was, but to no avail.[20] It is possible, however, that Piaggio served in a volunteer organization or the merchant marine.

Piaggio's mansion in Mississippi City was heavily damaged in a hurricane in 1947 and a large barge deposited in the front yard had to be removed in pieces after being cut up with oxy-acetylene torches.[21] The mansion was totally destroyed by hurricane Camille in 1969. After this disaster, the remains of the mansion were cleared away, and nothing was left of the empire of Piaggio. The ships were gone except for some pitiful hulks, and the shipyard in Orange had burned.

What can we conclude about this man who made good in America, as did many of his fellow countrymen? He learned to be a successful businessman in the forestry industry, built ships, sent lumber to Italy during World War I, and was generous when it came to crew pay, manning of his ships, and charitable causes. In his time, he was very well thought of, both personally and professionally, in Gulfport and Orange, according to several reports.

The reasons for his possible loss of fortune is unknown except that the market for lumber probably evaporated after the war even faster than it developed. Several ISC ships carried cargoes other than lumber at the war's end, witness the petroleum cargoes, the grains, and the tramp adventures of the *City of Beaumont*. The profusion of ties rotting on an island off the coast of Mobile, Alabama, were probably manufactured for the war. The Piave mill in Mississippi may have been heavily invested in by Piaggio.

In addition, according to the obituary, Piaggio had been ailing since the previous April (some nine months) and possibly longer. His declining health may have prevented him from fighting another battle with finances that he might otherwise have coped with. The earlier statement that Piaggio may have embezzled the Italian government was never hinted at elsewhere, and nothing in any of the extensive file research indicated any irregularity. This comment was most likely a local rumor, possibly based on envy and prejudice.

Piaggio was only forty-seven years old at his death, and no children were mentioned in the obituary. His will left all of his property to his wife, with no children listed.[22] The will did not describe the estate.

Despite his apparent financial woes at the end, Piaggio was successful for instigating and completing the biggest cargo sailing ship construction program in the history of the world.

THE LEGACY OF JOHN LEONARD BLUDWORTH

Bludworth was the master carpenter for the eleven barkentines. After these were completed, Bludworth moved back to the Galveston area, continuing work with boats. For a time he worked for Gulf Fisheries.

One of his tasks was disposing of some of the beautiful two-masted schooners built at Essex, Massachusetts, earlier in the century, as they came to the end of their useful life and mechanically powered vessels began to take over. The disposal was accomplished by towing the vessels out into the Gulf of Mexico and scuttling them.

In 1927, he operated the Bludworth Shipyard on Brays Bayou in Harrisburg. His four sons and at least one grandson continued in the shipbuilding and repair business. These were John L. Bludworth, Jr., Martin Bludworth, Dannie Bludworth, and Harold Bludworth. John L. Bludworth, Jr. founded the J. Bludworth, Incorporated, shipyard at Corpus Christi, Texas, in 1979, still in operation.

As of 1998, the Bludworth Bond Shipyard, along the ship channel and in Texas City, was still operated by Harold Bludworth and Lennie Bond, a relative. The John Bludworth Marine, Incorporated, a shipyard on the ship channel, was also in operation in 1998. This yard is owned and operated by Johnny Bludworth, a grandson of John L. Bludworth, and Johnny's son is involved in the operation, continuing the family tradition. Recently, Johnny Bludworth opened another yard on Pelican Island (adjacent to Galveston), just a few hundred feet from where his grandfather's yard was in the early 1900s.

Like the earlier Bludworths at Rockport, many of the later Bludworths were active in racing sailboats on Galveston Bay, and Martin Bludworth was renowned countrywide for his racing skills in the Flying Dutchman, one of the very demanding Olympic classes. Perhaps all of this is a legacy of the ships built at Orange, but one has the strong feeling that this is a maritime family, and, regardless of the past, the Bludworths were destined to build, repair, and race boats and maintain their ties to the sea.

THE INTERNATIONAL SHIPBUILDING COMPANY CREWS

The International Shipbuilding Company crews should be mentioned, even though little is known about them. Some conclusions can be reached based on the ship design and careers.

First, the barkentines. Eleven of these magnificent ships sailed at least once and required more than just schooner sailors. The barkentines had to have a few sailors that were competent square-rigger men, even though they only had one mast with square sails. Square sails require more work aloft, and the time to go up is usually the most threatening time, such as when sudden storms hit and some or all of the sails must be furled.

Four of the ships built at Orange burned while in port, and one was sunk by a German submarine, but none of the fourteen ships were lost in a storm, foundered, or were involved in a collision at sea while registered in Texas. One did run aground on the Bahama Islands Banks, but it was repaired. At least one other ship, the *City of Dallas*, burned at Genoa, Italy, on August 4, 1919, eleven days after its transfer to the Italian flag. This was less than a year after its completion on September 25, 1918.[23]

Several of the ISC ships made at least one transatlantic trip to Genoa, Italy, and quite a few made trips to other European, Balkan, and South American ports. In this much time at sea, some storms must have been encountered and some rigging failures occurred, and yet the ships pulled through. The vessels lost to fire occurred in port, possibly caused, at least some of the time, by the auxiliary engines, the gasoline on board, and the hazardous cargoes. One fire was reported at sea, and it was, with diligent effort, extinguished.

Statistics concerning the fate of the 458 four-masted schooners from the East and Gulf Coast yards are representative of what might have been expected of large sailing ships of this era.[24] The causes of the losses follow:

    29 collision
    160 stranding
    27 burning
    20 enemy action
    53 sold to foreign flag
    14 reduced to barges
    36 broken up or abandoned
    98 abandoned at sea or foundered
    21 went missing

All but the last two causes were man-made, and the so-called human error factor was prevalent in the first three causes. The last two were owing to the ship and crew's inability to overcome the stress of weather while at sea. The ISC ships had four burnings in port, one loss to enemy action, and several of the other causes, but none was abandoned at sea or went missing. Other than the bad fire record, the ISC ships did quite well, a tribute to both the construction and seamanship by the crews. Two ships were abandoned or foundered, but this was after they had left ISC and, in both cases, had been drastically altered and had the engines removed.

It is quite possible that, despite their disadvantages, use of the engines saved the ship and crew on one or more occasions while sailing for ISC, but that information is gone.

Documentation was found for three four-masted schooners that were built by other yards in the East Texas area as a result of World War I. These were built to the American, rather than the Italian, war calendar, so were somewhat later than several of the ISC ships. One four-masted schooner, the *Elmir Roberts*, was built at Orange, Texas, by the Southern Drydock and Shipbuilding Company for the Elmir Roberts Corporation, 42 Broadway, New York, New York. L. E. Weaver was the master carpenter for this ship, and his granddaughter, Mrs. Jerry W. Harris of Orange, Texas, provided the photograph (figure 10.1) of the *Elmir Roberts*. This picture shows typical internal construction techniques in use at the time.

More of the Story

First, note the thick wooden members close to the bilges, which will go from the sister (assistant) keelsons to the bilges and then up the sides of the hull. They vary in thickness, from four inches at the bottom, increasing to twelve inches at the bilges, and perhaps to ten inches on the sides. These members are called floor ceiling, bilge ceiling, and side

fig. 10.1. Elmir Roberts *under construction.* Courtesy Mrs. Jerry W. Harris

ceiling, according to their location. Also along the centerline of the vessel is the buildup of what will be a massive keelson. See also the *Bertha L. Downs.*[25]

The vessel had a net tonnage of 695 and was just slightly larger all around than the *City of Pensacola*. She had a 200 horsepower oil-burning Fairbanks-Morse engine and only carried 1,700 gallons of fuel, or enough for less than four days' continuous running.[26] Application for official number was made August 16, 1918, and listed a crew of ten; however, the Certificate of Registry No. 26 was not issued until January 25, 1919, and it listed a crew of six, again demonstrating a lack of consistency in filling out the forms.[27] The document was a duplicate copy that was transmitted in place of the original, which apparently had been lost. This document was surrendered at Port Arthur, Texas, on September 15, 1919. Reason surrendered: "Vessel lost at sea on August 22, 1919. Burned 41° 5'N, 62°18' W; 12 on board no life lost." This position is a little more than four hundred miles east of Cape Cod, Massachusetts. Another source indicated the ship had loaded salvage ammunition at Paulliac, located on the west coast of France about forty miles up a waterway toward Bordeaux (shown in figure 8.2), so it was miraculous that no lives were lost.[28] It is possible that the ship delivered a load of timbers to an American or foreign port prior to its untimely end. In another photograph provided by Mrs. Harris, the ship is at a timber dock where large numbers of floating timbers are alongside. The ship had lumber ports and the visible port side lumber port is open, which at least circumstantially indicates lumber-loading intentions.

The last two four-masted Texas schooners were the *Albert D. Cummins* and the *Marie F. Cummins*, built by the Beaumont Shipbuilding and Drydock Company of Beaumont. These ships were constructed for the A. D. Cummins Company, Incorporated, of Wilmington, Delaware. The two like vessels were 190 feet long, or slightly larger than the other four masters discussed.[29] They had no engines, so net tonnage was more than 1,000 (over 300 more than the *Elmir Roberts* and more than 400 tons better than the *City of Pensacola*) and called for a crew of eight, excluding master. One can readily see big advantages from both the cargo and crew standpoints. A 30 to 40 percent increase in cargo capacity, along with a 40 percent reduction in crew, is very significant.

These ships managed to stay out of trouble until both were abandoned at Wilmington, Delaware, on December 4, 1937.[30] The vessels were not kept around this long for sentimental reasons; this owner knew how to make money hauling bulk cargoes using small, low-paid, economically fed crews. It was the height of the Depression, and most men would do any work, no matter how small the pay, simply to survive. The

hulls ended up at Philadelphia, Pennsylvania, where they were reportedly burned for scrap in the summer of 1947.[31]

Based on the research conducted, these and the ISC ships were the
only four- and five-masted sailing vessels ever built in Texas. It is of interest to note that after the loss of the *City of Mobile* not another one of
the ISC ships was lost to fire, even though several of them had engines
at least for awhile. The *City of Beaumont* came close but survived and the
two four-masted schooners (no engines) built at Beaumont, Texas, were
documented until 1937. The *City of Dallas* burned but after transfer to
the Italian flag. The *Elmir Roberts* with one engine and built at Orange,
Texas, also burned on her return trip to France. Can one blame the fires
on the engines or perhaps poor design of the exhaust system? Only circumstantially, for we simply do not have enough facts to pinpoint the
fire causes with any certainty.

THE HULKS

Some of the ships had a significant afterlife, receiving considerable attention in some circles. The surrender statements indicated that *Smith
and Terry No. 4* ex *City of Austin* was dismantled and abandoned at Port
Johnson, Bayonne, New Jersey, on August 15, 1935, and the *H. W. Brown*
ex *Macerata* followed on February 13, 1936. One reference indicated
that the *City of Austin* was renamed the *Mortara* while in Italy.[32] It was
officially renamed the *Smith and Terry No. 4* after returning to the
United States from Italy.

The Port Johnson hulks served as models for the renowned marine
artist John Noble. One of his lithographs, *Mortara Genova*, shows a
stern view of a hulk in the ice. He wrote:

> A barkentine of weird and monstrous proportions lies listed on the
> silted purlieu of a boneyard. Several such five-masters—bearing
> the looks of ships seen in dreams—were built on the Gulf Coast.
>
> The *Molfetta* was one of twelve five-masted wooden barkentines
> built by Piaggio on the Gulf Coast in the 1919–20 era (*Mortara,
> Marsala*, etc.). They were huge, nearly 300 feet long, and some
> had strange Italianate sterns. They were obsolete upon launching,
> as the war shipping was over by then, and squareriggers needed
> larger crews. . . .[33]
>
> The *Mortara Genova*, a five-masted barkentine built for Italy
> during the first World War, was an ugly-duckling kin to the coast
> schooners. She found her end in a northern ice field, having never
> seen her "home" port, Genoa.[34]

The maiden voyage of the *City of Austin* (pre-*Mortara*) was to Genoa, Italy, and her Certificate of Registry was returned from there. Most wooden vessels are ugly ducklings several years after abandonment and the ravages of weather, no maintenance, and scavengers. Note, on the other hand, the *Buccaneer* ex *City of Beaumont* residing and being admired on the Manhattan waterfront for several years because she was kept painted and properly maintained. The reference contains several photographs and copies of Noble's work that have the ISC barkentines as the main subject or in view.

Noble was a fine artist, but along with most of the rest of the world, he had all of the ships being built later than they really were and never accomplishing anything, when, in fact, several useful trips were made. Presumably, Noble is stating the home port along with the vessel name when he uses *Mortara Genova*.

Previous trips, based on official documents, indicate that two barkentines went to Buenos Aires with packaged petroleum products, and one with lumber. At least five other barkentines made one or more trips, usually loaded with more than two million board feet of lumber to Genoa, Italy, and one trip that we know of (cargo unspecified) was made to Funchal, Madeira. This same ship, *City of Galveston*, made at least one more trip from the Gulf Coast to England, probably with lumber, and then to Genoa, Italy, where she was eventually dismantled. The maiden voyage of the *City of Beaumont* covered approximately 15,000 miles, going to the Black Sea, and 82 miles up the Danube River with many intermediate cargo deliveries and loadings. She then sailed the East Coast for several years before becoming a showboat.

After going to the Italian flag and then returning to the U.S. flag, some of the other barkentines made several years' contribution in the coastal trade as barkentines or converted to schooners. Several successful trips were made by the schooner *City of Orange* and one successful delivery by the *City of Pensacola*.

At least 15 million board feet of lumber were estimated to have been delivered to Italy, in addition to bulk cargo deliveries made to other ports while the ships belonged to ISC. This does not take into account any of the deliveries made by the several other ships leased by Piaggio.

American-named ships were named for American cities (seven Texan), and Italian-named ships were named for Italian cities. The names used by Noble in describing his lithographs came from this source, right off the ships sterns probably. Why the Italian ship names all started with an "M" was not revealed but was perhaps analogous to the German Flying P Line Series. Alvise Bragadin's letterhead does not list any Italian ship names, including the *Monfalcone* or the *Macerata*.

Two five-masted barkentines were built at Pascagoula, Mississippi, by ISC, bringing the total to fourteen, rather than twelve, barkentines built on the Gulf Coast. The ending for these two barkentines—the *City of Biloxi* and the *City of Pascagoula*—is unknown. The *City of Waco's* ending was also questionable. A telegram from the deputy collector at Gulfport, Mississippi, to the commissioner of navigation, dated September 8, 1919, stated that agents for *City of Biloxi*, under the Italian flag, wanted to know the procedure for changing a name, if permissible.[35]

The *City of Austin* came back from the Italian flag but kept or resumed its original name, *City of Austin*, until changing to the *Smith and Terry No. 4*. The American documentation only indicated that two hulks of the ships built at Orange ended up abandoned at Port Johnson, although it is possible that two or three of the other barkentines could have been abandoned at Port Johnson at some point.

Even after becoming hulks, these and other ships in the boneyard served some useful and charitable purposes. The longleaf yellow pine was taken from the ships for firewood as a means to survive the cold nights. Even the artist Noble participated, using or selling timbers for his own support.[36]

Scavengers also retrieved the scrap metals, sails and manila, and the masts were cut down for use as fender booms. Noble, rightfully so, admired these pirates, who were not "thieves of great villany," and who saved "tons of iron, lead, and copper that would have been lost to the coming generations without them." At the end of the 1970s, Noble saw the last seamen leave Sailers' Snug Harbor, and the last wrecks in Port Johnson were burned to the waterline by the Army Corps of Engineers, who he felt "should be more closely watched."[37]

The most enduring was the *City of Beaumont*, and the Texas Seaport Museum at Galveston has been instrumental in collecting considerable information about this ship and retrieving hardware from her remains.

In an article in *Sea History*, Norman Brouwer wrote that the *City of Beaumont* was one of sixteen similar vessels produced by shipyards in Texas and Mississippi during World War I. Only one five-masted barkentine had been built in this country before then, the *David Dows*. During the war, three more were built at Aberdeen, Washington, and seven others were converted from steamers under construction in California shipyards, explaining Karppi's reference to some barkentines built on the West Coast.

Brouwer went on to mention that the foremast doubling was moved to San Francisco sometime in the 1960s where it is displayed below decks in the museum ship *Balclutha*. Other relics of the ship have been acquired by South Street (the New York City Maritime Museum), including the wheel and steering gear and the poop deck capstan.[38]

Some informal notes made by the late Karl Kortum (former director of the National Maritime Museum, San Francisco, California) provide some interesting insights into these museum acquisitions:

> About 1963 Sterling Hayden told me of seeing a barkentine alongside the railroad tracks at Hastings-on-Hudson. I immediately asked him: "Is the foremast still standing?" "Yes it is."
>
> Hastings-on-Hudson is about thirty miles up-river from the Empire State Building. If the foremast still stood that meant that the portion of the mast where the lower mast overlaps the topmast, complete with a half-circular wooden top platform, was intact— the last square-rigged mast doubling in America. Lord Nelson was shot by a French sharp-shooter located in the top of the REDOUBTABLE but that distant, tragic event was not my reason for being interested.

The writer went on to explain that he was looking at the *Great Britain* in the Falklands, but it was British so he went after an American bird-in-the-hand—the doubling and top on the Hudson River. Later he cased the ship, the *City of Beaumont*, and eventually obtained his doubling and top. He stated that the ship had Douglas fir spars, undoubtedly shipped down by rail from Oregon or Washington. John Noble, the artist, served as a hand for the independent Bill Van Frank, the salvor, when the mast doubling was removed from the ship.[39]

The *Buccaneer* ex *City of Beaumont* attracted the attention of the *New York Times* in 1988. The occasion was a visit by Peter H. Brink, executive director of the Galveston Historical Society, who stated, "We're interested in it because it was a Texas ship, and we want to give people an idea of the size and scale of these incredible ships." Brink was made aware of the ship by Karl Kortum. Kortum said that he had "no worry" that the ship could be sectioned and moved. He added that the expense "wouldn't be too costly for Texas." Brink conceded that "there once was a time when Texans thought they could do anything," but "we've become more conservative in recent years."[40]

A letter from Peter Stanford, president of the National Maritime Society, refers to the *City of Beaumont* maiden voyage letter. He was interested to learn that the engines were not strong enough to get through the Bosporus (which he heard runs 6 knots but finds hard to believe).[41]

Another source of useful information is "The *City of Beaumont* Survey," a report dated May 17, 1990, prepared for the Galveston Historical

Foundation, and performed by four individuals from the University of Lowell at Lowell, Massachusetts. One possible error in this report, however, is the claim that some of the wood in the hull was fir, including the deck planking. Both economically and logistically, this was very unlikely. All other references indicate the ships were built of southern yellow pine, and the only fir used was for the spars. Drawings for the *Bertha L. Downs* launched at Bath, Maine, in 1908, called for all long leaf yellow pine except for oak frames and a few other minor exceptions. The differences seen in decay rates can result from heartwood versus sapwood, and variance between different species of southern yellow pine, which is the generic term for at least four species.

The report provides dimensions for various components. For example, the chainplates were 4-by-5/8-inch bar stock more than 10 feet long (bottoms hidden by water). Chainplates were 28 inches on center; the rigging screws (turnbuckles) were 67 inches long by 3 1/2 inches in diameter, and the shrouds were 1 3/4 inches in diameter. The barkentines had twelve shrouds and backstays on the foremast. The cast-iron rudder stock was 18 inches in diameter, with an estimated length of 26 feet. A mast stub was measured at 28 inches in diameter and was stated to be white pine.[42] White pine is the state tree for Maine, and shipbuilders in that state as well as in the rest of New England, had long ago used most of the available white pine trees for masts.[43] By all accounts, the New Englanders and Texans used Douglas fir for the spars, which came from Oregon and Washington.

The final result of the studies was the practical one, and that included bringing several portable pieces, but no massive sections, of the ship's hardware to the Texas Seaport Museum at Galveston. Three sets of the *City of Beaumont*'s mooring bitts are on display at the entrance to the museum. Other items are warehoused, awaiting future use. The Port of Beaumont also has some mooring bitts and other small pieces of the ship.

Figure 10.2 shows the hulk of the ship in the early 1990s. The photograph was taken at Hastings-on-Hudson. The open lumber ports identify this as a ship built to haul lumber, although how often that was her cargo is unknown.

Some of the wood retrieved from the ship was turned over to Robert Haas of Lumberton, Texas, for model construction. A small amount was used in a six-foot-long model of the *City of Beaumont* that is on display at the Clifton Steamboat Museum at Beaumont, Texas, along with a piece of wood from the hull. Haas also built a smaller model for the Texas Seaport Museum at Galveston and another model of the ship for the Port of Beaumont, using retrieved wood.

*fig. 10.2. Hulk of
the* City of Beau-
mont. Courtesy
Texas Seaport
Museum

A letter dated October 7, 1994, tells the final story:

> I thought all of you would want to know that the BUCCANEER, originally the CITY OF BEAUMONT, is no more. The enclosed page (or copy of same) from the latest issue of our *Hastings Historian* depicts the demise of this once proud barkentine.Please inform others who might be interested.[44]

The page referred to shows the cleanup of the site by a salvage company.

This, then, was the last of the fourteen fabulous ships built by Texans of Texas materials. They hauled some cargo, had some adventures, were manned by both ruffians and heroes, but, most of all, made major contributions to the maritime history of Texas.

The amazing thing is that not one of these ships ended her career in Texas, or lies rotting on our shores, or sank in one of our bays or estuaries.

The Wooden Steamships

A writer for *Harper's Weekly*, George Creel, said "Ships will win the war,—We must build a bridge of ships across the sea."[1] So ships were built out of steel, wood, and even concrete.

The United States Shipping Board was organized on January 30, 1917, under the Shipping Act of September 7, 1916, and was almost immediately faced with the necessity of creating a large fleet to transport men and materials needed in World War I. The board seized, requisitioned, or purchased vessels, and began a huge program of shipbuilding. The board's principal instrument for the performance of these functions was the Emergency Fleet Corporation, in Washington, D.C.[2] This war-born bureaucracy finally died October 25, 1936, in name at least, when absorbed by the newly organized United States Maritime Commission.

During World War I, nine shipyards along the Texas Gulf Coast received contracts to build wooden steamships for the United States Shipping Board. These ships were paid for by the government and owned by the Emergency Fleet Corporation after completion. The ships were built of pine to a standard design, and all of the yards were in the Orange, Beaumont, and Houston area, except for one yard at Rockport almost two hundred miles from the nearest pine forest. The steam screw, *Nacogdoches*, named by the first lady, Mrs. Woodrow Wilson, was built in Houston and was about the same size as the barkentines. Her capacity was 600 to 900 tons less, however, because of the large engine room, space for 500 tons of coal, and quarters for a crew of 55 men. This large crew was attributable partly to having a government gun crew on board and partly to the need for a large engine room gang, as these ships burned thirty tons of coal a day. Besides a lot of machinery, plumbing, and pumps to look after, a lot of coal had to be shoveled by stokers.

These ships had a triple expansion steam engine of 1,400 horsepower that gave them a speed of 10 knots.[3] A 700 percent increase in power is required to double the speed because of the high energy needed to make waves and move more water out of the way of the hull. Triple expansion engines take the exhaust steam from the first cylinder and expand it twice more in two successively larger cylinders, with a corresponding increase in efficiency.

The ships were photographed at all stages of construction at the various shipyards, probably as a contract requirement. Gulf District No. 6 listed all of the Texas Gulf Coast shipyards involved in the program plus one yard at Morgan City, Louisiana.[4] Photographs were obtained from the pictorial library at College Park, Maryland, where the pictures are identified as to which yard they pertain to and sometimes hull number, but not by ship name. Research on these ships was handicapped by the lack of names, and most of the pictures are not identified. It is probable that a listing of the ships with a cross-index between the numbers and names is in existence somewhere. (Apparently none of the pictures had been acquired previously as they had to be numbered before I could order them.)

The magnitude of this shipbuilding endeavor was massive; it included both coasts in addition to twenty-three yards along the Gulf Coast, from Pensacola, Florida, to Rockport, Texas. Each yard had contracts for several ships. It was a prosperous time for the lumber industry and the shipbuilders. The United States Shipping Board was not involved in the funding for the construction of any of the sailing ships built in Texas; they merely controlled flag changes for all United States shipping.

ORANGE, TEXAS

Two yards building wooden steamships were located at Orange. One yard at Orange, the National Shipbuilding Company (not to be confused with ISC) built at least two of what were likely the longest wooden ships ever built. The other yard was the Southern Drydock and Shipbuilding Company located just opposite the International Shipbuilding Company (the sailing shipyard) on the Sabine River, as shown in figure 11.1. This figure shows one of the standard wooden steamships looking aft toward the bridge with a man holding a placard showing hull number 354. Each yard had a three-digit series of numbers for the ships built at that facility. The barkentine in the background built by ISC is not identified but is one of the later ships, as this steamship was not finished until late 1918 or 1919, and the wheelhouse on the barkentine was not a part of the design until after the *City of Dallas*.

Figure 11.2 shows some of the construction details of hull number 351. One can see the hatch frame timbers with dovetailing at the corners and scarfed joints where splices were required. Alongside is a four-

masted schooner, which could very well be the *Elmir Roberts*, built by this same company. The timeframe is about right, for this was well after the loss of the *City of Pensacola*. ISC is in the background with one of the later sailing ships on the ways with a gantry crane astride.

Figure 11.3 shows the National Shipbuilding Company, the other shipyard in Orange involved in building wooden steamships. Three ships can be seen on the ways and two more at the left center in the water. There are no gantry cranes in any of these yards building wooden steamships.

Figure 11.4 is a photograph also taken at the National Shipbuilding Company. The sign reads: "RECORD MADE FRAMING US HULL NO. 242 DAUGHTERY TYPE 79 FRAMES ERECTED IN 30 HOURS AND 35 MINUTES NATIONAL SHIP BLDG. CO. ORANGE, TEX." Some of the massive timbers in the frames can be seen along with the large C clamps used to hold parts together while being fastened. Two ships that came to light out of many built by the National Shipbuilding Company were the *War Marvel* and *War Mystery*.[5] The National Shipbuilding Company was building fourteen ships in late 1917 for the government, and at least some of them,

fig. 11.1. Wooden steamship with ISC barkentine on left. Courtesy National Archives

including the two named, were considerably larger than the Standard Wood Steamship design provided by the government. The Daugherty type was 330 feet long and had a deadweight tonnage of 5,000 tons compared to 267 feet and 3,600 tons for the standard ship.[6] The Gulf Coast Lumberman of March 1, 1918, described the ship, her launch, and the designer:

> Undoubtedly the biggest event of the kind that has taken place since the American nation started in to "Build ships and win the war", took place at Orange, Texas, at five o'clock on the afternoon of February 27th, when the National Ship Building Company of Texas, launched safely and majestically into the deep waters of the Sabine River, the largest ship built entirely of wood that has ever been launched in the history of the world.
>
> The fact that this IS the record wooden ship has sometimes been doubted, but so far as authorities on the subject can learn, this great ship of southern yellow pine, 330 feet in length, 48 foot beam, 27 feet mounded [*sic*] depth and with a tonnage of 5,000

*fig. 11.2. Ship at
Southern Drydock
and Shipbuilding
Company.
Courtesy
National
Archives*

tons, is actually and absolutely the largest wooden ship that ever took water.

The manner of her taking the water was unusual, and contributed to a most impressive ceremonial. When the stays that held her were still upright in many places, and just thirty minutes before President A. A. Daugherty [*sic*] of the National expected her to take the dip, she suddenly started into life. The whistle of the shipyard blew a shrill warning, and the nine hundred men who were helping in the launching preparations jumped clear of trouble. Smooth as glass, without a hitch or trouble, the great boat slid down her ways. As he [*sic*] struck the water, heading at great speed for the opposite side of the river, four great anchors that were held on trigger attachments, were turned loose, and her progress was so carefully checked that she was within forty feet of the opposite bank before she came to a dead stop. Then she swung upstream with the strong wind that was blowing, and floated beautifully—a masterpiece. . . .

"WAR MYSTERY" today holds the attention of the ship building authorities of the nation, for the reason that she is not of the standard Government pattern being built in the Government yards everywhere, but is considerably larger than the Govern-

fig. 11.3. National Shipbuilding Company of Texas. Courtesy National Archives

ment pattern, contains two hundred thousand feet of timber less than the Government pattern, is so specified that the timbers are much easier to cut than the Government standard, and—in the opinion of her builders and purchasers—is a much better, more practical and more valuable type of boat than the Government ship.

She was designed by Mr. A. A. Daughtery for the Cunard Line. Another of the same type for the same people is practically finished in the same yard, and will be launched within a month. The National Ship Building Company is also building six of the big ships at the present time, and expects to launch a ship at least every thirty days for some time to come.

This story would not be complete without slight mention of Mr. A. A. Daughtery, head of this big building concern. A splendid Irishman and a high class engineer of long experience, he brought to the ship building business the ability to promote and hold efficiency that makes the National yard at Orange the wonder of all beholders. They say that this is the most efficient yard

*fig. 11.4. Proud
workers pose for
photograph at
National Shipbuilding
Company.* Courtesy
National Archives

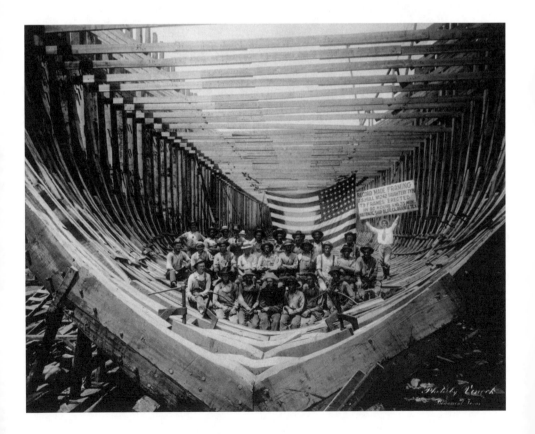

that is building ships in this country today, and it is certain that wonders have been wrought and are being wrought by this master of efficiency. He has succeeded in getting his crew of a thousand men thrilled with enthusiasm with regard to the work they are doing, and they are working for Uncle Sam every day, and to help lick the Kaiser.[7]

The claim that these vessels were the largest ships to ever be built out of wood in the United States was only true for the register length. One of the previous claimed champs was the six-masted schooner, *Wyoming*, built by Percy and Small at Bath, Maine, in 1909.[8] The net tonnage for the *Wyoming* was considerably larger than for the steamship since space was not required for propulsion, several hundred tons of coal, and the larger crew necessary on the steamship. With other yards in Orange, including ISC, a reporter contended that there were thirty-five ships under construction in November of 1917.[9]

BEAUMONT, TEXAS

Beaumont had four yards building wooden steamships. These were McBride and Law, Lone Star Shipbuilding Company, Beaumont Shipbuilding and Drydock Company, and J. N. McCammon.

Figure 11.5 shows the SS *Beaumont* built by McBride and Law at Beaumont. Since this ship was one of only a few for which papers were found, I will describe it from the official documentation. Her Application for Official Number was submitted at Port Arthur, Texas, November 28, 1918, some two weeks after World War I ended. The application indicated the rig was steam screw, her speed was 10 knots, she carried 550 tons of coal, and burned 24 tons per day. The deadweight capacity was 3,500 tons, and she drew 23.5 feet loaded. The gross tonnage was 2,551 and net was 1,528, with 1,000 tons taken up by the engine room, coal storage, and large crew, in this case only forty, excluding the master. Apparently, the gun crew was excluded, since the war was over. The ship was powered by a triple-expansion steam engine built by the Nordberg Manufacturing Company. The engine produced 1,400 horsepower at 94 rpm. Home port was Beaumont, Texas, and the ship was equipped with radio apparatus, with WXUA for call letters.[10]

According to the Certificate of Registry No. 40, issued April 28, 1919, at Port Arthur, the ship was owned by the United States of America, represented by the United States Shipping Board. Alex Maitland of Houston, Texas, district manager for the Emergency Fleet Corporation, took the oath and swore to these facts. The crew space was 167.57

tons, and the master's cabin was 9.06. The propelling power was allotted 816.51 tons and the bridge 190.64; there were several other deductions such as radio, anchor, and chart house. The register length was 267.3 feet, breadth 46 feet, and depth 23.6 feet. L. C. Weaver was the master carpenter, and the first ship's captain was Fred Bodungen.[11]

Another ship built at the same yard is shown in figure 11.6. The drydocked ship is having the seams caulked; one can only guess at how many feet of seams there were in each ship. The caulking after launching allowed the keel for another ship to be laid and construction started. The caulking was all done by hand and was usually oakum hammered in with a blunt tool, followed with hot tar payed into the seam. Cement was sometimes used for seams at lower levels.

fig. 11.5. The SS
Beaumont *with*
camouflage paint.
Courtesy
National
Archives

The SS *Oneco* received her Certificate of Registry on September 14, 1918, at Port Arthur, Texas. The master carpenter was S. G. Reed, and it was built at the Beaumont Shipbuilding and Drydock Company in Beaumont.[12] All of her dimensions were close to those given for the SS *Beaumont.*

The SS *Swampscott*, built at the same yard, had her Application of

Owner or Master for Official Number submitted at Port Arthur, Texas, on September 27, 1918.[13] She received the first Certificate of Registry No. 19, on May 9, 1919.[14] There did not appear to be any great hurry to get these ships into operation since the war was over; however, she did go to sea. All of these ships had radio apparatus.

fig. 11.6. Dry-docked ship at Beaumont. Courtesy National Archives

HOUSTON, TEXAS

Houston had two yards building ships for the government, the Universal Shipbuilding Company and the Midland Bridge Company.

Figure 11.7 shows a launched ship almost to the other side of the channel. This picture was taken at the Universal yard, Galena, Texas. The date on the picture indicates the launch took place October 27, 1919, more than eleven months after the end of World War I.

One of the ships built by Universal was the *Nacogdoches*, and the Application for Official Number was submitted May 29, 1918, to the Port of Galveston, Texas.[15] This was another Ferris standard design with dimensions and capacities close to, but not the same as, the SS *Beaumont*.

RSAL SYPYARD 9-27-1

*fig. 11.7. Launched
ship in water.
Courtesy
National
Archives*
Number of crew was listed as 55, which included the gun crew, and the
owner was listed as the United States Shipping Board. The engine was
from the Worthington Pump and Machinery Company.

The manager of the Division of Wood, Composite, and Concrete
Ship Construction was a James Heyworth. He sent a memorandum
dated April 1, 1918, to the chairman of the United States Shipping Board
confirming the contents of a telegram to Lord, an official of the Universal Shipbuilding Company at Houston: "Chairman Hurley suggests
that at the suggestion of Senator Sheppard, Miss Nina Cullinan, daugh-

ter of Hon. John S. Cullinan, Houston, Texas, be selected as sponsor for your ship to be launched April ninth or tenth STOP The name to be 'Nacogdoches' STOP You to make all other arrangements."[16] This is another indication of the importance attached to these launchings. These events were well attended, as numerous pictures show. No Certificate of Registry was issued for the *Nacogdoches*.

ROCKPORT, TEXAS

The selection of Rockport as a location to build wooden ships is somewhat baffling, since the East Texas piney woods are more than 200 miles away. The area has many twisted, windblown live oaks, but they would not be useful in large ship construction. A newspaper article did throw some light on the subject, with possible exaggerations:

The 31st of July will long be remembered in Rockport and Southwest Texas as commemorating the biggest shipping event ever to happen and this occasion is due to the persistence of F. W. and

fig. 11.8.
Heldenfels shipyard
at Rockport.
Courtesy
National
Archives

C. A. Heldenfels, who after being refused for military service by the Government on the grounds that there were plenty of single men for the army and that men with large families stay behind, F. W. Heldenfels immediately took up with the shipping department of the merchant marine the idea of constructing wooden vessels on the Texas coast west of Houston and was told to get out and secure a site and this he did. First he went to Corpus Christi and his proposition was turned down. Then Aransas Pass was approached with towns along the Brazos River with no results. Finally Rockport was given the opportunity to come in on the deal and after an inspection by the representative of the Shipping Bureau and the port declared sufficient for all the requirements in so far as the depth of water was concerned. Then it was that the citizens of Rockport came forward with a bonus of $7,500 on each ship, making a total of $30,000, being the difference in freight rates on material to Brazos River points and Rockport. Rockport had strong competition in this item alone to keep the yard from going further east. In addition to the above sum the people of

*fig. 11.9. Four hulls
under construction.*
Courtesy National
Archives

Rockport gave a site of thirteen acres to Heldenfels Bros., free of any cost with the only stipulation that the shipyards were to remain a permanent fixture for five years.[17]

The July 31 occasion was the launching of the first ship, the *Baychester*. As was the case for many other ships up the coast, she was completed after the war had been over for several months. The Heldenfels Brothers obtained contracts to build eight ships; however, by the end of the war, only four were under way, since the first keel was not laid until January 1918. After the war, the decision was made to utilize the ships in South American trade. This plan was further changed to allow for completion of the first two ships, with the second two to be converted into barges.[18]

Figure 11.8 shows the yard at Rockport. The massive timber storage area is shown in the picture. These materials were transported from East Texas by railroad or barge or a combination of both.

Figure 11.9 provides a closer view of the construction. This is a bow view of the 600 series hulls, which was the number series allotted to this yard.

fig. 11.10. Scene toward bow. Courtesy National Archives

*fig. 11.11. Scene
toward stern.*
Courtesy Na-
tional Archives

The scene in figure 11.10 is closer to the real work. Power tools were used in the shop area, but here the workers are using two-man crosscut saws to make some massive construction blocks. The chain saw or practical handheld electric power saws had not yet been developed. The worker on the left is driving a large bolt to fasten the strakes of the ship's bottom to its lower timbers.

Figure 11.11 shows a scene inside one of the hulls toward the stern. Massive, cut timbers make up the intricate structural members of the stern. The shaft hole is lower and left of center.

Included in the list of dignitaries for the first launching were Governor W. P. Hobby with his staff, the lieutenant governor, and the cabinet. Mrs. Woodrow Wilson agreed to name the first vessel, and Mrs. F. W. Heldenfels was chosen to sponsor the *Baychester*.

For about two years, Rockport was crowded to the utmost to accommodate the shipyard employees. At one time, the Heldenfels Brothers employed approximately 900 people. Even the old bank building was converted into a hotel to house them.[19]

No documentation could be found for any of the ships built at Rockport, indicating they were finished too late, along with hundreds of others.

Figure 11.12, though not of a ship from a Texas yard, is the best finished ship view found of the Standard Wood Steamship Design. Instead of cranes, ships in this era through the 1950s used a mast-and-boom system operated by steam winches for cargo handling. The masts were supported by side stays, with turnbuckles for adjustment similar to those on sailing vessels. The dense coal smoke is coming from another ship behind the *Panga*. Almost everything about coal-fired ships was dirty from the coal dust and sooty smoke.

As noted, many of these ships were still being built in the latter part of 1919, a year after the war ended, and that was true on the other two coasts as well as the Gulf Coast. Indications were that Texas yards turned out more than 20 wooden steamships in 1918 and more than 100 in 1919. The total output in the United States during this period was 589 wooden steamships. The steel ship division turned out 1,200 ships during this time, but the tonnage was over three times as much, because the steel ships were generally larger.[20] Had the war lasted longer, the wooden steamships might have made a significant contribution to the American war effort.

fig. *11.12. The SS* Panga *from Pascagoula, Missis-sippi.* Courtesy National Archives

S/S "PANGA" July 14, 1919, ready for service. Dierks-Blodgett Shipbldg. Co Pascagoula, Miss.

Texas Wooden Ship Careers

In this chapter the careers and disposition of some of the wooden steam-ships built in Texas are discussed. The government was rather late in get-ting the wooden steamship program started and then due to bureaucracy and inertia had even more difficulties getting it stopped. It seems that one ship always has to have more bad luck than the rest and we find one such in this chapter. Most of the ships' names allowing National Archive research came from one source.[1]

THE SS *WAR MYSTERY*

The first communication concerning the SS *War Mystery* was a telegram dated June 29, 1918, from the Southern Pine Association. This was to the British Naval attaché, at the British Embassy, Washington, D.C. As stated earlier, this ship, called the Daughtery design, was 337 feet long (reported as 330 elsewhere), some 70 feet longer than the standard gov-ernment design. The telegram stated that the design of the 5,000-ton wooden merchant boat had been adopted by the U.S. Emergency Fleet Corporation. The association asked for permission for a representative named Frost to go on the maiden trip from Orange to some American port. The telegram also indicated the ship was built for the Cunard Company (British), which explains why no American documentation was found for this vessel.[2]

Captain Arthur Snaggs, R.N. British Naval attaché, answered the telegram June 29, 1918. The commander-in-chief, North American and West Indies Station, informed the attaché that permission could be granted only if direct application were made by the U.S. Shipping Board to the British commander-in-chief through the attaché. This seemed to discourage the association, as nothing further occurred; the ship prob-ably sailed by the time the answer got back, as the Shipping Board Law Division did not receive it until July 9, 1918.[3]

The next letter sheds a bit more light on the transfer of flag. This was from the commissioner of navigation to the U.S. Shipping Board, dated May 9, 1922: "This office requests you to forward copies of the orders authorizing the transfer of the steamers WAR MARVEL and WAR MYSTERY built by the National Shipbuilding Company of Orange, Tex., for the Cunard Steamship Line Company of London, England. These vessels were transferred on July 9, 1918 and August 26, 1918, respectfully."[4]

THE SS *LONE STAR*

Another ship heard about was the *Lone Star*, built by the Lone Star Shipbuilding Company of Beaumont. A long letter from the acting commissioner for navigation to the collector of customs, Port Arthur, dated August 31, 1918, gave an indication as to when the ship would be nearing completion. The figures used for ascertaining her tonnage were compared to those for sister ships at Tacoma, Washington, and Portland, Maine, and although the results were similar, the official preferred the Tacoma figures. He stated that if the numbers had not yet been carved in the vessel, the Tacoma figures should be used. R. E. Latimer, collector at Port Arthur, replied October 1, 1918, that the numbers had not been carved, and they would use the Tacoma figures.[5]

The acting shipping commissioner, Harry Pinert, wrote a letter to the Customs Service at Jacksonville, Florida, in March, 1919, concerning the SS *Lone Star*.[6] The letter indicated that wages were to be computed from and inclusive of the date the crew would be required to be on the vessel by the ship's articles. Another letter on the same subject dated August 5, 1919, was from the comptroller of the Department of Commerce to Navigation. The comptroller called the previous letter evasive and erroneous, and it caused the master to pay part of the crew twice for October 31. Now, the shipping board was going to have to pay for this unnecessary expenditure. The commissioner of navigation replied and upheld the decision of the deputy collector. This was voyage one for the SS *Lone Star*, and she had stopped in Jacksonville for repairs.[7]

What these ships were doing for the government several months after the war was over is not known, but a few of the ships were put to some limited use.

THE SS *ONECO*

The Beaumont Shipbuilding and Dry Dock Company submitted the Application of Owner or Master for Official Number for this vessel on

August 9, 1918, at Port Arthur, Texas.[8] She received her Certificate of Registry, on September 14, 1918, at Port Arthur.[9]

On April 30, 1919, PE No. 16 was surrendered, and Certificate of Registry No. 42 was issued as a result of a property change when the vessel was transferred from the shipyard to the United States Shipping Board.[10]

On February 14, 1919, the New Orleans Dry Dock and Ship Building Company had the first bad news on this ship. The essence of the letter was that, after receiving the SS *Oneco*, they discovered that the shaft had something wrong with it and the ship was returned to the owners (this may have meant "builders"). A bill for repairs to the ship, dated October 31, 1918, amounted to about $20,000, but additional repairs were required that increased the bill to $30,000. The president of the New Orleans company wrote to John A. Donald, vice president of the U.S. Shipping Board, a personal acquaintance of the writer located in Philadelphia, Pennsylvania. His complaint was that he could not get the district representative for the shipping board, named Maitland (in Houston), to respond to his telegrams or letters. The question was, should they enter an attachment for the bill, since the yard had no insurance on the ship should it burn. The builder forwarded all of the approved bills to Maitland with the expectation that the shipping board would pay. The writer was looking for advice on how to get a settlement.[11]

The next letter on this matter, dated February 28, 1919, was from the general counsel for the U.S. Shipping Board, Emergency Fleet Corporation, Philadelphia, to the commissioner of the U.S. Shipping Board in Washington, D.C. He felt that the bill was owed jointly by the Fleet Corporation and the Beaumont yard, but a controversy existed as to the proper division. He went on to state that there was no reason to withhold payment to the New Orleans company, and he asked the finance division to verify the bill and pay it promptly; that seemed to have settled this matter after only two weeks.[12]

The next document, written a little less than a year later, was headed "London, January 8, 1920," and was from surveyors of ship damage to Underwriters' representatives: "THIS IS TO CERTIFY that the undersigned, by virtue of the above appointment, attended on board the above vessel on the 9th of January 1920 and subsequent dates, as she then lay afloat at Hartpool and afterwards at West Hartpool, in order to survey and assess the damages the vessel is alleged to have sustained in consequence of collision with the *S.S. "O N E G A"* [*sic*] of Beaumont, in the Old Harbour at Hartpool, on or about the 7th January 1920, when the 'Risvaer' was lying moored at the buoys and the 'Onega was proceeding to sea.'"[13]

The main damages inflicted by the *Oneco* on the steel ship consisted of two bulwark plates considerably indented, two shell plates and one bulwark plate slightly indented, seven stanchions bent, two lengths of bulwark main rail buckled, and sundry other items of a lesser nature. The estimated cost was £254.3.3 or approximately $1,200.

Soon the SS *Oneco* got involved in another set of problems. These communications are all in the same file.[14] The SS *Oneco* left England, and the next event took place at Gibraltar. A cablegram was sent to the legal department of the shipping board from Amshibo (American Shipping Board), in London. The message indicated that the salvors of the SS *Oneco* were claiming a bill of 1.5 million pesetas, reduced to 600,000 pesetas, for three tugs that provided sixteen hours of service. The SS *Oneco* apparently ran aground near Gibraltar, and the master agreed to discuss the terms of settlement when the vessel reached a safe anchorage. The communication recommended that the matter be arbitrated at Gibraltar. An interoffice memorandum dated March 29, 1920, from the director of insurance, B. K. Ogden, signed by S. Peacock to the admiralty counsel at the shipping board in Washington, asked for advice on the matter. That office concurred that arbitration in Gibraltar would be desirable.

Another cablegram dated March 30, 1920, from Amshibo, London, states, "Your 3090 ONECO will be offered auction in London April 21st and please forward bill of sale and Certificate of Registry so they can be filled out after the sale." The next cable on this matter was dated November 30, 1920, and was from Amshibo, stating that, "Our endeavor to sell vessel as is and where is without result Blands original offer of 7500 pounds warranted free of all liens is still open Shall we accept?" Salvors claimed 12,000 pounds on the basis of official valuation of the vessel, refused arbitration, and threaten court proceedings. Gibraltar representatives were of the opinion that they would accept 2,500 pounds. Amshibo requested authority to offer this amount. It is easy to see why Bland wanted a warranty against all liens.

A cable from admiralty counsel in Washington on December 3, 1920, said authority was granted and that it was inadvisable to sell the vessel before the salvage matter was settled. Amshibo's cable to the admiralty counsel in Washington on December 27, 1920, stated that the salvage claim of 2,500 pounds has been settled but there was still an outstanding claim for towage. The sender requested authority to pay the tug *San Jose* not more than 350 pounds and 850 pounds to the tug *Courage*. The other news in the cablegram was that Bland had withdrawn his original offer of 8,500 pounds. Amshibo further stated that the Amshibo director for Spain cabled to "Disposal ship any price not inconsistent with Boards best interests."

During this same period, other departments were trying to get the ship sold. This was indicated in a memorandum dated August 23, 1920, from W. W. Nottingham, an assistant counsel to J. Harry Philbin, acting manager of ship sales, both officials of the U.S. Shipping Board:

> The Board resolution of August 4th having authorized the sale of the wreck of the Steamer "oneco" at a price not less than $30,340.00, I see no objection to accepting the offer of Bland and Company amounting to 850 pounds cash [sic 8500 pounds]. This price is in excess of the minimum price set by the Board and the fact that certain claims are due against the vessel should not be considered in accepting this offer, as regardless of what price the Board receives for the vessel, these claims must be taken care of. I therefore recommend that you submit this matter to the Chairman for approval and cable London authority to fill in and deliver the bill of sale previously forwarded to them covering this vessel.[15]

On August 31, 1920, an interoffice memorandum indicated that the board on August 26, 1920, by formal resolution, approved the sale of the wrecked wooden SS *Onesco* to Bland and Company of London, England. The sale price was 8,500 pounds cash on delivery; sold "as is, where is."

The next letter, dated November 12, 1920, was to the general counsel, Washington, D.C., from Joseph E. Sheedy, European manager, both elements of the U.S. Shipping Board. The subject was "SS 'oneco'-Collision Spanish Barque 'manola'":

> Replying to the letter of November 10th from the Admiralty Counsel, there seems to be some misunderstanding as to the circumstances surrounding the sale of the "oneco". The original offer of £8,500 was made by Messrs. Bland & Co. on the understanding that the vessel would be warranted free from all liens. The Board at that time wished to sell with a clear title because of the outstanding claims. Finally, in March, a second offer of £3500 was accepted. The bill of sale warranted the vessel free from all liens. The discrepancy between the first and second offer was due chiefly, we believe, to the drop in the market; it was not due to any change in the understanding with Messrs. Bland & Co. as to the terms of the sale.

The letter also discusses the *Risvaer* claim that went from about 200 pounds to an excessive demurrage claim of 3,000 pounds and was being disputed. With reference to the collision with the *Manola*, the writer suggested it would be difficult to prove in court that 52 pounds of damage was much of a consideration in selling a wreck for the low price stated. The Spanish were not cooperating, and the only recourse would have been either to arrest the vessel or bring an action against the owners in Spain. The writer did not think that would have been advisable, since they did not have any repair bills to back up the claim.

An unrelated legal matter also came up October 11, 1921. In a letter from a New York company, the American Steamship Owners Mutual Protection and Indemnity Association, the writer informed the Shipping Board that he had been retained by certain members of the crew of the *Oneco* and the owners, agents, and operators to recover damages. The crew members had signed on at various ports in Texas for a trip to foreign ports, not to exceed twelve months, and to return to the United States. At Gibraltar, the time expired October 14, 1920, and the crew was sent back to New York City on the steamship *President Grant*, arriving November 14, 1920. They were not paid for another twenty-five days, and they then made claim of two days' pay for each day of the twenty-five days. The writer also indicated that the crew was paid off at the office of J. H. W. Steele and Company, 50 Broad Street, without having a representative of the United States Shipping Commissioner's office present, in violation of statutes.[16]

Another letter dated November 10, 1921, was to J. H. Sheedy, manager of the U.S. Shipping Board in London, from G. R. Snider, admiralty counsel, concerning the Spanish vessel collision. Snider wanted to pass on the liability for the SS *Risvaer* to the buyer, that got such a bargain but was afraid the vessel was sold with a warranty against all claims. With regard to the Spanish collision, Snider stated he would like for the manager to make further efforts to collect the money if the expense would not eat up the monies recovered.

The next communication was necessary to introduce one of the primary players in the selling process for the SS *Oneco*. That letter, dated July 22, 1921, was from Vice Admiral A. P. Niblick, commander, U.S. Naval Forces Operating in European Waters, and his flagship was the USS *Pittsburgh*, a cruiser at the time, at Le Havre, France. Niblick was a man of considerable stature, and his letter went to Edward P. Farley, U.S. Shipping Board in Washington, D.C.:

Replying to your letter of 30 June, 1921, as to Mr. F. B. Bostwick of Gibraltar, I wish to state that he is an American dentist who has lived for many years in Spain. He has an office in Gibraltar and lives at Algeciras across the Bay. During the war he was the only American citizen not in military service who was doing business in Gibraltar. He was, however, employed by me in Naval Intelligence Service. When I was in Gibraltar in February 1921 last and again in May 1921, he told me a great many of the things which the Shipping Board was doing which he did not think was in the best interests of the Government. I advised him to submit the complaints direct to the Shipping Board itself.

I am not aware of the nature of the letter which he wrote nor am I in a position to judge of the merits of the case, but in a general way I regard Dr. Bostwick as a very keen, wide-awake American.[17]

This letter was written almost a year after approval of the sale. It would appear that, besides being a dentist, Bostwick was a part-time spy and ship broker.

On December 7, 1920, Dr. Bostwick did write a scathing, five-page letter to the U.S. Shipping Board in Washington. He started out by confirming a cable he sent December 2, 1920:

> Incredible delay which has cost and is costing Government thousands delivery steamer Oneco Bland Company's offer accepted August seventeenth please cable satisfaction obtained from London Gibraltar representatives.
>
> Broker Bostwick and Bland, Gibraltar

The letter goes on to complain about a Captain Griswald, who asked him if he knew of anyone who wanted a bargain in the way of a steamer, the *Oneco*, for 8,000 pounds. Bostwick thought he did and asked the captain to hold it. He got Bland to make an offer of 8,000 pounds, and the next day the captain raised the price 500 pounds. Bland still wanted the ship and so made a firm offer of the 8,500 pounds. The captain procrastinated for several weeks and then told Bostwick he had offered the ship to other parties for 7,000 pounds more than the Bland offer. Bostwick was quick to tell him that was not an honorable or straightforward thing to do and asked what the people of the United States would think of such proceedings. The captain wanted to offer a substitute steamer, and the runaround continued until the date of the letter, which was December 7, 1920:

> All these months, until Monday 1st, when the vessel was brought inside the harbour and tied up to the wharf, this vessel has lain out in the Bay with steam up and a crew all of which has cost thousands of dollars unnecessarily for had the matter been treated in a business-like way it would have been brought inside the harbour

and tied up the very first week so as to cut down expenses. When lying outside it was ran into by another vessel and damaged, the repair of which means more expense to the Government as I understand the vessel which caused the damage got away without being arrested.

Dr. Bostwick went on to say that the shipping board was the laughing stock of that part of the world, which was rather humiliating, but he did not wonder that people would laugh. The general impression was that nobody seemed to know what to do or how to do it. Dr. Bostwick stated that he was a native of Ohio but had lived in that part of the world for eighteen years. For references, he mentioned Senator Atalee Pomerene and Admiral Niblack. He also mentioned that the way some of the American steamers had been laid up there for weeks and months was another thing that, he thought, would bear investigation.

The problems that ISC had disposing of several ships were minor compared to just this one vessel. Finally, on December 8, 1921, the American consul at Gibraltar, Spain, had the honor to transmit Register No. 42 for the steamship *Oneco* that was sold at that port on March 7, 1921, for the sum of 3,500 pounds. The purchasers were Messrs. Bland and Company, and the transaction took over a year. The ship's new name was *Gibel-Zalag*. The date Register No. 42 was surrendered was December 8, 1921. Reason surrendered: "Vessel sold to aliens (British flag) March 7, 1921."[18]

The disposal of the ship did not end the matter. On February 22, 1922, the merchants and owners of the schooner *Manola* wrote a letter from Bilboa. The vessel more likely was a schooner rather than a barque, as the Americans had called it. The letter indicated that a certificate issued by a judge had been delivered to them by the Comandancia de Marina of Bilbao on Claims of the Commandancia de Marina at Algeciras, but the intent of the letter was unclear. They did say: "That, in accordance with our captain's advices the American vessel *Oneco* is solely liable for the said collision." The *Oneco* was at anchor when the collision occurred, but this was not mentioned in the letter.

Handwritten comments on an inconsequential letter dated February 13, 1923, indicated that on August 31, 1923, the case was closed, that damages for £322.4.9 and costs for £222.14.6 had been paid. This probably pertained to the *Risvaer*, or the salvors' claims.

The vessel had at least five changes of master: three at New Orleans, Louisiana, one at Mobile, Alabama, and one at Huelva, Spain.[19]

The last letter pertaining to the *Oneco* was dated May 8, 1925, and was from the attorney general of the Department of Justice to the chairman of the U.S. Shipping Board. The message was that approval was being given to pay £19.1.4, to Messrs. Thomas Cooper and Company for legal services rendered from November 18, 1920, to and including November 4, 1924, in connection with the claim against the owners of the *Manola* for alleged damages to the wooden steamer *Oneco* on November 12, 1920.[20] Thus ended the American career of the Texas-built *Oneco*.

THE SS *BEAUMONT*

The SS *Beaumont* was built by McBride and Law at Beaumont, Texas, and they were listed as the owner on the Application for Official Number. L. C. Weaver was listed as the master carpenter, and the first master was Fred Bodungen. Nothing else was found concerning this ship until the Certificate of Registry No. 40 was surrendered at Port Arthur, April 16, 1926. Reason surrendered: "Vessel sold to be scrapped."[21]

THE SS *SWAMPSCOTT*

The first Certificate of Registry No. 19, issued September 28, 1918, at Port Arthur, listed the builder, Beaumont Shipbuilding and Dry Dock Company, as the owner. The first master was J. L. Warren, and the master carpenter was S. G. Reed, with Beaumont the hailing port. A new Certificate of Registry No. 44, was issued May 9, 1919, for property change when the ship was purchased by the U.S. Shipping Board.[22]

The *Swampscott* apparently was being used to transport lumber to England, according to a cablegram dated August 2, 1919. The ship had sixty-four consignments of lumber, and there was no quayage space for sorting and delivery, causing a grave detention to the steamer. The sender recommended that, in the future, either stowage should be obtained or the consignments should be separated, so they could be discharged over the side to barges.[23] Two more rather confusing communications were made on this subject without any clear resolution.

The vessel had at least three changes of masters, two at the Port of New York, New York, and one at the Port of New London, Connecticut.[24] The Register No. 44 was surrendered at Norfolk, Virginia, on December 31, 1923. The reason was "Scrapped 12/29/23 file 130116N."

THE SS *NACOGDOCHES*

The SS *Nacogdoches* got an Official Number, on May 29, 1918, but apparently no Certificate of Registry was issued. The transcript of information provided by a Cox of Philadelphia in a telephone call made March 18, 1919, to Senator Charles A. Towne, 100 Broadway, representing Captain Walcom, reads, "BASCO and NACOGDOCHES those two vessels are being built by the Universal and are very badly built. It is a question as to what can be done with them. A Survey has been ordered made as to what amount of additional work is necessary on them, but it cannot be determined yet what will have to be done with them."[25] In the same conversation Cox indicated that several ships were finished but did not have rudders, as they apparently had a separate rudder manufacturer who was behind in his deliveries. The preceding information was from Cox to the senator.

The next interoffice memorandum, dated August 8, 1922, was from the Material Sales Division to the director of sales. "I find I am in error with reference to the ship 'TCHEFUNCPA' being located at Beaumont. She is at Madisonville, La. and is seventy-nine percent complete as a hull and is understood to be land-locked."

How this could happen is a mystery. One also has to wonder at how some of the ships' names were selected. The writer went on to say that the *Nacogdoches* was at Beaumont, that it was 99 percent completed, and that he wondered if it were included in the Pendleton sale. He had been advised that there were winches and windlasses on many of the hulls at Beaumont but no propelling machinery.[26] The *Nacogdoches* was built at Houston, and it would be interesting to know how she got to Beaumont.

A telegram was sent September 18, 1922, concerning Beaumont ships to the Emergency Fleet in Washington. The Pendleton Brothers were removing hulls in lots of eight to include all hulls, except for the *Nacogdoches* and the *Basco*. The *Basco* was leaking so badly they were having trouble keeping her afloat and would either have to beach it or put it on the marine railway for repairs. The sender wanted a wire back, indicating what action to take.[27] The war has been over for almost four years, and the wooden steamship program was still costing the government a lot of money.

The next memo dated September 29, 1922, was from the manager of ship sales to the Materials Sales Division, and the subject was the ships *Basco* and *Nacogdoches*. He stated that these two ships were included in the fleet of 228 wooden composite vessels sold to George D. Perry of San Francisco. Payment for the ships had been made and paperwork executed, evidencing delivery of the ships to Perry. If additional expenses were incurred because the ships had not been taken over promptly, the writer wanted to know so that collection could be made from the purchasers.[28] Just this one sale of 228 wooden ships underscored the magnitude of the construction program and the subsequent problem of disposing of these monstrous acquisitions. Very few were going to be used; the ship breakers were buying them for next to nothing and removing winches, engines if installed, and any other usable hardware. Too many steel ships had been left over from the shipbuilding frenzy for there to be any market for wooden steamships.

That was the end of the story for the wooden steamships. No Captain Rupert Wry, no fires, no German submarines, nothing too exciting—just a lot of bureaucracy and wasted money.

By comparison, the ISC program, even though it was sail, was a huge success all the way down to their system of naming the ships. Piaggio started his shipbuilding business early and made several deliveries of East Gulf Coast pine lumber to Italy. Other cargo deliveries were made to France and South America, and of the ships not struck by disaster, it is possible that much more than we know about was accomplished.

When it came time to get out of shipping, Piaggio and his associates did an excellent job of getting around the bureaucracy of the United States Shipping Board, who had to approve their flag changes. Several of the ships wound up on the East Coast, one on the West Coast, and went on to perform for several years.

WOODEN STEAMSHIP HULKS

It was thought that some of the wooden steamships were abandoned near the region where they were built. Dennis Gooch of Orange spoke of hulks that could be seen when a norther blew the water out, but he was of the opinion that they were wooden barges. He provided pictures of what he had seen, and most, at least, did indeed appear to be barges. They were located on the east side of Pavel Island about two miles southeast of Harbor Island. He indicated that there were other older hulks on the east side of the old Sabine River channel close to Conway Bayou. These could be wooden steamship hulks; however, such information is more appropriately in the realm of marine archeology rather than document research.

TEXAS DESERVES CREDIT

When this book was started, I had at least two major objectives. First I wanted to thoroughly document a significant period of Texas maritime history that had already been mostly forgotten. Second, I wanted to verify that Texans were excellent boat and shipbuilders when the need arose. Only a fraction of what maritime Texans accomplished has been covered in this book, but this epic period was their shining hour in the design and construction of large wooden ships.

We often hear about and see pictures of the great fishing schooners and sailing ships of the New England states, but Texas's maritime heritage, in those circles at least, generally has been considered insignificant. That simply is not true. Perhaps, in what might be considered an uncharacteristic turn for Texans, they didn't see the need to brag about their boats and sailing ships. It is not bragging, however, to say that this was undoubtedly the first and last time that sailing ships were built on a multiple hull production basis in a yard that was better equipped for the job with materials, equipment, and expertise than any other sailing shipyard in the world. As a result, fourteen magnificent sailing ships were built in a little more than three years, and that construction feat included eleven five-masted barkentines.

Notes

CHAPTER I. FOURTEEN FABULOUS SHIPS

1. Maxwell and Baker, *Sawdust Empire*, 181.
2. Hugh McCulloch, letter of the Secretary of the Treasury to the Collectors of Customs, Mar. 18, 1867, RG 41. Started annual list of merchant vessels.
3. Certificate of Enrollment No. 1, Oct. 23, 1895, RG 41.
4. Ansted, *Dictionary of Sea Terms*, 306.
5. Merchant Vessels of the United States, 1947, USPO, Washington, D.C. Explanation of terms and abbreviations. Other years provide the same information.
6. Certificate of Enrollment No. 1, June 1, 1903, RG 41.
7. Chapelle, *American Small Sailing Craft*, 332, 335.
8. Ibid., 51.
9. Certificate of Registry No. 1, May 29, 1901, RG 41.
10. Merchant Vessels of the United States, 1900.
11. Certificate of Enrollment No. 169, issued at New York, N.Y., July 28, 1896; and Certificate of Enrollment No. 30, issued at Galveston, Tex., Nov. 26, 1907, RG 41.
12. Leather, *Gaff Rig*, 259.
13. Certificate of Enrollment No. 25, issued at Galveston, Tex., Nov. 28, 1902 (*Bonita*); and Certificate of Enrollment No. 20, issued at Galveston, Tex., Nov. 12, 1902, (*Cuba*), RG 41.
14. Certificate of Enrollment No. 9, issued at Galveston, Tex., Nov. 11, 1897, RG 41.
15. "Fishing schooner return trip," *Galveston Daily News*, Apr. 20, 1900.
16. Duplicate Certificate of Enrollment No. 51, Feb. 9, 1907, RG 41.
17. License for Vessel Under Twenty Tons No. 117, issued at Galveston, Tex., June 5, 1883, RG 41.
18. *Mermaid*, License of Vessel Under Twenty Tons No. 30, issued at Galveston, Tex., Sept. 27, 1881; *Hard Times*, Certificate of Enrollment No. 11, issued at Galveston, Tex., Jan. 3, 1880, RG 41.
19. *Dolphin*, License of Vessel Under Twenty Tons No. 82, issued at Galveston, Tex., Mar. 27, 1907; *St. George*, License of Vessel under Twenty Tons No. 16, issued at Port Arthur, Tex., Mar. 17, 1910; *Elida*, License of Vessel Under Twenty Tons No. 18, issued at Galveston, Tex., Aug. 5, 1889, RG 41.
20. Henson, *History of Baytown*, 73.
21. Ibid., 66, 67.
22. Ibid., 67.

23. Permanent Enrollment No. 3, issued at Galveston, Tex., July 27, 1872, RG 41.
24. McGuire, *Julius Stockfleth*, 1.
25. "Effects of the Great Cold Wave," *Galveston Daily News*, Jan. 9, 10, and 11, 1886.
26. Ibid.
27. Certificate of Enrollment No. 70, Feb. 16, 1893, RG 41.
28. Albert Blaha, Passenger Lists for Galveston, Houston, 1985, Texas Seaport Museum, Galveston, Tex.
29. Caney and Reynolds, *Reed's Marine Distance Tables*, 10.
30. Application of Owner or Master to Collector of Customs for Official Number, submitted at Galveston, Tex., Jan. 20, 1886; Inspector's Certificate of Official Number, Tonnage, &c., issued at Galveston, Tex., Feb. 11, 1886, RG 41.
31. License of Vessel Under Twenty Tons No. 21, surrendered at Galveston, Tex., Mar. 17, 1944, RG 41.
32. Annual List of Merchant Vessels of the United States, 1900, Houston Public Library, Houston, Tex.
33. Kenyon, *From Arrows to Astronauts*, 8, 28–32.
34. Vela and Edwards, *Reaching for the Sea*, 31.
35. Certificate of Registry No. 5, Sept. 7, 1915; and PE 20, Mar. 22, 1916, RG 41.
36. Caney and Reynolds, *Reed's Marine Distance Tables*, 117–18.
37. Temporary Certificate of Registry No. 17, surrendered at New York, N.Y., June 27, 1927, RG 41.
38. Museum of the Gulf Coast, Port Arthur, Tex., photograph files.
39. Baker, *Maritime History*, 2:777.
40. Maxwell and Baker, *Sawdust Empire*, 185.
41. Botting, *U-Boats*, 36.
42. Carse, *Twilight of Sailing Ships*, 122–25.
43. Ibid., 49, 50.
44. Morris, *Four Masted Schooners*, 5.

CHAPTER 2. THE FIRST THREE SHIPS

1. Morris, *Four Masted Schooners*, 57.
2. "Pre-launch news of the *City of Orange*," *Galveston Daily News*, Nov. 14 and 15, 1916.
3. Application for Official Number, Mar. 17, 1917, RG 41.
4. Certificate of Registry, Apr. 23, 1917, RG 41.
5. Carse, *Twilight of Sailing Ships*, 39.
6. Morris, *Four Masted Schooners*, 47.
7. Ibid., 47.
8. Baker, *Maritime History*, 2:794, 795.
9. Ibid., 795.
10. Ibid., 685.
11. Maxwell and Baker, *Sawdust Empire*, 184.

12. Mantell, *Engineering Materials Handbook*, 29–12.

13. Fairbanks-Morse, Instructions No. 2600.

14. International Shipbuilding Co., letter to Capt. Rupert Wry, Mar. 9, 1918, RG 41, File No. 99749.

15. Peter Stanford, "On the Naming of Masts," *Sea History*, no. 79 (Autumn 1996): 35.

16. Certificate of Registry No. 3, for *City of Houston*, issued July 28, 1917, at Port Arthur, Tex., RG 41.

17. Certificate of Registry No. 10, for *City of Pensacola*, issued Sept. 6, 1917, at Port Arthur, Tex., RG 41.

18. For the interested reader, many fine details of the construction of a four-masted schooner are presented in Greenhill and Manning, *Bertha L. Downs*.

CHAPTER 3. ELEVEN BARKENTINES

1. Ansted, *Dictionary of Sea Terms*, 13.

2. Carse, *Twilight of Sailing Ships*, 57.

3. Laing, *American Ships*, 406.

4. Hennessy, *Sewall Ships*, preface, vii.

5. Baker, *Maritime History*, 777, 778.

6. Hennessy, *Sewall Ships*, 14, 17.

7. Morris, *Four Masted Schooners*, 25.

8. "Regatta at Rockport," *Rockport Pilot*, Aug. 31, 1893.

9. "Challenge Cup Winner," *Rockport Pilot*, Sept. 4, 1894.

10. Consolidated Enrollment and License, No. 22, issued at Galveston, Tex., May 18, 1914, RG 41.

11. Surrender Statement on Consolidated Enrollment and License No. 106, surrendered at New Orleans, La., June 14, 1960, RG 41.

12. Nathan R. Lipfert, Library Director, Maine Maritime Museum, Bath, Maine, letter to author, July 28, 1997.

13. Application of Owner or Master for Official Number, RG 41.

14. Fairbanks-Morse, Instructions Nos. 2600 & 2514.

15. Mary Anna Crary Anderson, notes prepared and provided to the author, June 6, 1997.

16. Fairbanks-Morse, Instructions No. 2514.

17. Greenhill and Manning, *Bertha L. Downs*, 21.

CHAPTER 4. THE MAIDEN VOYAGE
OF THE *CITY OF ORANGE*

1. Telegram, Attached to Application of Owner or Master for Official Number, RG 41.

2. File No. 93582, RG 41.

3. Caney and Reynolds, *Reed's Marine Distance Tables*, 58.

4. Carse, *Twilight of Sailing Ships*, 99.

5. Morris, *Four Masted Schooners*, 53.

6. File No. 96297, RG 41.

7. Maxwell and Baker, *Sawdust Empire*, 188.

8. File No. 96297, RG 41.

9. Ansted, *Dictionary of Sea Terms*, 221.

10. File No. 96297, RG 41.

11. Ibid.

12. File No. 96333, RG 41.

13. Morris, *Four Masted Schooners*, 47.

14. File No. 96333, RG 41.

15. Ibid.

16. Ibid.

CHAPTER 5. THE *CITY OF ORANGE* AT GIBRALTAR AND OTHER PLACES

1. File No. 96531, RG 41.

2. Ibid.

3. Ibid.

4. Ibid.

5. Hohman, *History of American Merchant Seamen*, 30–33.

6. File No. 96531, RG 41.

7. Ibid.

8. Hohman, *History of American Merchant Seamen*, 7.

9. Baker, *Maritime History*, 2:653, 654.

10. Botting, *U-Boats*, 33.

11. Hohman, *History of American Merchant Seamen*, 20.

12. File No. 96531, RG 41.

13. Ibid.

14. Ibid.

15. Ibid.

16. Ibid.

17. Ibid.

18. Ibid.

19. Ibid.

20. File No. 103399, RG 41.

21. File No. 103396, RG 41.

22. File No. 104556, RG 41.

23. Ibid.

24. File No. 106308, RG 41.

25. Ibid.

26. Stanford, "On the Naming of Masts," 35.

27. File No. 106308, RG 41.

28. Ibid.

29. Temporary Consolidated Enrollment and License No. 19, RG 41.

30. Temporary Certificate of Registry No. 17, issued Aug. 6, 1918, at Port Arthur, Tex., RG 41.

CHAPTER 6. THE NEXT TWO SHIPS

1. Certificate of Registry No. 3, Official No. 215216, July 28, 1917, RG 41.
2. Temporary Certificate of Registry No. 1, issued at Port Arthur, Tex., July 2, 1919, RG 41.
3. Morris, *Four Masted Schooners*, 142.
4. Temporary Certificate of Registry No. 1, surrendered at Gibraltar, Spain, November 3, 1919, RG41.
5. Certificate of Registry No. 10, Official No. 215246, May 5, 1918, RG 41.
6. File Number 96367, RG 41.
7. Certificate of Registry No. 10, surrendered at Port Arthur, Tex., May 5, 1918.
8. File No. 93521, RG 41.
9. Ibid.
10. Ibid.
11. Ibid.
12. *Encyclopaedia Britannica*, s.v. "Spain."
13. File No. 93521, RG 41.
14. Ibid.
15. Ibid.

CHAPTER 7. TWO BARKENTINES GO SOUTH

1. Certificate of Registry No. 43, Mar. 12, 1918, RG 41.
2. File No. 99749, RG 41.
3. Ibid.
4. Indorsements of Change of Master, *City of Gulfport*, ON 215942, RG 41.
5. File No. 99749, RG 41.
6. Ibid.
7. Ibid.
8. Ibid.
9. Ibid.
10. Ibid.
11. Ibid.
12. File No. 104718, RG 41.
13. Caney and Reynolds, *Reed's Marine Distance Tables*, 92.
14. File No. 104718, RG 41.
15. "A case is two five gallon tinned cans in a wood crate" (Nathan R. Lipfert, Library Director, Maine Maritime Museum, Bath, Maine, telephone conversation, Dec. 3, 1996).
16. File No. 105991, RG 41.
17. Surrender statement on Certificate of Registry No. 43, Mar. 12, 1918, RG 41.
18. File No. 105231, RG 41.

19. Certificate of Registry No. 6, Official No. 216350, RG 41.
20. Treasury Department, New York, N.Y., letter to Collector of Customs, New York, N.Y., July 29, 1919, File No. 106308, RG 41.
21. American Consulate, Montevideo, Uruguay, letter to Secretary of State, Washington, D.C., File No. 106308, RG 41.
22. Acting Secretary of State, letter to the Secretary of Commerce, May 22, 1919, File No. 106308, RG 41.
23. File No. 106308, RG 41.
24. Ibid.
25. Certificate of Registry No. 6, RG 41.
26. File No. 106308, RG 41.
27. Ibid.
28. Ibid.
29. American Consulate, Montevideo, Uruguay, letter to Secretary of State, Washington, D.C., May 28, 1919, File No. 106308, RG 41.
30. Ibid.
31. File No. 106308, RG 41.
32. Ibid.
33. Ibid.
34. Ibid.
35. Ibid
36. Ibid.

CHAPTER 8. THE *CITY OF BEAUMONT*

1. Certificate of Registry No. 8, issued at Port Arthur, Tex., July 22, 1918, RG 41.
2. W. B. Butler, letter to Mary Anna Crary (Anderson), Nov. 23, 1919. Full letter from Peabody Essex Museum, Salem, Mass. Edited and abridged copy also available at Tyrrell Historical Library, Beaumont, Tex. Several photographs of the *City of Beaumont* and the *Buccaneer* along with the mascot picture of Mary Anna Crary are also available from the Peabody Museum.
3. International Shipbuilding Company, letter to United States Shipping Board, June 29, 1919, U.S.S.B. General files, File No. 1091, RG 32.
4. Ibid., File No. 4463.
5. Certificate of Registry No. 8, surrendered Feb. 27, 1920, and No. 10, issued at Wilmington, Del., RG 41.
6. Certificate of Registry No. 10, surrendered May 19, 1922, and No. 121, issued at New York, N.Y., RG 41.
7. Consolidated Enrollment and License No. 121, surrendered Sept. 21, 1925, and No. 34, issued at Baltimore, Md., RG 41.
8. Consolidated Enrollment and License No. 34, surrendered Jan. 10, 1927, and No. 41, issued at New York, N.Y., RG 41.
9. Consolidated Enrollment and License No. 41, surrendered Mar. 31, 1927, and No. 57, issued at New York, N.Y., RG 41.

10. Consolidated Enrollment and License No. 57, surrendered Aug. 2, 1927, and No. 5 issued at New York, N.Y., RG 41.

11. Consolidated Enrollment and License No. 5, surrendered Aug. 2, 1928, and No. 9, issued at New York, N.Y., RG 41.

12. Consolidated Enrollment and License No. 9, surrendered June 24, 1932, and No. 226, issued at Los Angeles, Calif., RG 41.

13. Peter Stanford, "The USS *Constitution*," *Sea History*, no. 44 (Summer 1987): 12.

14. CDR Tyrone G. Martin USN (Ret.), *A Most Fortunate Ship*, 313, 316.

15. Consolidated Enrollment and License No. 226, surrendered May 20, 1933, and No. 474, issued at New York, N.Y., RG 41.

16. Consolidated Enrollment and License No. 474, surrendered July 11, 1933, and No. 15, issued at New York N.Y., RG 41.

17. Consolidated Enrollment and License No. 15, surrendered Aug. 31, 1933, and No. 2 issued at New York, N.Y., RG 41.

18. Consolidated Enrollment and License No. 2, surrendered Jan. 17, 1939, at New York, N.Y., RG 41.

19. Boardman, "Buccaneer," 4.

20. Ibid., 4.

21. Gary Kriss, "Texas Wants Old Ship in Hastings," *New York Times*, Nov. 27, 1988.

22. Surrender Statement on Consolidated Enrollment and License No. 2, RG 41.

CHAPTER 9. EIGHT MORE BARKENTINES

1. Certificate of Registry No. 18, Sept. 25, 1918, RG 41.

2. United States Shipping Board General Files, File No. 1091–4463, Subject: *City of Lafayette*, RG 32.

3. Karppi, "Shipbuilding on Harbor Island," 9.

4. Temporary Certificate of Registry No. 19, ON 217160, surrendered at Genoa, Italy, June 30, 1919, RG 41.

5. Application of Owner or Master for Official Number, submitted at Port Arthur, Tex., Sept. 11, 1918, RG 41.

6. Special Deputy Collector, New York, N.Y., letter to Commissioner of Navigation, July 11, 1919, RG 41.

7. Photograph Collection No. TMM-556, Texas Maritime Museum, Rockport, Tex.

8. Consolidated Enrollment and License, No. 97, surrendered at New York, N.Y., Apr. 6, 1923, and No. 99 issued, RG 41.

9. Consolidated Enrollment and License, No. 99, surrendered at Norfolk and Newport News, Va., May 25, 1923 and Temporary No. 74 issued, RG 41.

10. Temporary Consolidated Enrollment and License No. 74, surrendered at New York, N.Y., July 25, 1923, and No. 8 issued, RG 41.

11. Consolidated Enrollment and License No. 8, surrendered at New York, N.Y., Apr. 8, 1924, and No. 84 issued, RG 41.

12. Consolidated Enrollment and License No. 84, surrendered at New York, N.Y., Mar. 18, 1928, and No. 59 issued, RG 41.

13. Final Consolidated Enrollment and License No. 59, surrendered at New York, N.Y., Aug. 15, 1935, RG 41.

14. Karppi, "Shipbuilding on Harbor Island," 9.

15. Certificate of Registry No. 28, surrendered at Port Arthur, Tex., July 7, 1920, and Temporary No. 2 issued.

16. File No. 113841, RG 41.

17. Caney and Reynolds, *Reed's Marine Distance Tables*, 93.

18. Secretary of State, letter to Department of Commerce Dated, Mar. 26, 1920, File No. 113841, RG 41.

19. File No. 113841, RG 41.

20. Temporary Certificate of Registry No. 2, issued at Port Arthur, Tex., July 7, 1920, for the *City of Galveston* of Wilmington, Del., RG 41.

21. File No. 116690, RG 41.

22. Hohman, *History of American Merchant Seamen*, 33.

23. File No. 116690, RG 41.

24. File No. 120442, RG 41.

25. Ibid.

26. Ibid.

27. Surrender of Temporary Certificate of Registry No. 2, Oct. 13, 1922, RG 41.

28. Consolidated Enrollment and License No. 43, surrendered Nov. 28, 1923, New York, N.Y., RG 41.

29. United States Shipping Board, General Files, File No. 1091–4463, Subject: Ships—General, City of Lafayette, No. 218275, RG 32.

30. Ibid.

31. Ibid.

32. Photograph Collection No. TMM-556, Texas Maritime Museum, Rockport, Tex.

33. Karppi, "Shipbuilding on Harbor Island," 10.

34. Application of Owner or Master for Official Number, at Port Arthur, Tex., Nov. 18, 1919, RG 41.

35. Certificate of Registry No. 31, issued and surrendered at Port Arthur, Tex., on same date of Dec. 29, 1919, and temporary Certificate of Registry No. 32 issued, RG 41.

36. Temporary Registry No. 32, surrendered at New York, N.Y., and PE No. 122 issued May 22, 1922, RG 41.

37. Consolidated Enrollment and License No. 122, surrendered at New York, N.Y., Apr. 24, 1924, and PE No. 83 issued, RG 41.

38. Consolidated Enrollment and License No. 83, surrendered at New York, N.Y., June 25, 1924, and PE No. 165 issued, RG 41.

39. Consolidated Enrollment and License No. 165, surrendered at Boston, Mass., Aug. 29, 1924, and PE No. 19 issued, RG 41.

40. Consolidated Enrollment and License No. 19, surrendered at New York, N.Y., Mar. 5, 1929, and PE No. 43 issued, RG 41.

41. Consolidated Enrollment and License No. 43, surrendered at New York, N.Y., Feb. 13, 1936, RG 41.
42. Karppi, "Shipbuilding on Harbor Island," 10.
43. Application of Owner or Master for Official Number, submitted at Port Arthur, Tex., Dec. 29, 1919, RG 41.
44. Certificate of Registry No. 3, surrendered Nov. 29, 1921, at New Orleans, La., and PE No. 39 issued, RG 41.
45. Certificate of Registry No. 39, surrendered Dec. 3, 1923, at Los Angeles, Calif., and PE No. 73 issued, RG 41.
46. Karppi, "Shipbuilding on Harbor Island," 11.
47. Consolidated Enrollment and License No. 73, surrendered Jan. 25, 1924, at Los Angeles, Calif., and PE No. 102 issued, RG 41.
48. Certificate of Registry No. 102, surrendered Apr. 30, 1928, at Los Angeles, Calif., and PE No. 270 issued, RG 41.
49. Consolidated Enrollment and License No. 270, surrendered Oct. 13, 1928, at Los Angeles, Calif., and PE No. 84 issued, RG 41.
50. Consolidated Enrollment and License No. 84, surrendered Nov. 17, 1928, at Los Angeles, Calif., "Exempt-not in trade," RG 41.

CHAPTER 10. MORE OF THE STORY

1. Karppi, "Shipbuilding on Harbor Island," 3.
2. Land transaction books 114, 118, 120, 123, and 124, at Harrison County Courthouse, Gulfport, Miss. Courtesy of Murella Hebert Powell, Local History and Genealogy Librarian, Biloxi Public Library, Biloxi, Miss.
3. Thompson, "Five Miracles," 14.
4. Ben Earles, interview by R. Wayne Pyle, Mississippi Oral History Program, University of Southern Mississippi, 1981.
5. *Encyclopaedia Britannica*, s.v. "automobile."
6. Brieger, *Hometown Mississippi*, Biloxi Public Library, Biloxi, Miss., 149.
7. William J. Brown, letter to Secretary of State, Mar. 17, 1922, concerning lawsuit initiated by Mr. Piaggio, 311.6554 EL4, National Archives at College Park, Md.
8. Baker, *Maritime History*, 2:882.
9. Earles, interview.
10. "Bridging the Atlantic 1917," *Orange Leader Sunday Magazine*, Sept. 30, 1973.
11. U.S. Shipping Board General Files 1091–4463, Subject: *City of Lafayette* (Cross Reference), RG 32.
12. Kenneth Heger, letter, Nov. 5, 1996, Archives II Reference Branch, NNR297–1336, Register of the Department of State, National Archives, College Park, Md.
13. Record of funeral for Henry Nino Piaggio, Rieman Funeral Home, Gulfport, Miss., No. 90, Dec. 20, 1921, 2.
14. Karppi, "Shipbuilding on Harbor Island," 4.

15. Diamond Jubilee Photo Album, Gulfport-Harrison County Library, Gulfport, Miss.

16. Mr. Henry Piaggio obituary, *Biloxi Daily Herald*, Dec. 20 1921.

17. Murella Hebert Powell, Biloxi Public Library, letter to author, July 1, 1997.

18. "Piaggio Villa to be turned into Sanitarium," *Harrison County Times*, Aug. 23, 1924.

19. Record of funeral for Henry Nino Piaggio.

20. Richard W. Peuser, letter to author, May 16, 1997, Archives I Reference Branch, NA, Washington, D.C., reply to NWDTI-97-10877-RWP. An additional search was made by Peuser in July looking at other records, but to no avail. In his opinion, Piaggio was not in any American military service during the Spanish American War. Peuser, telephone conversations with author, July 16 and 17, 1997.

21. Thompson, "Five Miracles," 3.

22. Harrison County Records, Will Book 5, page 60, No. 6902, will filed Jan. 26, 1922.

23. Karppi, "Last Sailing Ships," 66.

24. Morris, *Four Masted Schooners*, 57.

25. Greenhill and Manning, *Bertha L. Downs*, 71.

26. Application of Owner or Master for Official Number, submitted at Port Arthur, Tex., August 19, 1918, File No. 1101648, RG 41.

27. Duplicate Certificate of Registry No. 26, ON 216798, RG 41.

28. Morris, *Four Masted Schooners*, 122.

29. Temporary Certificate of Registry Nos. 65 and 74, ON 219916 and ON 220195, issued May 1, 1920, and June 16, 1920, at Port Arthur, Tex., RG 41.

30. Consolidated Enrollment and License No's 24 and 25, surrendered December 4, 1937, at Wilmington, Delaware.

31. Morris, *Four Masted Schooners*, 99 and 154.

32. Photo Collection, TMM-564, Texas Maritime Museum, Rockport, Tex.

33. Urbin, *Hulls and Hulks*, 236.

34. Ibid., 114.

35. File No. 107659, RG 41.

36. Urbin, *Hulls and Hulks*, 166.

37. Ibid, 76.

38. Brouwer, *"City of Beaumont."*

39. Unsigned, undated paper, considered valid based on other information and copies of historical photographs included in the article. Karl Kortum was director of the National Maritime Museum at San Francisco, California, and was known to have been instrumental in getting the mast doubling from the *Buccaneer* for display in the *Balclutha* at San Francisco. Document found at Texas Seaport Museum, Galveston, Texas, under *City of Beaumont*, Ships Research Files.

40. Gary Kriss, "Texas Wants Old Ship in Hastings," *New York Times*, Nov. 27, 1988.

41. Peter Stanford, letter to Walter Rybka, Nov. 30, 1988, copy at Texas Seaport Museum, Galveston, Tex.
42. City of Beaumont Survey, May 17, 1990, by personnel of the University of Lowell, Continuing Education, Lowell, Mass., copy at Texas Seaport Museum, Galveston, Tex.
43. Little, *Audubon Society Field Guide to North American Trees*, 296.
44. Mary Allison, President Hastings Historical Society, letter to South Street Seaport, National Maritime Historical Society, Hudson River Maritime Museum, Peabody Museum, Texas Gulf Historical Society, San Francisco Maritime Museum, Galveston Historical Society. Copy at Texas Seaport Museum, Galveston, Tex.

CHAPTER 11. THE WOODEN STEAMSHIPS

1. Maxwell and Baker, *Sawdust Empire*, 181.
2. Administrative Histories of RG 32/41, p. 1 of Introduction to Records of the United States Shipping Board.
3. Application of Owner or Master for Official Number, submitted May 29, 1918 at Galveston, Tex., RG 41.
4. Finding Aid to Textual or Blueprint Records in RG 32, National Archives, College Park, Md.
5. United States Shipping Board Files, Ships Correspondence-General, File No. 1091–1611, *War Mystery*, RG 32.
6. Maxwell and Baker, *Sawdust Empire*, 190, 193.
7. "Gulf Coast Lumberman" in *Las Sabinas*, book 1, volume viii (Feb. 19, 1982): 21, 23. *Las Sabinas* is the official quarterly publication of the Orange County Historical Society.
8. Baker, *Maritime History*, 2:886.
9. Maxwell and Baker, *Sawdust Empire*, 192.
10. Application of Owner or Master for Official Number, Nov. 28, 1918, RG 41.
11. Certificate of Registry No. 40, RG 41.
12. Certificate of Registry No. 16, RG 41.
13. Application of Owner or Master for Official Number, ON 217000, File No. 102381, RG 41.
14. Certificate of Registry No. 19, ON 217000, RG 41.
15. Application of Owner or Master for Official Number, ON 216401, submitted May 29, 1918, at Galveston, Tex., RG 41.
16. File No. 5944, RG 36.
17. Story on the Wooden Steamships Construction at Rockport, Tex. *San Antonio Express*, July 27, 1919.
18. "Ship-Building Industry," *A Glimpse at Our Past* (June 13–21, 1970), presented by Aransas County Centennial Incorporated.
19. Ibid.
20. Maxwell and Baker, *Sawdust Empire*, 194.

1. As previously mentioned, it is difficult to do research on vessels without their names. Most of the ships' names that led to the following information came from one source: Maxwell and Baker, *Sawdust Empire*, ch. 12.

2. File No. 1091–1611, Ships Correspondence—General, War Mystery, RG 32.

3. Ibid.

4. Ibid.

5. File No. 101856, RG 41.

6. File No. 108189, RG 41.

7. Ibid.

8. Application of Owner or Master for Official Number, RG 41.

9. Certificate of Registry No. 16, ON 216765, issued Sept. 14, 1918, surrendered Apr. 30, 1919, at Port Arthur, Tex., and PE 42 issued, RG 41.

10. Certificate of Registry No. 42, issued Apr. 30, 1919, at Port Arthur.

11. USSB, File No. 1091, RG 32.

12. Ibid.

13. Ibid.

14. USSB, File No. 585–1629, RG 32.

15. USSB, File No. 1091–4369, RG 32.

16. Ibid.

17. Ibid.

18. Certificate of Registry no. 42, surrendered Dec. 8, 1921, at Gibraltar, Spain, File No. 126393, RG 41.

19. Indorsements of Change of Master, RG 41.

20. USSB, File No. 585–1629, RG 32.

21. Certificate of Registry No. 40, RG 41.

22. Certificate of Registry No. 44, RG 41.

23. Amshibo, London, cablegram to U.S. Shipping Board, File No. 1091–4365, RG 32.

24. Indorsements of Change of Master, RG 41.

25. USSB, File No. 1091–4369, RG 32.

26. Ibid.

27. Ibid.

28. Ibid.

Bibliography

PUBLISHED WORKS

Allen, Oliver E. *The Windjammers*. Alexandria, Va.: Time-Life, 1978.

Ansted, A. *A Dictionary of Sea Terms*. 3rd ed. 1985. Reprint, revised by Peter Clissold. Glasgow, Scotland: Brown, Son, and Ferguson, 1991.

Baker, T. Lindsay. *Lighthouses of Texas*. With paintings by Harold Phenix. College Station: Texas A&M University Press, 1991.

Baker, William Avery, *A Maritime History of Bath, Maine, and the Kennebec River Region*. Vols. 1 and 2. Portland, Maine: Anthoensen, 1973.

Boardman, Bob. "The *Buccaneer*: A Faded Beauty with a Questionable Past." *Hastings Historian* 19, no. 1 (Winter 1990).

Botting, Douglas. *The U-Boats*. Alexandria, Va,: Time-Life, 1979.

Brouwer, Norman. *"City of Beaumont."* *Sea History* Spring 1973.

Caney, R. W., and J. E. Reynolds. *Reed's Marine Distance Tables*. 7th ed. Surrey, England: Thomas Reed, 1992.

Carse, Robert. *The Twilight of Sailing Ships*. New York: Grosset and Dunlop, 1965.

Chapelle, Howard I. *American Small Sailing Craft: Their Design, Development, and Construction*. New York: Norton, 1951.

Greenhill, Basil, and Sam Manning. *Bertha L. Downs*. Annapolis, Md.: Naval Institute Press, 1995.

Henson, Margaret Swett. *The History of Baytown*. 2nd ed. N.P.: Bay Area Heritage Society, 1991.

Hennessy, Mark W. *The Sewall Ships of Steel*. Augusta, Maine: Kennebec Journal Press, 1937.

Hohman, Elmo Paul. *History of American Merchant Seamen*. Hamden, Conn.: Shoe String Press, 1956.

Karppi, Frank O. "The Last Sailing Ships Built in Texas." *Texas Gulf Historical and Biographical Record* 16, no. 1 (November, 1980): 55–68.

Kenyon, Delores. *From Arrows to Astronauts*. League City, Tex.: National Association of Conservation Districts, 1976.

Laing, Alexander. *American Ships*. New York: American Heritage Press, 1971.

Leather, John. *Gaff Rig*. 2nd ed. Camden, Maine: International Marine Publishing, 1989.

Little, Elbert L. *The Audubon Society Field Guide to North American Trees: Eastern Region*. New York: Knopf, 1980.

Mantell, Charles L., ed. *Engineering Materials Handbook*. New York: McGraw-Hill, 1958.

Martin, CDR Tyrone G. USN (Ret.) *A Most Fortunate Ship.* Old Saybrook, Conn.: Globe Pequot Press Inc., 1980.

Maxwell, Robert S., and Robert D. Baker. *Sawdust Empire: The Texas Lumber Industry, 1830–1940.* College Station: Texas A&M University Press, 1983.

McGuire, James Patrick. *Julius Stockfleth, Gulf Coast Marine and Landscape Painter.* San Antonio and Galveston: Trinity University Press and Rosenberg Library, 1976.

Morris, Paul C. *Four Masted Schooners of the East Coast.* Orleans, Mass.: Lower Cape, 1975.

Safford, Jeffrey J. *Wilsonian Maritime Diplomacy, 1913–1921.* Newark, N.J.: Rutgers University Press, 1978.

"Ship-Building Industry." *A Glimpse at Our Past* (June 13–21, 1970). Presented by Aransas County Centennial Incorporated. Card Catalog No. F-392.A7 FS. Texas Maritime Museum. Rockport, Tex.

Stanford, Peter. "On the Naming of Masts." *Sea History* 79 (Autumn 1996): 35.

———. "The USS *Constitution.*" *Sea History* 44 (Summer 1987): 10.

Thompson, Ray M. "The Five Miracles of Joe Famiglio." *Down South* (September-October 1957): 3, 14, 31.

Underhill, Harold A. *Masting and Rigging: The Clipper Ship and Ocean Carrier.* 1946. Reprint, Glasgow, Scotland: Brown, Son, and Ferguson, 1988.

Urbin, Erin. *Hulls and Hulks in the Tide of Time: The Life and Work of John A. Noble.* Staten Island, N.Y.: John A. Noble Collection, Publishers, 1993.

Vela, Lee, and Maxine Edwards. *Reaching for the Sea: The Story of the Port of Houston.* Houston: Port of Houston Authority, 1989.

Works Projects Administration. *Houston: A History and Guide.* Houston: Anson Jones Press, 1942.

UNPUBLISHED WORKS

Fairbanks-Morse. Instructions No. 2514 for installing and operating Type "C-O" Heavy Duty Marine Oil Engines, 150 and 200 H.P. Direct Reversible. Fairbanks Morse, Beloit, Wis., 1918.

———. Instructions No. 2600 for installing and operating Type "C-O" Heavy Duty Marine Oil Engines, 75 and 100 H.P. Fairbanks Morse, Beloit, Wis., 1919.

Karppi, Frank O. "Shipbuilding on Harbor Island." Paper presented at Heritage House Museum, Orange, Tex.

Earles, Ben. Interview by Pyle, R. Wayne. Mississippi Oral History Program. Vol. 190. University of Southern Mississippi, 1981.

RELATED MARITIME RECORDS AT THE NATIONAL ARCHIVES OF THE UNITED STATES, WASHINGTON, D.C.

Records listed below are from the following sources: Records Group 32 (RG 32), Records of the United States Shipping Board; and Records Group 41 (RG 41), Records of the Bureau of Marine Inspection and Navigation.

List of Merchant Vessels of the United States. Issued for each year since 1868. Lists all U.S. vessels over five tons in alphabetical order. Gives length, breadth, and depth of hold. The location built and district along with rig and tonnage figures are also given. Key information in these books to finding other records is the Official Number (ON). Washington, D.C.: U.S. Printing Office, n.d.

Inspectors Certificate of Official Number, Tonnage, Etc. RG 41. Required to insure that the Official Number and net tonnage is carved in the main beam or otherwise permanently marked there. Also to insure that vessel name is on each bow and name and home port are on the stern with letters not less than four inches in length in light on dark ground or dark on light ground (state color).

Request by Owner or Master for Official Number. RG 41. Lists measurements and other pertinent information. This was also the only government document found listing engine horsepower, fuel consumption, quantity, draft loaded and in ballast, and the deadweight tonnage. The official number is the key to other ship documentation.

Certificates of Registry. RG 41. Required for all vessels over five tons engaged in Foreign Trade.

Certificate of Enrollment. RG 41. Required for Vessels in the Coastal or Fishing Trade over 20 tons.

License, required for vessels 5 to 20 tons in coastal or fishing trade. RG 41.

Indorsements for Change of Master. RG 41.

Consolidated Certificate of Enrollment and License. RG 41. One enrollment is used unless a change occurs and the license is renewed each year by Indorsements of Renewal.

Permanent Enrollment, PE, term for Certificate of Registry or Consolidated Enrollment and License issued at home port.

General Correspondence Files. RG 41. General Correspondence Files 1906–1934. By ship name.

United States Shipping Board, General Files, Records of the United States Shipping Board by subjects and ship name, RG 32.

Ships' documentation files are held in Official Number files in the relevant Records Group (RG). The RG for ship documenation depends on the years as follows:

Records Group 41 (1867–1942)

Records Group 36 (1942–56)

Records Group 26 (1956–72)

All of the ships' documentation in this book fell in the time frame of RG 41. With the Official Numbers provided in the tables of the book and repeated for the following ships, one can request all documents, first and last documents, or a selected document. Correspondence files are not a part of the Official Number Files.

Correspondence files are held in the Bureau of Marine Inspection and Navigation (BMIN), 1906–34, General Correspondence Files, and are still in

RG 41. The time frame of 1906–34 encompassed all of the National Archive (BMIN) correspondence cited in this book.

Correspondence was not researched for the small vessels of chapter 1, and it is unlikely that much was generated or saved from that period.

Subject and file numbers for the ships researched is provided for the sailing ships listed (in order built) and are in the General Correspondence Files in RG 41 unless otherwise noted:

City of Orange, ON 214819

All correspondence pertaining to:

Clearance without licensed officers. File No. 93582

Action of Captain Wry in throwing cargo of lumber overboard in Gulf of Mexico. File No. 96297

Shanghaiing of D. W. Patterson at Key West Florida. File No. 96333

Charge against Rupert Wry, master, for abusing W. A. White. File No. 96531

Effects of Ben Hagdahl. File No. 103399

Death and effects of Peter Nestaby. File No. 103396

Transfer to Italian flag on arrival in Italy. File No. 104556

Destruction of vessel by fire. File No. 106308

City of Houston, ON 215246

No correspondence.

City of Pensacola, ON 215584

All correspondence pertaining to:

Problem obtaining steam licensed officers. File No. 96367

The sinking of the ship. File No. 93521

City of Gulfport, ON 215942

All correspondence pertaining to:

Captain Wry allowing unlawful passenger. File No. 99749

Death at sea of seaman. File No. 104718

Loss of the ship due to fire. File No. 105231

Crew discharge due to change in ship's articles. File No. 105991

City of Mobile, ON 216350

Loss of ship due to fire. File No. 106308

City of Beaumont, ON 216473

No correspondence.

City of Dallas, ON 216909

No correspondence.

City of Austin, ON 217160

No correspondence.

City of Galveston, ON 217482

All correspondence pertaining to:

Ship blown out to sea at Funchal, Madeira. File No. 113841

Inability to obtain required number of A. B. Seamen. File No. 116692

Dismantling of the ship. File No. 120442

City of Orleans, ON 217696

No correspondence.

City of Lafayette, ON none issued

All correspondence pertaining to this ship was under U.S. Shipping Board General File No. 1091–4463, Subject Ships—general, RG 32.

City of Waco, ON none issued
  No correspondence.

Macerata, ON 192862
  No correspondence.

Monfalcone, ON 219468
  No correspondence.

The three four-masted schooners built at Orange and Beaumont, Texas were not researched for correspondence.

The wooden steamships referred to in the book are listed below along with their Official Number if available. Correspondence came from U.S. Shipping Board (USSB) General Files RG 32 or Bureau of Marine Inspection and Navigation General Correspondence (BMIN) 1906–34, Files, RG 41.

SS *Beaumont*, ON 217313
  No correspondence.

SS *Lone Star*, ON not found

  Ship measurements. BMIN General Correspondence Files, File No. 101856 RG 41.

  Crew pay discrepancy. BMIN General Correspondence Files, File No. 108189, RG 41.

SS *Nacogdoches*, ON 216401

  Disposition of the ship. USSB Correspondence Files, General, File No. 1091– 4369, Subject Ships, RG 32.

SS *Oneco*, ON 216765

  Correspondence pertaining to admeasurement sheets. BMIN General Correspondence Files, File No. 101561, RG 41.

  USSB, General Files, File No. 553–2200, Subject Ships—Collisions, SS *Oneco*, SS *Risvaer*, RG 32.

  Salvors claims. USSB, General Files, File No. 553–2200, Subject Ships, RG 32.

  Collision of the Spanish ship *Manola* with the SS *Oneco*. USSB, General Files, File No. 553–1629, Subject Ships—Collisions, RG 32.

  Documents pertaining to the sale of the ship. USSB, General Files, File No. 1091–4369, Subject Ships, RG 32.

  Transmittal of Certificate of Registry after sale of SS *Oneco*. BMIN General Correspondence Files, File No. 12693, RG 41.

SS *Swampscott*, ON 217000

  Lumber unloading and quayage problems in British port. USSB General Correspondence—General, File No. 1091–4369, RG 32.

SS *War Mystery*, ON not issued, sold to Cunard Steamship Company, British flag.

  Request to British attaché to go on first trip and transfer of ship to Cunard Steamship Line. USSB, Ships Correspondence—General *War Mystery* (Steam Screw) File No. 1091–1611, RG 32.

Index

Note: Pages with illustrations are indicated by italics.